# THE AMERICAN NOVEL AND ITS TRADITION

# THE AMERICAN NOVEL AND ITS TRADITION

Richard Chase

THE JOHNS HOPKINS UNIVERSITY PRESS
Baltimore and London

A part of the first section of Chapter I originally appeared in *Commentary* (Copyright
1955 by The American Jewish Committee).
The section of Chapter VIII that concerns
G. W. Cable's *The Grandissimes* appeared in
the *Kenyon Review* (Copyright 1956 by Richard Chase).

The Johns Hopkins University Press, Baltimore, Maryland 21218
The Johns Hopkins Press, Ltd., London

Library of Congress Cataloging in Publication Data

Chase, Richard Volney, 1914–1962.
The American novel and its tradition.

Reprint of the 1st ed. published
by Doubleday, Garden City, N.Y.
Bibliography:   p. 247.     Includes index.
1.   American fiction—History and criticism.
I.   Title.     [PS371.C5   1980]     813′.009     79–3702
ISBN 0–8018–2303–X

# Contents

# Introduction

IN this study of the American novel, I have arranged my
chapters chronologically from Charles Brockden Brown to
Faulkner. But the book is an essay in definition and appreciation, and although it often takes a historical view, it is
not a detailed literary history. My main and, as it seems,
inevitable theme is the relation between the romance, or
romance-novel, and the novel proper. I have limited the
discussion to a relatively small number of novels, in order
to consider them at some length. The choice of novels has
been guided partly by my theme, but it has necessarily
been somewhat arbitrary. I have not mentioned, or have
mentioned only in passing, a good many which I might
have included but for various reasons did not. Certain
books, such as *The Scarlet Letter, Moby-Dick, The Portrait
of a Lady, Huckleberry Finn,* and *The Sound and the Fury,*
may be expected to appear in almost any study of the
American novel, and I have included these. In the last fifteen years much criticism and scholarship have been devoted to these novels, and I have thought it possible to
write of them in the spirit of summary and generalization
and in this way to take advantage of the large body of recent criticism, even though I am forced to differ with certain established opinions.

A variety of motives has entered into the choice of the
other novels I consider. I have had in mind in almost every
case the originality and "Americanness" of the novel in
question, though I do not deny that the precise nature of
these qualities is often debatable, nor that certain novels I

marginal handwritten note: "novel vs. romance"

do not discuss may be said also to have these qualities. In at least one instance—Cooper's *Satanstoe*—the opportunity of cultural definition rather than formal or aesthetic definition has determined the choice. In every other case the choice has been influenced by the novel's offering the opportunity of both. Finally, I picked two novels not only for their relevance to the general argument but because they are unfortunately unknown to most readers—G. W. Cable's *The Grandissimes* and Howells's *The Vacation of the Kelwyns*.

As for my main purpose, it is: to assess the significance of the fact that since the earliest days the American novel, in its most original and characteristic form, has worked out its destiny and defined itself by incorporating an element of romance. This purpose has led me to propose a native tradition of the novel. I understand this tradition, inevitably, as springing from England, but as differing from the English tradition by its perpetual reassessment and reconstitution of romance within the novel form.

Thus I am interested mainly in defining the leading characteristics of the American romance-novel, as it may be called—that freer, more daring, more brilliant fiction that contrasts with the solid moral inclusiveness and massive equability of the English novel. As Thoreau says, the imagination has a place for "wildness" as well as for the more solid and domesticated virtues, just as "nature has a place for the wild clematis as well as the cabbage." True, cabbages may be made to grow in the American soil and the wild clematis in the English. But as it has turned out, the element of romance has been far more noticeable in the American novel than in the English.

Thoreau's words suggest something of what "romance" means as it was applied to the American novel by such different writers as Cooper, Hawthorne, James, and Frank Norris in their prefaces and essays and, as, following their lead, I use it in this book. I try to define "romance" in the first chapter. For the moment, let me say that the word

viii

*define romance*

must signify, besides the more obvious qualities of the picturesque and the heroic, an assumed freedom from the ordinary novelistic requirements of verisimilitude, development, and continuity; a tendency towards melodrama and idyl; a more or less formal abstractness and, on the other hand, a tendency to plunge into the underside of consciousness; a willingness to abandon moral questions or to ignore the spectacle of man in society, or to consider these things only indirectly or abstractly.

Obviously the romance is by nature disqualified to perform some of the classic offices of the novel. Henry James, as it now seems, did not adequately respond to *The Scarlet Letter*, although his treatment of it in his biography of Hawthorne is the starting point of any sane criticism. He seems never to have heard of *Moby-Dick*, and if he had read it there is no doubt that he would have found it lacking in certain of the novelistic virtues. He would have found that it lacked the sense of life as it is actually lived, that it did not establish the continuity between events and the characters' sense of events, that there was a general lack of that "experience" which James defines as "our apprehension and our measure of what happens to us as social creatures." Like other romance-novels, *Moby-Dick* is thus somewhat disqualified for engaging the moral imagination in the sort of close involvement with real life which makes the context for moral ideas in such novels as those of Balzac, George Eliot, and James himself.

To keep the record straight, let me say that I agree with the usual modern opinion that James is the greatest American novelist and critic of the novel. There is no doubt, however, that James in practice—say, in *The Portrait of a Lady*, as well as in a novel like *The Princess Casamassima*, which has a strong element of melodramatic romance, or *The Wings of the Dove*, which is a kind of lyric pageant—was more the romancer than his own theories, strictly applied, would have allowed him to be. But what I am most interested in in this book is that farther realm of fiction which the American novelists have explored and occupied—moved, as they have been, by what James himself called a "rich passion for extremes." In this trans-Jamesian realm of fiction there are certain special virtues. Among them are the "intellectual energy" that Brockden Brown prized, the profundity described by Melville as "the blackness of darkness," a certain intrepid and penetrating dialectic of action and meaning, a radical skepticism about ultimate questions.

These are not the qualities usually thought of in relation to the romance or romance-novel. They are not to be found in Scott or Stevenson, even less in Margaret Mitchell, Kenneth Roberts or the many other American writers who, distantly following Scott, have romanticized episodes of the American past. Nor in the general history of literature has romance been distinguished, among the perennial literary forms, for its intellectual and moral power. On the contrary, it has on this score generally been inferior to greater forms such as tragedy and comedy—in ancient and medieval as well as in modern times.

Nevertheless the best American novelists have found uses for romance far beyond the escapism, fantasy, and sentimentality often associated with it. They have found that in the very freedom of romance from the conditions of actuality there are certain potential virtues of the mind, which may be suggested by such words as rapidity, irony, abstraction, profundity. These qualities have made romance a suitable, even, as it seems, an inevitable, vehicle for the intellectual and moral ideas of the American novelists. They have used romance to introduce into the novel what one may roughly describe as the narrow profundity of New England Puritanism, the skeptical, rationalistic spirit of the Enlightenment, and the imaginative freedom of Transcendentalism. In doing so they have created a brilliant and original, if often unstable and fragmentary, kind of literature.

It follows that the usual depreciation of romance on intellectual and moral grounds is not always justifiable. (It also follows that the *over*estimation of the novels of Hawthorne, Melville, and Faulkner by many recent critics, on the ground that these novels have the harmony and authority of the greatest tragic and religious literature, is not justifiable either. But this is a matter that may be postponed to later pages.) It is not necessarily true that in so far as a novel departs from realism it is obscurantist and disqualified to make moral comments on the world. As applied to many novels, there is no doubt that this view contains much truth. Still, one may put in a provisional claim for a particular kind of rationality in the romance-novel. The very abstractness and profundity of romance allow it to formulate moral truths of universal validity, although it perforce ignores home truths that may be equally or more important. One may point to the power of romance to express dark and complex truths unavailable to realism. The inner facts of political life have been better grasped by romance-melodramas, as they may be called—such as those of Dostoevski and Malraux—than by strictly realistic fiction.

Admittedly, the "intellectual energy" of Brown's *Wieland*, of *Moby-Dick*, or of *The Octopus* doesn't guarantee intellectual clarity. The compulsion to plunge directly to "the very axis of reality," a compulsion Melville finds, and praises, in both Hawthorne and Shakespeare, leads to some desperate gambits. And the intense desire to drive everything through to the last turn of the screw or twist of the knife, which distinguishes American writers from English, often results in romantic nihilism, a poetry of force and darkness.

But it is not my primary aim either to defend or attack the American novel on intellectual or moral grounds. I do not suggest that whatever is is right. I do suggest, however, that the romance-novel *is*. It used to be thought that the element of romance in American fiction was destined to disappear, perhaps had to all intents and purposes already disappeared, as a result of the rise of modern realism which set in after the Civil War. It used to be thought, also, that this was a good thing, romance being regarded as a backward tendency of the comparatively unenlightened youth of our culture. But the fact seems to be that the history of the American novel is not only the history of the rise of realism but also of the repeated rediscovery of the uses of romance, and that this will continue to be so. In view of this fact about American literature, it becomes of some interest to describe how, in certain instances, this process of the amalgamation of realism and romance has been going on. And that is what I try to describe in the ensuing pages.

Let me note again my general awareness of the difficulty of making accurate judgments about what is specially American in American novels or American culture. Yet without a certain rhetorical boldness, such as appears in the first part of the first chapter, nothing of interest can be said at all on this score. In the first chapter, I try to bring out certain contrasting characteristics of the American novels as opposed to the English, in an attempt to account for the obvious fact that although most of the great American novels are romances, most of the great English novels are not—the fact, in other words, that the tradition of romance is major in the history of the American novel but minor in the history of the English novel. But elsewhere I would have it understood that when I speak of what is true of the American novels, I do not at all imply that in one way or another the same may not be true of the English, French, or Russian novels. It would be tedious to say this repeatedly in the ensuing pages, and so I have left it unsaid. My only purpose is to define some of the leading qualities of the American novel. My method is not comparative but descriptive, except at the beginning of the book, and in one or two other places, where comparison (or contrast) appears to facilitate description.

In conclusion, I should like to thank Andrew Chiappe and R. W. Flint for their careful reading of the manuscript of this book and for the several helpful suggestions which they offered for its improvement.

# THE AMERICAN NOVEL AND ITS TRADITION

# Chapter I

# THE BROKEN CIRCUIT

## A Culture of Contradictions

THE imagination that has produced much of the best and most characteristic American fiction has been shaped by the contradictions and not by the unities and harmonies of our culture. In a sense this may be true of all literatures of whatever time and place. Nevertheless there are some literatures which take their form and tone from polarities, opposites, and irreconcilables, but are content to rest in and sustain them, or to resolve them into unities, if at all, only by special and limited means. The American novel tends to rest in contradictions and among extreme ranges of experience. When it attempts to resolve contradictions, it does so in oblique, morally equivocal ways. As a general rule it does so either in melodramatic actions or in pastoral idyls, although intermixed with both one may find the stirring instabilities of "American humor." These qualities constitute the uniqueness of that branch of the novelistic tradition which has flourished in this country. They help to account

1

for the strong element of "romance" in the American "novel."

By contrast, the English novel has followed a middle way. It is notable for its great practical sanity, its powerful, engrossing composition of wide ranges of experience into a moral centrality and equability of judgment. Oddity, distortion of personality, dislocations of normal life, recklessness of behavior, malignancy of motive—these the English novel has included. Yet the profound poetry of disorder we find in the American novel is missing, with rare exceptions, from the English. Radical maladjustments and contradictions are reported but are seldom of the essence of form in the English novel, and although it is no stranger to suffering and defeat or to triumphant joy either, it gives the impression of absorbing all extremes, all maladjustments and contradictions into a normative view of life. In doing so, it shows itself to derive from the two great influences that stand behind it—classic tragedy and Christianity. The English novel has not, of course, always been strictly speaking tragic or Christian. Often it has been comic, but often, too, in that superior form of comedy which approaches tragedy. Usually it has been realistic or, in the philosophical sense of the word, "naturalistic." Yet even its peculiar kind of gross poetic naturalism has preserved something of the two great traditions that formed English literature. The English novel, that is, follows the tendency of tragic art and Christian art, which characteristically move through contradictions to forms of harmony, reconciliation, catharsis, and transfiguration.

Judging by our greatest novels, the American imagination, even when it wishes to assuage and reconcile the contradictions of life, has not been stirred by the possibility of catharsis or incarnation, by the tragic or Christian possibility. It has been stirred, rather, by the aesthetic possibilities of radical forms of alienation, contradiction, and disorder.

The essential difference between the American novel and the English will be strongly pointed up to any reader of

2

F. R. Leavis's *The Great Tradition*. Mr. Leavis's "great tradition" of the novel is really Anglo-American, and it includes
not only Jane Austen, George Eliot, Conrad, and Henry
James but, apparently, in one of its branches Hawthorne
and Melville. My assumption in this book is that the American novel is obviously a development from the English
tradition. At least it was, down to 1880 or 1890. For at
that time our novelists began to turn to French and Russian
models and the English influence has decreased steadily
ever since. The more extreme imagination of the French
and Russian novelists has clearly been more in accord with
the purposes of modern American writers than has the English imagination. True, an American reader of Mr. Leavis's
book will have little trouble in giving a very general assent
to his very general proposition about the Anglo-American
tradition. Nevertheless, he will also be forced constantly to
protest that there is another tradition of which Mr. Leavis
does not seem to be aware, a tradition which includes most
of the best American novels.

Ultimately, it does not matter much whether one insists
that there are really *two* traditions, the English and the
American (leaving aside the question of what writers each
might be said to comprise) or whether one insists merely
that there is a radical divergence within one tradition. All I
hold out for is a provisional recognition of the divergence
as a necessary step towards understanding and appreciation
of both the English and the American novel. The divergence
is brought home to an American reader of Leavis's book
when, for example, he comes across the brief note allotted
to the Brontës. Here is Leavis's comment on Emily Brontë:

> I have said nothing about *Wuthering Heights* because
> that astonishing work seems to me a kind of sport . . .
> she broke completely, and in the most astonishing way,
> both with the Scott tradition that imposed on the novelist
> a romantic resolution of his themes, and with the tradi-
> tion coming down from the eighteenth century that de-

3

manded a plane-mirror reflection of the surface of "real" life. Out of her a minor tradition comes, to which belongs, most notably, *The House with the Green Shutters.*

Of course Mr. Leavis is right; in relation to the great tradition of the English novel, *Wuthering Heights* is indeed a sport. But suppose it were discovered that *Wuthering Heights* was written by an American of New England Calvinist or Southern Presbyterian background. The novel would be astonishing and unique no matter who wrote it or where. But if it were an American novel it would not be a sport; it has too close an affinity with too many American novels, and among them some of the best. Like many of the fictions discussed in this book *Wuthering Heights* proceeds from an imagination that is essentially melodramatic, that operates among radical contradictions and renders reality indirectly or poetically, thus breaking, as Mr. Leavis observes, with the traditions that require a surface rendering of real life and a resolution of themes, "romantic" or otherwise.

Those readers who make a dogma out of Leavis's views are thus proprietors of an Anglo-American tradition in which many of the most interesting and original and several of the greatest American novels are sports. *Wieland* is a sport, and so are *The Scarlet Letter* and *The Blithedale Romance, Moby-Dick, Pierre,* and *The Confidence Man, Huckleberry Finn, The Red Badge of Courage, McTeague, As I Lay Dying, The Sun Also Rises*—all are eccentric, in their differing ways, to a tradition of which, let us say, *Middlemarch* is a standard representative. Not one of them has any close kinship with the massive, temperate, moralistic rendering of life and thought we associate with Mr. Leavis's "great tradition."

The English novel, one might say, has been a kind of imperial enterprise, an appropriation of reality with the high purpose of bringing order to disorder. By contrast, as Lawrence observed in his *Studies in Classic American Litera-*

*ture,* the American novel has usually seemed content to
explore, rather than to appropriate and civilize, the remarkable and in some ways unexampled territories of life in the
New World and to reflect its anomalies and dilemmas. It
has not wanted to build an imperium but merely to discover
a new place and a new state of mind. Explorers see more
deeply, darkly, privately and disinterestedly than imperi-
alists, who must perforce be circumspect and prudential.
The American novel is more profound and clairvoyant than
the English novel, but by the same token it is narrower
and more arbitrary, and it tends to carve out of experience
brilliant, highly wrought fragments rather than massive
unities.

For whatever reason—perhaps the nagging scrupulosity
of the Puritan mind has something to do with it—the American novel has sometimes approached a perfection or art unknown to the English tradition, in which we discover no
such highly skilled practitioners as Hawthorne, Stephen
Crane, Henry James, or Hemingway. These writers, often
overestimated as moralists, seem content to oppose the disorder and rawness of their culture with a scrupulous art-
consciousness, with aesthetic forms—which do, of course,
often broaden out into moral significance.

In a well known passage Allen Tate refers to the "complexity of feeling" that everyone senses in the American
novel and that, as Mr. Tate says, "from Hawthorne down
to our own time has baffled our best understanding." The
complexity of the American novel has been much exaggerated. With the exception of one or two of James's novels
no American fiction has anything like the complexity of
character and event of *Our Mutual Friend,* for example.
In *The Scarlet Letter* or *Moby-Dick* the characters and
events have actually a kind of abstracted simplicity about
them. In these books character may be deep but it is narrow and predictable. Events take place with a formalized
clarity. And certainly it cannot be argued that society and

5

the social life of man are shown to be complex in these fictions.

*but true complexity of feeling ✓*

But of course Tate says "complexity of feeling," and he is right about that. The states of feeling, and the language in which they are caught, are sometimes very intricate in American novels. Yet these musing tides of feeling and language that make such a rich poetry in our fiction often seem to be at variance with the simplified actions and conceptions of life our novels present. The origins of this apparent anomaly must be sought in the contradictions of our culture.

Marius Bewley takes up Tate's remark in an essay called "Fenimore Cooper and the Economic Age" and traces this "complexity of feeling" to a "tension" which he finds not only in Cooper but in Hawthorne and James. It is, he thinks, a political tension in its origins, although as embodied in the works of these authors, it assumes many forms. This tension, he says, "was the result of a struggle to close the split in American experience, to discover a unity that —for the artist especially—almost sensibly *was not there.* What was the nature of the division that supported this conflict? It took on many forms concurrently; it was an opposition between tradition and progress or between the past and the future; between Europe and America, liberalism and reaction, aggressive acquisitive economics and benevolent wealth. These same divisions existed in Europe also, but there they were more ballasted by a denser social medium, a richer sense of the past, a more inhibited sense of material possibilities."

Mr. Bewley's apt discussion of the matter needs to be amended in one fundamental way. The kind of art that stems from a mind primarily moved by the impulse toward aesthetic and cultural unities and thus "struggles to close the split in American experience" as an artist might wish to close it—this kind of art is practiced often, though not always, by Henry James, but less often by Hawthorne and Cooper, and much less often by Faulkner, Melville, and Mark Twain. The fact is that many of the best American

6

novels achieve their very being, their energy and their form, from the perception and acceptance not of unities but of radical disunities.

Like many readers of American literature, Bewley makes the mistake of assuming both that our writers have wanted to reconcile disunities by their art and their intelligence and that this is what they *should* have wanted to do. Behind this assumption is a faulty historical view, as well as a certain overplus of moralism, which neglects to observe that there have been notable bodies of literature, as well as of painting and sculpture, that have proposed and accepted an imaginative world of radical, even irreconcilable contradictions, and that with some important exceptions, the American novel (by which I mean its most original and characteristic examples) has been one of these bodies of literature.

*world of contradictions*

Surely Cooper (as will be noted later) is not at his best in a novel like *Satanstoe,* which is a "culture-making" novel and in which his mind is moved by an image of aesthetic and political harmony. On the contrary he is at his best in a book like *The Prairie,* where the search for unity is not at the center of the stage and he can accept without anxiety or thought the vivid contradictions of Natty Bumppo and his way of life—those contradictions which, as Balzac saw, made him so original a conception. In this book Cooper is not inspired by an impulse to resolve cultural contradictions half so much as by the sheer romantic exhilaration of escape from culture itself, into a world where nature is dire, terrible, and beautiful, where human virtues are personal, alien, and renunciatory, and where contradictions are to be resolved only by death, the ceaseless brooding presence of which endows with an unspeakable beauty every irreconcilable of experience and all the irrationalities of life.

Mr. Bewley is not alone in assuming it to be the destiny of American literature to reconcile disunities rather than to pursue the possibility it has actually pursued—that is, to discover a putative unity *in* disunity or to rest at last among

7

irreconcilables. In *Democracy in America* Tocqueville tried to account for a number of related contradictions in American life. He noted a disparity between ideals and practice, a lack of connection between thought and experience, a tendency of the American mind to oscillate rather wildly between ideas that "are all either extremely minute and clear or extremely general and vague."

Tocqueville sought a genetic explanation for these disparities. He pointed out that in aristocratic societies there was a shared body of inherited habits, attitudes and institutions that stood in a mediating position between the individual and the state. This, he observed, was not true in a democracy, where "each citizen is habitually engaged in the contemplation of a very puny object: namely, himself. If he ever looks higher, he perceives only the immense form of society at large or the still more imposing aspect of mankind. . . . What lies between is a void." Tocqueville believed that this either/or habit of mind also owed much to the sharp distinctions made by Calvinism and its habit of opposing the individual to his God, with a minimum of mythic or ecclesiastical mediation. He found certain advantages in this "democratic" quality of mind, but he warned Americans that it might produce great confusion in philosophy, morals, and politics and a basic instability in literary and cultural values, and that consequently Americans should try to discover democratic equivalents for those traditional habits of mind which in aristocracies had moderated and reconciled extremes in thought and experience.

Tocqueville knew that the dualistic kind of thought of which he spoke was specifically American only in the peculiar quality of its origin and expression. He saw that with the probable exception of England, Europe would characteristically concern itself during the nineteenth century with grand intellectual oppositions, usually more or less of a Hegelian order. But even though the tendency of thought Tocqueville predicated belonged to Western culture generally, one is nevertheless struck by how often American

8

writers conceive of human dilemmas according to his scheme, and how many make aesthetic capital out of what seemed to him a moral and intellectual shortcoming.

In his studies of the classic American writers, D. H. Lawrence presented his version of the contrariety, or, as he said, "duplicity" of the American literary mind by saying that he found in writers like Cooper, Melville, and Hawthorne "a tight mental allegiance to a morality which all their passion goes to destroy," a formulation which describes perfectly the inner contradiction of such products of the American imagination as the story of Natty Bumppo. In general Lawrence was thinking of an inherent conflict between "genteel" spirituality and a pragmatic experientialism which in its lower depths was sheer Dionysian or "Indian" energy and violence. Acute enough to see that the best American artistic achievements had depended in one way or another on this dualism, he seemed ready nevertheless to advocate, on moral grounds, a reconciliation of opposites, such as he thought he discerned in the poems of Whitman.

In short, like all the observers of American literature we are citing in these pages, Lawrence was trying to find out what was wrong with it. He is a sympathetic and resourceful reader—one of the best, surely, ever to turn his attention to the American novel. But he thinks that the American novel is sick, and he wants to cure it. Perhaps there is something wrong with it, perhaps it is sick—but a too exclusive preoccupation with the wrongness of the American novel has in some ways disqualified him for seeing what, right or wrong, it *is*.

Finally, there is the division of American culture into "highbrow" and "lowbrow" made by Van Wyck Brooks in 1915 in his *America's Coming-of-Age*. Brooks's essay is a great piece of writing; it is eloquent, incisive, and witty. But we have lived through enough history now to see its fundamental error—namely, the idea that it is the duty of our writers to heal the split and reconcile the contradictions in our culture by pursuing a middlebrow course. All the

9

evidence shows that wherever American literature has pursued the middle way it has tended by a kind of native fatality not to reconcile but merely to deny or ignore the polarities of our culture. Our middlebrow literature—for example, the novels of Howells—has generally been dull and mediocre. In the face of Brooks's desire to unite the highbrow and the lowbrow on a middle ground, there remains the fact that our best novelists have been, not middlebrows, but either highbrows like James, lowbrows like Mark Twain, Frank Norris, Dreiser, and Sherwood Anderson, or combination highbrow-lowbrows like Melville, Faulkner, and Hemingway. Here again American fiction contrasts strongly with English. The English novel at its best is staunchly middlebrow. The cultural conditions within which English literature has evolved have allowed it to become a great middlebrow literature—the only one, it may be, in history.

Let us in all candor admit the limited, the merely instrumental value of the terms used in the last paragraph. They work very well, and are in fact indispensable, in making large cultural formulations. But in applying them to individual authors the terms must be constantly reexamined. We might ask, for example, whether from one point of view both Hawthorne and James performed the unlikely feat of becoming great middlebrow writers. Both of them, at any rate, achieve a kind of contemplative centrality of vision within the confines of which their minds work with great delicacy and equanimity. In so far as they do this, one certainly cannot chide them for shying away from some of the more extreme contradictions, the more drastic forms of alienation, the more violent, earthy, or sordid ranges of experience which engage the minds of Melville and Faulkner, and in fact most of our best writers. Yet to achieve a "contemplative centrality of vision" certainly requires an action of the mind; whereas the word "middlebrow," although suggesting centrality of vision, inevitably suggests, judging by our American literature, a

view gained by no other means than passivity and the re-
fusal of experience.

To conclude this brief account of the contradictions
which have vivified and excited the American imagination,
these contradictions seem traceable to certain historical
facts. First, there is the solitary position man has been
placed in in this country, a position very early enforced by
the doctrines of Puritanism and later by frontier conditions
and, as Tocqueville skillfully pointed out, by the very institutions of democracy as these evolved in the eighteenth
and nineteenth centuries.

*solitary*

Second, the Manichaean quality of New England Puritanism, which, as Yvor Winters and others have shown, had
so strong an effect on writers like Hawthorne and Melville
and entered deeply into the national consciousness. From
the historical point of view, this Puritanism was a back-
sliding in religion as momentous in shaping the imagination
as the cultural reversion Cooper studied on the frontier.
For, at least as apprehended by the literary imagination,
New England Puritanism—with its grand metaphors of election and damnation, its opposition of the kingdom of light
and the kingdom of darkness, its eternal and autonomous
contraries of good and evil—seems to have recaptured the
Manichaean sensibility. The American imagination, like the
New England Puritan mind itself, seems less interested in
redemption than in the melodrama of the eternal struggle
of good and evil, less interested in incarnation and reconciliation than in alienation and disorder. If we may suppose
ourselves correct in tracing to this origin the prevalence in
American literature of the symbols of light and dark, we
may doubtless suppose also that this sensibility has been
enhanced by the racial composition of our people and by
the Civil War that was fought, if more in legend than in
fact, over the Negro.

*Manichaean*

More obviously, a third source of contradiction lies in the
dual allegiance of the American, who in his intellectual culture belongs both to the Old World and the New. These are

speculative ideas which I can only hope to make concrete and relevant in the succeeding pages. I would hope to avoid, at the same time, the rather arid procedure that would result from trying to find a "contradiction" behind every character and episode.

## Novel vs. Romance

Nothing will be gained by trying to define "novel" and "romance" too closely. One of their chief advantages is that, as literary forms go, they are relatively loose and flexible. But especially in discussing American literature, these terms have to be defined closely enough to distinguish between them, even though the distinction itself may sometimes be meaningless as applied to a given book and even though, following usage, one ordinarily uses the word "novel" to describe a book like Cooper's *The Prairie* which might more accurately be called a "romance" or a "romance-novel."

Doubtless the main difference between the novel and the romance is in the way in which they view reality. The novel renders reality closely and in comprehensive detail. It takes a group of people and sets them going about the business of life. We come to see these people in their real complexity of temperament and motive. They are in explicable relation to nature, to each other, to their social class, to their own past. Character is more important than action and plot, and probably the tragic or comic actions of the narrative will have the primary purpose of enhancing our knowledge of and feeling for an important character, a group of characters, or a way of life. The events that occur will usually be plausible, given the circumstances, and if the novelist includes a violent or sensational occurrence in his plot, he will introduce it only into such scenes as have been (in the words of Percy Lubbock) "already prepared to vouch for it." Historically, as it has often been said, the novel has

12

served the interests and aspirations of an insurgent middle class.

By contrast the romance, following distantly the medieval example, feels free to render reality in less volume and detail. It tends to prefer action to character, and action will be freer in a romance than in a novel, encountering, as it were, less resistance from reality. (This is not always true, as we see in what might be called the static romances of Hawthorne, in which the author uses the allegorical and moral, rather than the dramatic, possibilities of the form.) The romance can flourish without providing much intricacy of relation. The characters, probably rather two-dimensional types, will not be complexly related to each other or to society or to the past. Human beings will on the whole be shown in ideal relation—that is, they will share emotions only after these have become abstract or symbolic. To be sure, characters may become profoundly involved in some way, as in Hawthorne or Melville, but it will be a deep and narrow, an obsessive, involvement. In American romances it will not matter much what class people come from, and where the novelist would arouse our interest in a character by exploring his origin, the romancer will probably do so by enveloping it in mystery. Character itself becomes, then, somewhat abstract and ideal, so much so in some romances that it seems to be merely a function of plot. The plot we may expect to be highly colored. Astonishing events may occur, and these are likely to have a symbolic or ideological, rather than a realistic, plausibility. Being less committed to the immediate rendition of reality than the novel, the romance will more freely veer toward mythic, allegorical, and symbolistic forms.

# The Historical View

Although some of the best works of American fiction have to be called, for purposes of criticism, romances rather than

13

novels, we would be pursuing a chimera if we tried, except provisionally, to isolate a literary form known as the American prose romance, as distinguished from the European or the American novel. In actuality the romances of our literature, like European prose romances, are literary hybrids, unique only in their peculiar but widely differing amalgamation of novelistic and romance elements. The greatest American fiction has tended toward the romance more often than the greatest European fiction. Still, our fiction is historically a branch of the European tradition of the novel. And it is the better part of valor in the critic to understand our American romances as adaptations of traditional novelistic procedures to new cultural conditions and new aesthetic aspirations. It will not damage our appreciation of the originality and value of *Moby-Dick* or *The Blithedale Romance* to say that they both seem to begin as novels but then veer off into the province of romance, in the one case making a supreme triumph, in the other, a somewhat dubious but interesting medley of genres and intentions.

Inevitably we look to the writings of James Fenimore Cooper, for it was he who first fully exemplified and formulated the situation of the novelist in the New World. His first book, *Precaution*, was a novel of manners, somewhat in the style of Jane Austen. Considering this a failure, he wrote *The Spy*, a story of the Revolution, in which, following Scott, he put his characters in a borderland (in this case between the American and British armies) where the institutions and manners of society did not obtain. He sketched out in Harvey Birch the semilegendary hero who would find his full development in Natty Bumppo. As for characterization and realism of presentation, he contented himself with what he called in *Notions of the Americans* "the general picture" and "the delineation of principles"—this being, as he said, all that could be expected of the American writer, given the "poverty of materials" and the uniformity of behavior and public opinion. He introduced an element of melodrama, believing that this might be

14

suitable to scenes set in the American forest, even though we had no mysterious castles, dungeons, or monasteries. He introduced also a certain "elevation" of style and a freedom in arranging events and attributing moral qualities to his characters. It is thus apparent that if American conditions had forced Cooper to be content with "the general picture" and "the delineation of principles" this was, if a step away from the novel form proper, a step *toward* the successful mythic qualities of the Leather-Stocking tales. Here was proof of Tocqueville's idea that although the abstractness and generality of the democratic imagination would make unavailable some of the traditional sources of fiction, this abstractness would in itself be a new source of mythic ideality.

In Cooper's books we see what was to be the main drift of American fiction. Responding to various pressures, it would depart markedly from the novelistic tradition. When it did so, it would—with variations that may be observed in such writers as Hawthorne, Melville, Mark Twain, Faulkner, and Hemingway—become either melodrama or pastoral idyl, often both.

Although Cooper gave an indubitably American tone to romance he did so without ceasing to be, in many ways, a disciple of Scott. Another disciple of Scott, and to a lesser extent of Godwin, was Cooper's near contemporary, the South Carolina journalist and romancer William Gilmore Simms. This author is no less convinced than Cooper that romance is the form of fiction called for by American conditions. Historical romance was his particular *forte,* and his *Views and Reviews* (1845) contains an interesting investigation of the materials available to the American romancer. In his prefatory letter to *The Yemassee,* his most popular tale of Indian warfare (first published in 1835), Simms defines the romance as the modern version of epic:

> You will note that I call *The Yemassee* a romance, and not a novel. You will permit me to insist on the dis-

15

tinction . . . What are the standards of the modern Romance? What is the modern Romance itself? The reply is immediate. The modern Romance is the substitute which the people of the present day offer for the ancient epic. The form is changed; the matter is very much the same; at all events, it differs much more seriously from the English novel than it does from the epic and the drama, because the difference is one of material, even more than of fabrication. The reader who, reading *Ivanhoe*, keeps Richardson and Fielding beside him, will be at fault in every step of his progress. The domestic novel of those writers, confined to the felicitous narration of common and daily occurring events, and the grouping and delineation of characters in the ordinary conditions of society, is altogether a different sort of composition; and if, in a strange doggedness or simplicity of spirit, such a reader happens to pin his faith to such writers alone, circumscribing the boundless horizon of art to the domestic circle, the Romances of Maturin, Scott, Bulwer, and others of the present day, will be little better than rhapsodical and intolerable nonsense.

When I say that our Romance is the substitute of modern times for the epic or the drama, I do not mean to say that they are exactly the same things, and yet, examined thoroughly . . . the differences between them are very slight. These differences depend upon the material employed, rather than upon the particular mode in which it is used. The Romance is of loftier origin than the Novel. It approximates the poem. It may be described as an amalgam of the two. It is only with those who are apt to insist upon poetry as verse, and to confound rhyme with poetry, that the resemblance is unapparent. The standards of the Romance . . . are very much those of the epic. It invests individuals with an absorbing interest—it hurries them rapidly through crowding and exacting events, in a narrow space of time—it requires the

16

same unities of plan, of purpose, and harmony of parts, and it seeks for its adventures among the wild and wonderful. It does not confine itself to what is known, or even what is probable. It grasps at the possible; and, placing a human agent in hitherto untried situations, it exercises its ingenuity in extricating him from them, while describing his feelings and his fortunes in the process.

Loosely written as it is, this statement, with its echoes of Aristotle's *Poetics*, remains something of a classic in the history of American criticism, its general purport being one which so many of our prose fictionists have accepted. American fiction has been notable for its poetic quality, which is not the poetry of verse nor yet the domestic or naturalistic poetry of the novel but the poetry of romance. In allying romance to epic Simms was reflecting his own preoccupation with panoramic settings, battles, and heroic deeds; doubtless he had also in mind, vociferous nationalist that he was, the power of epic to mirror the soul of a people. There are many American fictions besides *The Yemassee* which remind us of epics, large and small: Cooper's *Prairie*, *Moby-Dick*, *The Adventures of Huckleberry Finn*, Faulkner's *As I Lay Dying*, for example. Yet on the whole, American fiction has approximated the poetry of idyl and of melodrama more often than of epic.

Not all of Simms's own romances have the epic quality. *Confession: or the Blind Heart* (1841), *Beauchampe* (1842), and *Charlemont* (1856) are "tales of passion" and have to do with seduction, murder, revenge, and domestic cruelty. They are dark studies in psychology that reflect Godwin and the Gothic tradition at the same time that in their pictures of town life, lawyers, court trials, and local customs they forecast later Southern writers, such as Faulkner and Robert Penn Warren. Simms's tales of passion, however, are fatally marred by the carelessness and crudity with which they are thrown together, and it was in the work of Hawthorne that for the first time the psychological possibilities of romance were realized.

As we see from the prefaces to his longer fictions, particularly *The Marble Faun,* Hawthorne was no less convinced than Cooper and Simms that romance, rather than the novel, was the predestined form of American narrative. In distinguishing between forms, his Preface to *The House of the Seven Gables* makes some of the same points Simms had made:

> When a writer calls his work a romance, it need hardly be observed that he wishes to claim a certain latitude, both as to its fashion and material, which he would not have felt himself entitled to assume, had he professed to be writing a novel. The latter form of composition is presumed to aim at a very minute fidelity, not merely to the possible, but to the probable and ordinary course of man's experience. The former—while, as a work of art, it must rigidly subject itself to laws, and while it sins unpardonably so far as it may swerve aside from the truth of the human heart—has fairly a right to present that truth under circumstances, to a great extent, of the writer's own choosing or creation. If he think fit, also, he may so manage his atmospherical medium as to bring out or mellow the lights, and deepen and enrich the shadows, of the picture. He will be wise, no doubt, to make a very moderate use of the privileges here stated, and especially, to mingle the marvellous rather as a slight, delicate, and evanescent flavor, than as any portion of the actual substance of the dish offered to the public. He can hardly be said, however, to commit a literary crime, even if he disregard this caution.

As Hawthorne sees the problem confronting the American author, it consists in the necessity of finding (in the words of the Introduction to *The Scarlet Letter*) "a neutral territory, somewhere between the real world and fairy-land, where the Actual and the Imaginary may meet, and each imbue itself with the nature of the other." Romance is, as we see, a kind of "border" fiction, whether the field of action is in the neutral territory between civilization and the wilderness, as in the adventure tales of Cooper and Simms, or whether, as in Hawthorne and later romancers, the field of action is conceived not so much as a place as a state of mind—the borderland of the human mind where the actual and the imaginary intermingle. Romance does not plant itself, like the novel, solidly in the midst of the actual. Nor when it is memorable, does it escape into the purely imaginary.

In saying that no matter what its extravagances romance must not "swerve aside from the truth of the human heart," Hawthorne was in effect announcing the definitive adaptation of romance to America. To keep fiction in touch with the human heart is to give it a universal human significance. But this cannot be done memorably in prose fiction, even in the relatively loose form of the romance, without giving it a local significance. The truth of the heart as pictured in romance may be more generic or archetypal than in the novel; it may be rendered less concretely; but it must still be made to belong to a time and a place. Surely Hawthorne's romances do. In his writings romance was made for the first time to respond to the particular demands of an American imagination and to mirror, in certain limited ways, the American mind. In order to accomplish this Hawthorne had to bring into play his considerable talent for psychology. Cooper was not a psychologist of any subtlety and outside of the striking conception of the stoic inner life of Natty Bumppo, he gave to romance no psychological quality that might not find its close analogue in Scott. Although no one would mistake a fiction of Simms for one of Scott, Simms's originality was circumscribed by his apparent belief, as stated in the quotation above, that American romance would differ from earlier forms only because it had different material rather than a "particular mode" of rendering this material. His claim to originality was severely limited by the crudity and indecision of his literary form and of his psychological insights.

In the writings of Brockden Brown, Cooper, and Simms we have the first difficult steps in the adaptation of English romance to American conditions and needs. Following these pioneers we have had, ever since, two streams of romance in our literary history. The first is the stream that makes the main subject of this book and includes Hawthorne, Melville, James, Mark Twain, Frank Norris, Faulkner, Hemingway, and others who have found that romance offers certain qualities of thought and imagination which the American fiction writer needs but which are outside the province of the novel proper. These are writers who each in his own way have followed Hawthorne both in thinking the imagination of romance necessary and in knowing that it must not "swerve aside from the truth of the human heart."

The other stream of romance, justly contemned by Mark Twain and James, is one which also descends from Scott, and includes John Esten Cooke's *Surry of Eagle's Nest* (1886), Lew Wallace's *Ben Hur* (1880), Charles Major's *When Knighthood Was In Flower* (1899), and later books like *Gone with the Wind* and the historical tales of Kenneth Roberts. Although these works may have their points, according to the taste of the reader, they are, historically considered, the tag-end of a European tradition that begins in the Middle Ages and has come down into our own literature without responding to the forms of imagination which the actualities of American life have inspired. Romances of this sort are sometimes defended because "they tell a good story"—as opposed to the fictions of, say, Faulkner and Melville, which allegedly don't. People who make this complaint have a real point; yet they put themselves in the position of defending books which have a fatal inner falsity.

The fact is that the word "romance" begins to take on its inevitable meaning, for the historically minded American reader, in the writing of Hawthorne. Ever since his use of the word to describe his own fiction, it has appropriately signified the peculiar narrow profundity and rich interplay of lights and darks which one associates with the best American writing. It has also signified, to be sure, that common trait shared by the American romances which are discussed in this book and all other romances whatsoever—namely, the penchant for the marvelous, the sensational, the legendary, and in general the heightened effect. But the critical question is always: To what purpose have these amiable tricks of romance been used? To falsify reality and the human heart or to bring us round to a new, significant and perhaps startling relation to them?

## James on the Novel vs. the Romance

In the two preceding sections of this chapter, I have tried to formulate preliminary definitions of "romance" and the "novel" and then to look at the matter in a historical perspective. In order to amplify the discussion, in both the abstract and the concrete, it will be of value at this point to return, with the aid of Henry James's prefaces, to the question of definition. In doing so, I shall risk repeating one or two observations which have already been made.

The first four prefaces James wrote for the New York edition of his works set forth, or at least allude to, the main items of his credo as a novelist, and although they are perhaps well known, there may be some advantage in looking them over again before noticing what James had to say directly about the relation of the romance to the novel. The four prefaces are those to *Roderick Hudson, The American, The Portrait of a Lady,* and *The Princess Casamassima.*

We might take as a motto this sentence, from the Preface to *The Princess:* "Experience, as I see it, is our apprehension and our measure of what happens to us as social creatures." Although James himself does not overtly contrast

21

his procedure with that of romance until he comes to the Preface to *The American,* we shall be justified in ourselves making the contrast, since James is obviously seeking to show, among other things, how the imperfections of romance may be avoided. And thus we reflect that, in a romance, "experience" has less to do with human beings as "social creatures" than as individuals. Heroes, villains, victims, legendary types, confronting other individuals or confronting mysterious or otherwise dire forces—this is what we meet in romances.

When James tells us that the art of the novel is the "art of representation," the practice of which spreads "round us in a widening, not in a narrow circle," we reflect on the relative paucity of "representation" in the older American romances and their tendency towards a concentrated and narrow profundity. Again we hear that "development" is "of the very essence of the novelist's process," and we recall how in romances characters appear really to be given quantities rather than emerging and changing organisms responding to their circumstances as these themselves develop one out of another. For if characters change in a romance, let's say as Captain Ahab in *Moby-Dick* or the Reverend Dimmesdale in *The Scarlet Letter* change, we are not shown a "development"; we are left rather with an element of mystery, as with Ahab, or a simplified and conventionalized alteration of character, as with Dimmesdale. Similarly, the episodes of romance tend to follow each other without ostensible causation; here too there is likely to be an element either of mystery or convention. To "treat" a subject, James says, is to "exhibit . . . relations"; and the novelist "is in the perpetual predicament that the continuity of things is the whole matter, for him, of comedy and tragedy." But in a romance much may be made of unrelatedness, of alienation and discontinuity, for the romancer operates in a universe that is less coherent than that of the novelist.

As for the setting, James says that it is not enough merely

to report what it seems to the author to be, in however minute detail. The great thing is to get into the novel not only the setting but somebody's *sense* of the setting. We recall that in *The Scarlet Letter* the setting, although sketchy, is pictorially very beautiful and symbolically *à propos*. But none of the characters has a *sense* of the setting; that is all in the author's mind and hence the setting is never dramatized but remains instead a handsomely tapestried backdrop. In *Moby-Dick* the setting is less inert; it becomes, in fact, a kind of "enveloping action." Still, only in some of the scenes do we have Ishmael's sense of the setting; during most of the book Ishmael himself is all but banished as a dramatic presence.

The whole question of the "point of command" or "point of view" or "center of intelligence" is too complicated to go into here. Suffice it to say that the allotment of intelligence, the question of what character shall be specially conscious of the meaning of what happens to and around him so that we see events and people more or less through his eyes, thus gaining a sense of dramatic coherence—these questions are less and less pertinent as fiction approaches pure romance. Natty Bumppo need be conscious only of what the Indians are going to do next. Hawthorne's Chillingworth and Melville's Ahab are clairvoyantly conscious, but with a profoundly obsessive distortion of the truth. They are not placed in context in order to give concrete dramatic form to a large part of what the author sees, as is the "point of command" in a James novel; all we learn from them is how *they* see. And as I shall suggest in speaking of *The Blithedale Romance*, the dyed-in-the-wool romancer like Hawthorne merely proves that you mustn't have a central observer in your story, because if you do you simply point up the faults of romance and admit your incapacity to follow out a fully developed novelistic procedure. In the romance too much depends on mystery and bewilderment to risk a generally receptive intelligence in the midst of things. Too often the effect you are after depends on a universe

23

that is felt to be irrational, contradictory, and melodramatic —whereas the effect of a central intelligence is to produce a sense of verisimilitude and dramatic coherence.

One or two further items from the prefaces may point up the contrast. A character, especially "the fictive hero," as James says, "successfully appeals to us only as an eminent instance, as eminent as we like, of our own conscious kind." He must not be "a morbidly special case"—but in romance he may well be. Again, says James, when economy demands the suppression of parts of the possible story they must not be merely "eliminated"; they must be foreshortened, summarized, compressed but nevertheless brought to bear on the whole. But in the looser universe of the romance, we may think "elimination" will be less criminal and unexplained hiatuses and discontinuities may positively contribute to the effect. To take an obvious case, in *Moby-Dick* we are content to think the sudden elimination of Bulkington an interesting oddity rather than a novelistic blunder and we gladly draw on the poetic capital Melville makes of it.

As for the moral significance of the novel, James sees a "perfect dependence of the 'moral' sense of a work of art on the amount of felt life concerned in producing it." We must ask, he says, "is it valid, in a word, is it genuine, is it sincere, the result of some direct impression or perception of life." These questions bear less on the romance, one of the assumptions of which is that it need not contain a full amount of felt life, that life may be felt indirectly, through legend, symbol, or allegory. Nor does the romance need the sincerity of the novel; indeed, as Lawrence points out, American romances, especially, tend to make their effect by a deep "duplicity" or ironic indirection.

To come finally to James's specific comments on the question we are considering. In the prefaces he follows his own advice as that had been expressed twenty-odd years earlier in "The Art of Fiction"—he sees no reason, that is, why the practicing writer should distinguish between novel and ro-

24

mance. There are good novels and bad ones, novels that have life and those that haven't—and this, for the novelist, is the only relevant question. The implication is that the novelist will be also the romancer if the "life" he is rendering extends into the realm of the "romantic." But if we are not, except as critics and readers, to distinguish between novel and romance, we still have to distinguish, within the novel that may be also a romance, the "romantic" from the "real." And this James essays in his Preface to *The American*.

In rereading this early novel James found a large element of romance in the free and easy way in which he had made his semilegendary hero Christopher Newman behave on his European travels. Particularly, James thought, the picture of the Bellegard family was "romantic." James had made them reject Newman as a vulgar manufacturer when actually common sense tells us that "they would positively have jumped at him." And James comments that "the experience here represented is the disconnected and uncontrolled experience—uncontrolled by our general sense of 'the way things happen'—which romance alone more or less successfully palms off on us." At the same time James finds an unexpected pleasure in rereading *The American*, which somewhat compensates for the lapses of verisimilitude. And his description of this pleasure makes a fair definition of the pleasure of romance—"the free play of so much unchallenged instinct . . . the happiest season of surrender to the invoked muse and the projected fable."*

"The disconnected and uncontrolled experience," then, is of the essence of romance, and any adequate definition must proceed from this postulate. First, however, one may

---

* Cf. Melville's plea to his reality-minded readers for latitude in the depiction of character and incident. The ideal reader, he says, will "want nature . . . ; but nature unfettered, exhilarated, in effect transformed. . . . It is with fiction as with religion: it should present another world, and yet one to which we feel the tie." (*The Confidence Man*, Chapter 33.)

clear out of the way certain conventional but inadequate descriptions of romance. It is not "a matter indispensably of boats, or of caravans, or of tigers, or of 'historical characters,' or of ghosts, or of forgers, or of detectives, or of beautiful wicked women, or of pistols and knives"—although one might perhaps be a little readier than James to think that these things might be of service. Yet one follows him assentingly when he decides that the common element in sensational tales is "the facing of danger" and then goes on to say that for most of us the danger represented by caravans and forgers is certainly benign or impotent compared with the "common and covert" dangers we face in our everyday existence, which may "involve the sharpest hazards to life and honor and the highest instant decisions and intrepidities of action."

The "romantic" cannot be defined, either, as "the far and the strange," since, as such, these things are merely unknown, whereas the "romantic" is something we know, although we know it indirectly. Nor is a novel romantic because its hero or heroine is. "It would be impossible to have a more romantic temper than Flaubert's Madame Bovary, yet nothing less resembles a romance than the record of her adventures." Nor can we say the presence or absence of "costume" is a crucial difference, for "where . . . does costume begin or end."

James then arrives at the following formulation:

The only *general* attribute of projected romance that I can see, the only one that fits all its cases, is the fact of the kind of experience with which it deals—experience liberated, so to speak; experience disengaged, disembroiled, disencumbered, exempt from the conditions that we usually know to attach to it and, if we wish so to put the matter, drag upon it, and operating in a medium which relieves it, in a particular interest, of the inconvenience of a *related*, a measurable state, a state subject to all our vulgar communities.

And James goes on in words that are particularly illustrative of his own art:

> The greatest intensity may so be arrived at evidently—when the sacrifice of community, of the "related" sides of situations, has not been too rash. It must to this end not flagrantly betray itself; we must even be kept if possible, for our illusion, from suspecting any sacrifice at all.

In a fully developed art of the novel there is, as James says, a "latent extravagance." In novelists of "largest responding imagination before the human scene," we do not find only the romantic or only reality but a "current . . . extraordinarily rich and mixed." The great novelist responds to the "need of performing his whole possible revolution, by the law of some rich passion in him for extremes."

To have a rich passion for extremes is to grasp both the real and the romantic. By the "real," James explains, he means "the things we cannot possibly *not* know, sooner or later, in one way or another." By the "romantic" he means "the things that, with all the facilities in the world, all the wealth and all the courage and all the wit and all the adventure, we never *can* directly know; the things that can reach us only through the beautiful circuit and subterfuge of our thought and our desire."

We hear much in these prefaces of the novelist's rich and mixed "current," of the possible "revolution" of his mind among extremes, of the "circuit" of thought and desire. James speaks, too, of the "conversion" that goes on in the mind of the novelist's characters between what happens to them and their *sense* of what happens to them, and of "the link of connection" between a character's "doing" and his "feeling." In other words James thinks that the novel does not find its essential being until it discovers what we may call the circuit of life among extremes or opposites, the circuit of life that passes through the real and the ideal, through the directly known and the mysterious or the indirectly known, through doing and feeling. Much of the

27

best American fiction does not meet James's specifications. It has not made the circuit James requires of the "largest responding imagination." And the closer it has stuck to the assumptions of romance the more capital it has made, when any capital has been made, exactly by leaving the Jamesian circuits broken. That very great capital can be made in this way James does not acknowledge or know, and hence his own hostility, and that of many of his followers, to the more extreme forms of American fiction—those we associate, for example, with Brockden Brown, Poe, Melville, and Faulkner.

Nevertheless James's theory of the novel, his idea of the circuit of life which allows him to incorporate in his novels so many of the attributes of romance, is the most complete and admirable theory, as at their best James's are the most complete and admirable novels yet produced by an American. And it is against James's theory and often, though certainly not always, his practice that we have to test the achievements of his compatriots. But the danger is that in doing so we should lapse into an easy disapproval of that "rich passion . . . for extremes" which James praised on his own grounds but which may be seen operating to advantage on other grounds too.

# Chapter II

# BROCKDEN BROWN'S MELODRAMAS

*melodrama*

## *Wieland*

THE novels of Charles Brockden Brown are rather severely limited in their style, tone, and subject matter by the special genius of their author, a genius which was profound but narrow. Nevertheless these novels strikingly illustrate some of the generalizations made in the preceding chapter. Although there is little or no pastoral feeling in Brown, melodrama—the other main element of American romance, as this was defined above—is vividly present in his novels. Brown was the first writer of fiction in this country to use melodrama significantly and he was thus a genuine precursor of the later romance-novelists.

Between 1798 and 1801 Charles Brockden Brown wrote six novels—*Wieland, or The Transformation; Ormond; Edgar Huntly; Arthur Mervyn; Clara Howard;* and *Jane Talbot.* The general opinion that *Wieland* is the best of these productions is correct, for it is indeed a book full of beauty and horror. *Wieland* is also a very considerable intellectual accomplishment, although like Brown's other novels, it is an impetuous and uneven work. As a novelist Brown has many faults, and these faults are the ones usually associated with "Gothic" fiction, the genre with which Brown begins and from which he departs in certain ways that become significant in relation to the later development of the novel in America. One often finds in his books a sententious dullness alternating with rather ill-conceived sensational happenings and absurd posturings of character and rhetoric. Even in *Wieland* the writing tends to be hasty and careless. His plots, though undoubtedly exciting in *Wieland* and *Edgar Huntly,* are generally ill-made, and he leaves obvious mistakes and incongruities uncorrected. But Brown had an authentic genius that well merited the enthusiasm felt for his writing by Shelley, Keats, and Hazlitt, as well as by Cooper and Hawthorne. He was a minor master of shocking realism, as in his scenes of city life in Philadelphia. The portraits of Constantia Dudley in *Ormond* and of the heroines of his last two novels show his considerable knowledge of the feminine sensibility, and it may be that in this he was not surpassed among American novelists until the emergence of Henry James (which, however, is not saying much—in view of the general inability of American novelists such as Cooper, Hawthorne, and Melville to draw sympathetically realistic portraits of women). But Brown's true *forte* was melodrama of a sort that allowed him to advance beyond the Gothic novel and to inaugurate that peculiar vision of things we often find in American fiction—a vision of things that might be described as a heightened and mysteriously portentous representation of abstract symbols and ideas on the one hand and, on the other, of the involutions of the private psyche. Brown's genuine though abortive originality can be attributed to qualities which he himself said should appear in any successful novel: "force of mind" and "intellectual energy." These qualities, together with his sheer novelistic talent, entitle him to an important place at the beginning of the tradition of the American novel. He is, as Malcolm Cowley has noted, the originator of that strand of dark romance that runs through the tradition.

*Wieland* reflects, though not oppressively so, the influences which formed Brown's bookish mind. The radical spirit of the time into which he was born strongly appealed to him, and he early became acquainted with French philosophy and political doctrine. His ideas were further shaped by Godwin's *Political Justice* (1793) and Mary Wollstonecraft's *Rights of Women* (1792), and his fictions show an impassioned response to Godwin's novel *Caleb Williams* (1794). Besides considerable reading of the great English authors and of the Greeks and Romans (of whom, however, he shows only a provincial understanding) he was well versed in the sentimental novel of Richardson, the Gothic novels of Mrs. Radcliffe, and the so-called doctrinal novels of Bage and Holcroft. The culture of Rousseau and the poetic mysteries of romantic Germany permeate the rural seat of the Wieland family on the banks of the Schuylkill.

In the Richardsonian manner the story of *Wieland* is told in the form of an extended letter or memoir by a woman whose hand trembles at the enormity of the incidents she must relate but whose courage is sustained through the labors of composition by the duty to tell the truth and inculcate a moral. Clara Wieland, the sister of the ill-fated titular hero of the book, recounts how their father emigrated from Germany to America and after establishing a comfortable country estate outside Philadelphia, began to show signs of being overborne by the religious fanaticism that had succeeded the rigorous commercial training of his early years. On a hill near the house, overlooking the Schuylkill, he constructs a charming temple in the neo-classic manner, in which he prays at noon and at midnight. A baleful gleam being seen in this temple one night, his children discover that the elder Wieland has been killed either by an unknown assailant who struck him and set fire to his clothes or, more probably, by spontaneous combustion, a phenomenon the probability of which Brown attests to in a learned footnote.

In the ensuing years the younger Wieland lives in rustic tranquility with his wife Catherine, his sister, and his wife's brother, Pleyel. They devote themselves to reading, music, philosophic conversation, and the production of amateur theatricals. This pleasant intercourse is made profound by the reflective Wieland with his streak of Calvinism, lively by Pleyel, who speaks with the gay skepticism of the Enlightenment, and delightful by the sensibility and intellectuality of the ladies.

But then enters the real hero, or hero-villain, of the piece. After exclaiming, "O most fatal and potent of mankind. . . . My blood is congealed and my fingers are palsied when I call up thy image," the narrator describes Carwin as a man whose shambling gait at first proclaims him an uncouth rustic but whose heroic qualities are as quickly to be seen in the melancholy, pallid face and the sunken eyes with their "radiance inexpressibly serene and potent" as they are to be heard in the ravishing, mellifluous tones of his voice. There is about him an air of adventure, mystery, and eternal wandering, an air also of being pitiful and doomed—he is a close cousin of Schedoni in Mrs. Radcliffe's *Italian*.

Unknown to any but himself Carwin is an accomplished ventriloquist, and he begins to practice his art upon his new companions. The mysterious voices, produced by Carwin, which Wieland now begins to hear conspire with increasing signs that like his father he is falling victim to a religious madness. He hears a voice, not produced by Carwin, which he thinks is that of God and which demands that he kill his wife and children. This he does, and Brown adduces evidence that a local Pennsylvania farmer had actually killed his family under a similar misapprehension; also in the interest of scientific truth he cites evidence about the existence and efficacy of ventriloquism. One may agree with Whittier, who saw in *Wieland* an eloquent tract against religious fanaticism, that the "transformation scene" in which Wieland receives the command from God is "scarcely exceeded" in "sublime horror" by "the masters of Greek tragedy." But unfortunately the theme of the madness of a family loses in Brown's hands most of its tragic impact because the center of the stage is so much usurped by the putative seduction of Clara by Carwin.

Impelled by sensuality but more so by an uncontrollable curiosity, Carwin, after seducing Clara's maid, takes to snooping systematically among the diaries and other personal belongings which he discovers in her house. He terrifies her at night by simulating undiscoverable voices which threaten rape and murder. He poisons the mind of Pleyel, with whom she is in love, against her. But at the end Carwin saves her in her bedroom by uttering an apparently divine command to the shaggy maniac Wieland not to kill her, a mission which, having escaped from prison, he is about to accomplish. Wieland then kills himself with the penknife which Clara has been planning to use either on herself or on Carwin whenever he chooses to make the ultimate demand upon her, which, however, he never gets around to do.

Clara has had ambivalent opinions of Carwin all along and seems oddly drawn to him even when she suspects him of systematically warping her brother's mind and leading him to murder his wife and children. He has little difficulty in convincing her in an extended soliloquy in the last pages of the book that if he is a criminal he is a high-minded one whose actual crimes are venial, being merely the result of a certain necessary unscrupulousness in the choice of means to ends which are honorable or even utopian. She is ready to accept his bohemianism, his Rousseauistic emotional freebootery, his voyeurism, and his ventriloquial misdeeds because they seem to be akin to scientific method

33

and to be sanctioned by ends vaguely but excitingly suggestive of revolutionary moral and political ideals.

Of the nature of these ideals we learn something in a
fragment called *Memoirs of Carwin, the Biloquist*, apparently intended as a part of *Wieland* but not published until
1803–4. As a youth without prospects in Ireland, Carwin
had been taken up by the aristocrat Ludloe, a man of radical opinions who belongs to a revolutionary movement,
much akin to the inverted Jesuitry of the Society of the
Illuminati, which flourished clandestinely in Europe before
the French Revolution and in which Brown was interested.
With the air rather of a Nietzschean free spirit than of a
bourgeois libertarian, Ludloe teaches his pupil to practice
a self-interested immoralism in all immediate matters, to
disdain all bourgeois opinions and institutions, and to sub-
mit himself to those "years of solicitude and labour" after
which he may hope to soar "above vulgar heads," approximate "divine attributes, and prescribe the condition of a
large portion of mankind." The utopian villain represented
by Carwin and Ludloe is Brown's most striking modification of the conceptions of Godwin. Brown adopted something of Godwin's headlong style, his Gothic effects, his
sententiousness, and his theme of the impoverished protégé
and the villainous master. What Brown added was the
high-minded, utopian tone and an implied disapproval of
the way in which innocent persons, like Clara in *Wieland*
(and Constantia Dudley in *Ormond*), are cold-bloodedly
used as objects of experiment by relentlessly rational villains. Many changes were to be rung on this note, without
altering its original meaning, in the fictions of Poe, Hawthorne, and James.

To be sure, it is the humanitarian Brown who disapproves
of Carwin and Ludloe; on other sides of his character he
clearly admires them and thinks of them as persons who
will appeal to readers who have "soaring passions and intellectual energy" and will agree with him that in selecting
subjects for novels "the chief point is not the virtue of a

34

character. The prime regard is to the genius and force of mind that is displayed. Great energy employed in the promotion of vicious purposes, constitutes a very useful spectacle." Useful no doubt, but moral considerations aside, one notes that Brown could not help putting something of himself into his hero-villains. They share certain qualities of the novelist; Carwin "early discovered in himself a remarkable facility in imitating the voice and gestures of others"; they all have a consuming curiosity which makes them pitiless observers; and they tend to be adept at mystification and disguise.

*Carwin like Brown*

## Edgar Huntly

*Edgar Huntly* is an exciting novel, second in importance among Brown's works to *Wieland*. In this book Brown is able to practice again his skill at uniting swift action (of which there is more here than in the other novels) with abnormal psychological states, philosophical reflection, and a haunted nocturnal atmosphere. In his Preface, Brown proclaims his impatience with the Gothic novel and its European lumber of castles, monks, and dungeons and resolves to use native materials without loss of effect. Cast somewhat in the form of a detective story—formally at least, the question all the way through is who killed Waldegrave, the friend of Huntly—Brown's novel breaks into two loosely related parts. The first and less interesting recounts the origin of Clithero, a Carwin without intellectual talents who has fled to America from a scene of murder in Ireland (which is, one gathers, a nest of villainy). Although innocent, Clithero is insane and takes to walking about the countryside in his sleep, hiding in caves and sobbing; apparently by the power of suggestion, Huntly also becomes a sleepwalker, a device of which very effective use is made by the author. The second part of the book recounts the adventures of Huntly as he wanders in the woods seeking Clithero. There are stirring scenes, compounded of violence, horror, and shocking realism, and involving panthers and marauding Indians—nor is the force of the narrative lost by the rather obvious improbabilities. In the Preface to *The Spy* Cooper, who paid high tribute to *Wieland*, scoffed at Huntly's lurid encounter in a cave with the panther and the Indians. Yet the scene is fully the equal of some of Cooper's own, and there can be no doubt that the author of the Leather-Stocking tales profited by Brown's example. Indeed this scene and those related to it (beginning at Chapter XVI) are among the most original and influential in early American literature, as the reader may be led to think who compares Huntly's experience of waking up in the dark at the bottom of the cave and not knowing where he is with the similar happening in Poe's *The Pit and the Pendulum*. And certainly *Edgar Huntly*, with its setting of remote farms, of rugged hills, forested valleys, swift streams, bogs, fens, caves, precipices, sudden storms and night winds, hidden trails, and Indian retreats, successfully claims the American wilderness for fiction and does much to justify the author's idea that "he who shall examine objects with his own eyes, who shall employ the European models merely for the improvement of his taste, and adapt his fiction to all that is genuine and peculiar in the scene before him, will be entitled at least to praise of originality."

When he dissociates himself from "Gothic" romance in the Preface of *Edgar Huntly*, Brown of course refers to the works of writers like Mrs. Radcliffe, Monk Lewis, and Godwin. In *Wieland* he had used some of the more or less meretricious techniques of this second-rate, if also sometimes exciting and effective fiction. It is possible to think of *Edgar Huntly* as a Gothic fiction in the sense that it retains the Gothic tone, the highly wrought effect of horror, surprise, victimization, and the striving for abnormal psychological states, even though the action has been "naturalized," so to speak, by being staged in the American countryside.

In current usage the word "Gothic" is sometimes applied
to other American novels—for example, Melville's *Pierre* or
Faulkner's *Absalom, Absalom!* The term has taken on a
general meaning beyond the Mrs. Radcliffe kind of thing
and is often used rather loosely to suggest violence, mysteries, improbabilities, morbid passions, inflated and complex language of any sort. It is a useful word but since,
in its general reference, it becomes confused with "melodrama," it seems sensible to use "melodrama" for the general category and reserve "Gothic" for its more limited
meaning. The Gothic novel descended mainly from the
melodrama of the late Elizabethan and Jacobean stage.
And thus historically as well as morphologically, "Gothic,"
as it applies to the novel, appears to be a subdivision of
"melodrama."

## A Note on Melodrama

It has long been the custom of criticism to praise Brown
as a realist, to speak highly of his descriptions of city life
and the ravages of yellow fever in *Ormond* and *Arthur
Mervyn*, to commend his knowledge of the feminine sensibility, and to deprecate his sensationalism and his mysteries
wherever these are not carefully attributed to some natural
causation. This makes good sense, since Brown more often
than not intended to succeed, and often did so, as a realist.
And the principle that the history of the novel has been
and will be allied with the fate of realism in the arts generally is a necessary one. Nevertheless Brown's elevated
rhetoric and his melodramatic effects forecast much that is
admirable in Poe, Hawthorne, Melville, Faulkner, and even
James.

In his *Main Currents of American Thought* Parrington
regards the melodrama in Brown's novels as the dross which
unhappily sullies the gold of realism. He deplores the in-

fluence of this melodrama and is sorry that Brown thus contributed to "distorting the growth of native fiction for half a century." Like many modern critics of American literature, Parrington evidently regards a penchant for melodrama as evidence of retrograde views in morals and politics, although, if we remember the example of Euripides, Marlowe, and Dickens, we may think melodrama as good a vehicle for radical opinions as it proves to be for conservative ones in Dostoevski, Conrad, and James. The fact is that most people use the word "melodrama" only in the opprobrious sense. Yet melodrama is an ancient and honorable, if easily degraded, form, and the American novel cannot be understood without some attention to its methods.

The world of *Wieland* is melodramatically conceived. It is an abruptly dualistic, Manichaean world, there being a whiff of brimstone about the villain and of divinity in the titular hero. It is clear, furthermore, that the radical dichotomy of things will never be resolved by the merely formal belief of the characters in their deism and rationalism but can be escaped only by transcendent experiences of horror, heroism, love, or death. As is usual in melodrama, there is a cruel victimization. There is also a strict conventionalism which creates a tension between itself and the violent indeterminacy of events. In *Wieland* emotions are conventionalized; they are powerful but there are only a few of them, and the characters are always passing abruptly from the depths of despair and horror to heights of joy and rapture. The language too is highly formalized and often stilted. But whereas there is some sense in the complaint that Brown writes "he had not escaped the amorous contagion" instead of "he fell in love," this is really to miss the point. A stately and elevated language, like the measures of a classic ballet, is as useful in the aesthetic economy of the book as is the tireless rationalism of the conversation. The related complaint that Brown's characters are not realistic may also becloud the fact that the melodramatic

38

method demands characters of a somewhat abstract and conventionalized sort, so that in the extremities of the action they become less human beings than *loci* of the clash of ideas and forces. Finally, one may note a remarkable modernity in the fact that Brown conceives of politics as a melodramatic action, although he fails to make much use of this idea. It was to be further exploited, tentatively by Hawthorne in *The Blithedale Romance,* more fully by James in *The Princess Casamassima,* the only political melodrama by an American which will bear comparison with those of Dostoevski, Conrad, and Malraux.

Although not a writer of the first rank, Brown made an important contribution to the American novel. Not only did he "naturalize" the spirit of melodrama by showing how this form might be applied to native materials and a native setting and thus give a new tone and significance to the standard effects of melodramatic fiction. More important than this achievement was his demonstration of the uses—aesthetic, psychological, and intellectual—to which melodrama may be put. For it is in the skillful use of this relatively inferior art form for purposes beyond the rendition of extravagant and sensational happenings that the American novelists have excelled. They have known, for example, how to take advantage of the abstractness of melodrama and its capacity to evoke ultimates and absolutes, in order to dramatize theological, moral, and less frequently political ideology. In the capacity of this literary form to adduce opposites and contraries, they have seen the chance to create effective ironies. And in its capacity to elicit in its peculiarly striking way the dark side of consciousness they have discovered new ways to evoke complex mental and emotional states and new dramatic contexts for psychological and moral analysis.

The several uses to which melodrama may be put partly account for the anomaly noted in Chapter I, where the observation was made that many American novels have great "complexity of feeling" but that they also have simplified

*uses of melodrama*

characters and events. Melodrama has offered to the American novelists a simplified set of conventions, and all through our literary history there has been produced a vast body of inferior fiction by forgotten authors who made no use of this genre beyond the evocation of sensation or sentiment. But it is not enough to say of the great novelists—such as Hawthorne, Melville, James, and Faulkner, all of whom are dimly forecast in the novels of Brown—that they became great by *transcending* melodrama, thereby becoming genuinely tragic or comic writers. One must also add that they became great by discovering or rediscovering those special uses of melodrama noted above and that these uses of melodrama have enhanced an admittedly complex art. This is only to say that they have done in their concerted and characteristic way what the poets from Sophocles to Dante and Shakespeare and the novelists from Balzac and Stendhal to Dickens and Conrad have always known how to do.

The highest form of art is doubtless tragedy or that serious kind of comedy that approaches tragedy. But only occasionally and under the most favorable circumstances does tragedy emerge from the all but universal and perennial context of melodrama; for example, from many points of view a majority of the "tragedies" of the Athenian stage seem really to be melodramas. Roughly one may say that tragedy does not emerge out of melodrama until a notable and fully rounded character significantly resists the dire actions of the plot. The American novel abounds in striking but rather flatly conceived *figures*—from Natty Bumppo, Hester Prynne, and Captain Ahab on down to Henry Fleming, Frederic Henry, Joe Christmas, and Thomas Sutpen—but with certain exceptions mostly to be found in the novels of James, Dreiser and Faulkner, it has been poor in notable and fully rounded *characters*.

There are perhaps many reasons why melodrama should be so prominent in American literature. Some of them are suggested in Chapter I. Here one may point out that the "naturalistic" approach to the novel followed what may be called very generally the Calvinist approach of the pre-Civil-War writers. Since the naturalistic novel (see Chapter IX on Norris) is close to the spirit, though certainly not the letter, of deterministic science, what happened was that a new imagination emerged which seemed to be radically different from the older one but was in many ways similar to it—in the sense that both imaginations conceive of human beings not as heroes but as victims of dire, intractable, and contradictory forces.

To this may be added that melodrama is suitable to writers who do not have a firm sense of living in a culture. The American novelists tend to ideology and psychology; they are adept at depicting the largest public abstractions and the smallest and most elusive turn of the inner mind. But they do not have a firm sense of a social arena where ideology and psychology find a concrete representation and are seen in their fullest human significance. It is this thick collaboration of the strands of human experience which makes a "culture" and it is in this sense a culture or the illusion of one that makes the context of tragedy. Without it you have melodrama, which might be called tragedy in a vacuum. What generates significance in a tragedy is the resistance which a culture and the hero who is its type are able to offer to forces finally beyond human control. And the resistance must be active; it must bring the contradictions of experience to rest, even if at the moment of defeat, in a newly confirmed awareness of man's power of universally significant moral action. It cannot afford to be, like the resistance commonly depicted in American novels, passive, stoic, and private. Yet, as I have tried to point out, there are certain advantages in letting these forces go unresisted, advantages which in the hands of a master can ensure a brilliant and profound narrative art.

41

# Chapter III

# THE SIGNIFICANCE OF COOPER

Opinion as to the value of Fenimore Cooper's novels has varied markedly in this country, although abroad he has always enjoyed a reputation as an original American classic. In the past we have been embarrassedly self-conscious about Cooper, as we have been about American culture itself, a feeling made worse by Cooper's being the first of our major writers and, as such, presenting a special claim to significance. This claim has been amply requited in the standard histories of American literature, the authors of which, although they have generally pointed out the defects of Cooper's style, have not failed to respond favorably to the great dull imposing importance of his books.

It was this quasi-official overestimation of Cooper that √ irked and baffled Mark Twain. And the extreme disagreement about Cooper is well mirrored in the contrast between Mark Twain's "Fenimore Cooper's Literary Offenses" and the three adulatory utterances by Thomas Lounsbury, Brander Matthews, and Wilkie Collins he quotes at the beginning of his essay. Besides being a famous burlesque Mark Twain's essay is a serious though limited piece of criticism (which I will have occasion to mention later). Meanwhile, one is content to notice the abyss between Wilkie Collins's idea that "Cooper is the greatest artist in the domain of romantic fiction yet produced in America" and Mark Twain's specification of the literary rules Cooper violates. These rules require, among other things, that "the personages in the tale shall be alive, except in the case of corpses, and that always the reader shall be able to tell the corpses from the others. But this detail has been overlooked in the *Deerslayer* tale." Between these two extremes there have always been readers of Cooper who can enjoy him simply as a story-teller, a writer of romances and adventure tales, without worrying too much about literary offenses.

One reader who confesses to being able to read Cooper in this pleasurable way is D. H. Lawrence. And yet in his *Studies in Classic American Literature* Lawrence went on to explain not only the pleasure he found in Cooper but also the importance of Cooper as a kind of mythic demiurge or Homer of American literature. He saw in Natty Bumppo, Chingachgook, and their associates in the Leather-Stocking tales a new product of the poetic imagination. He saw that although the "American Scott" was influenced by the Waverley novels, he was an original and that his real descendants were not American Bulwer-Lyttons and American Stevensons but such writers as Melville. Lawrence's ideas*

* Opinion about Cooper during the last twenty years, when it has been interesting at all, has had to be in one way or another an elaboration or revision of Lawrence. Lawrence's approach to American literature, which may be described variously as historical, cultural, or mythic, has been congenial to those modern critics who have not devoted themselves merely to textual analysis. The recent critical effort has responded to the tone of the times, and the times have been all in favor of the reassessment of the American past and a consolidation of knowledge and

gained more credence because, without mentioning it, he clearly agrees with most of the allegations of Mark Twain's essay. He says, in effect, Yes, yes, that is all true, but observe that out of the welter of literary defects and absurdities there emerges an original conception of the life of man and its significance which will be mirrored again and again in the works of later American authors, not excluding *Huckleberry Finn.*

There are over thirty Cooper novels in which to observe literary offenses. None of them is free of the posturings, arid rhetoric, and inert inventories for which the author is notorious. He had some of the gifts of the true novelist and more of those of the romancer, and these gifts often serve him well over the short run. Usually his successes are scored in scenes of intense and violent action; he excels with ambuscades, combats, flights and pursuit, and all forms of forest melodrama. He is very good, too, at nocturnal terror and mystery. He is unsurpassed at rendering the panoramic effects suggested to him by the sea or by the American

---

opinion about it. The underlying spirit of this critical effort has been similar to that which inspired Van Wyck Brooks and his contemporaries during the decade or more after 1915 to "rediscover America" and to redefine the "usable past." This spirit was what moved Lawrence himself; his book, which had all the considerable advantages of being written by a sympathetic but critical foreigner, was published in 1922. History has fully justified the critics involved in this first period of reassessment and consolidation. Of the second period of historical criticism— that of the last fifteen years—it can at least be said that it has had the advantages of its defects. If the defects have been pedantry, academicism, lack of interesting moral and political ideas, and a tendency toward religiosity and gentility, the advantages have been the accomplishment of a good deal of useful scholarly and critical journeywork, a concertedness of effort, and an ability to place a convincing historical foundation under the valuable intuitions of writers like Lawrence, Brooks, and Constance Rourke. These critics and their contemporaries give an impression of brilliance but also of a sort of messianic instability and prophetic intuitiveness. It is now possible to see the American past in a somewhat more solid historical context.

45

forest and prairie. He can do acceptably well with a professional assassin on the sinister byways of Venice, as in *The
Bravo;* a prince living as a hermit in a Roman ruin in Germany, as in *The Heidenmauer,* with John Paul Jones elud-
ing the British men-of-war on the stormy North Sea, as in
*The Pilot;* with George Washington seen fleetingly at night
through the window of a cabin in the mountains, as in *The
Spy.* Above all, of course, he can do magnificently with
Natty Bumppo in the forest or on the lake or the prairie.

Usually his rendition of character and setting is unsatisfactory. In characterizing his people he makes the mistake
of reporting their etiquette instead of their manners and of
judging their propriety instead of their morals. His characters, especially his "females," as he always calls them, are
usually sticks. He offers us a great many details about the
ship, the house, the carriage, or the town his people are
in. And yet unless he has been able to set some swift in-
trigue or combat in motion, the setting remains—even when
thoroughly inventoried—scattered and inert, and fails to develop into that "enveloping action" which in a coherent
novel the setting should be.

Not only are Cooper's novels disorganized technically. It
was inevitable, given the time and place in which Cooper
wrote, that the culture his novels depict should also be disorganized. As Yvor Winters says, Cooper's writings are "a
mass of fragments . . . but the fragments are those of a
civilization." They are the fragments of a civilization in this
way at least: that they established for later writers certain
images of American culture and proposed certain ideological and aesthetic ways of understanding American life and
representing it. If Cooper is of only secondary importance
as an artist, he is of the first importance both as a creator
and critic of culture. In his novels and other writings he
was both the analyst and the visionary of American conditions. There was always in the back of his mind the idea
that each of his novels was a "letter to his countrymen"
(the title of one of his studies of the difference between

European and American culture). He wanted to be the spokesman of his country, as well as its severest critic, and he thought of his novels as public acts.

Exactly because he conceived of his duty as public and national, and also, of course, because he was among the first on the scene, Cooper was able to formulate some of the principal attitudes and dilemmas of American fiction. These we see expressed not only in the novels but also in the didactic cultural studies like *Notions of the Americans*. But for our purposes these attitudes and dilemmas can best be brought out by a consideration of two of Cooper's most characteristic novels, *Satanstoe* and *The Prairie*—reserving *The Prairie* for last (even though *The Prairie* is early and *Satanstoe* late Cooper) because it is a part of the Leather-Stocking series, for which Cooper was correct in thinking posterity would value him most highly.

## Satanstoe

This novel was published in 1845, the first volume of a trilogy which later included *The Chainbearer* (a reference to the measuring chain of land surveyors) and *The Redskins*. The trilogy was conceived as a protest against the Anti-Rent agitations of the 1840's, which threatened to break up the landed estates of Westchester and the Hudson Valley. Cooper wanted to demonstrate the social and cultural advantages to democracy of private estates and aristocratic families, and to this end he set out to recount the history of the Littlepage family. *Satanstoe* relates the fortunes of the family in colonial days and particularly, as the author says in his Preface, "the early career, the attachment, the marriage, etc., of Mr. Cornelius Littlepage." The Preface makes it all sound like a very formidable piece of history, but we are led to hope (and we are not entirely disappointed) that the hand of the novelist will be felt, by

47

the announcement that the author will stress the "capricious and uncalculated passions, motives, or impulses" of men and women rather than the "philosophical agencies" that interest historians.

The novel offers us a careful, loving, and interesting, if labored, study of manners in a very attractive provincial setting, plus a dangerous sleigh ride on the ice of the Hudson River (one of the best episodes in all of Cooper) and a skirmish between the young hero and the Hurons in the wilderness of northern New York after the battle of Ticonderoga.

The persons of the novel are types. There is Jason Newcombe, the Yankee-Puritan schoolteacher from Connecticut, who sums up the characteristics Cooper tended in satirical moments to associate with the New Englanders. Newcombe, although he has courage and a certain cold probity, is narrow-minded, canting, awkward, calculating, joyless, and quite without reverence for life, tradition, or station. By way of welcome contrast, Cooper introduces us to three different social groups. There is first the Westchester aristocracy, represented by the Littlepage family, to whom the young scion, Corny, was born in 1737 at the family manse, called Satanstoe. They are of English descent and they have the manners and sentiments of traditional landholders. They love their houses, their orchards, their Negro servants; they pay heartfelt homage to the Crown. Compared with the New Englanders, they live genially and easily. Their typical clergyman, the Reverend Mr. Worden, goes to cockfights, loves wine and gentlemanly frolics. Then there is the Rockland County Dutch-American aristocracy, the Van Valkenburgs, who live very much like the Littlepages but are appropriately stolid, sticklers for detail, given to rare spells of hard drinking and unbridled adventure. There is also the Albany aristocracy, represented by Guert Ten Eyck. These people resemble the Littlepages and Van Valkenburgs, except that being close to the frontier they are a little rougher and less educated.

48

The English soldier in the colonies is represented by Bulstrode; he is manly, clever, rich—a kind of ideal Englishman, in fact. But he lacks a certain delicacy or subtlety which the Americans have and which makes it impossible for him to understand why he is rejected by the heroine of the novel, Anneke Mordaunt. (Cooper instructs us to pronounce his heroine's name On-a-kay.) As for Anneke, she is one of the very few Cooper heroines who show any spark of life. She is appealing, virtuous, blushing, decorously ardent. But it takes a desperate situation in a log fortress surrounded by Hurons to extract from her an expression of passionate interest in the hero.

*Satanstoe* has a section about the genteel life in Manhattan which gives some sense of what that must have been like in pre-Revolutionary times. There is, for example, that standard delight of novelists, a scene involving amateur dramatics. Bulstrode excels at this pastime, but in his rough English way he does not perceive the maidenly disapproval of *The Beaux' Stratagem* manifested by Anneke's silence after the performance. Also in Manhattan the young people witness the Negro saturnalia known as the Pinkster festival and, presumably, react to it in various ways; but this is a great disappointment to the reader who, through an unpardonable novelist's error, is only told about the festival and not allowed to see it. (The same thing happens in *The Headsman,* where Cooper reports, somewhat more in detail to be sure, the Christianized pagan festival of the vine at Vevey but fails to *use* it to enrich our sense of the life in the novel, as a more coherent novelist would do— Hemingway, for example, with his festival of the bullfight at Pamplona in *The Sun Also Rises.*)

I have concentrated at what may seem too great length on the characters and social groups of *Satanstoe* because these are what Cooper himself is interested in. He is defending the way of life that makes these people possible and gives them their manners as well as their aristocratic sense of duty and honor. The plot is slight. It involves car-

49

rying out the duty of the Littlepages to take the long view of the destiny of the family. To this end, Corny and his companions brave the hardships of the forests and mountains in order to stake out a vast tract of land north of Albany. After doing this, and meeting with some of the predictable *contretemps* of the Huron-infested wilderness, Corny settles down with Anneke into the admirable (but unknown to them, doomed) way of life Cooper has given them.

Cooper was well aware of the formidable difficulties facing the novelist of manners and morals in America. In *Notions of the Americans* he complained, as Brockden Brown had before him and Hawthorne and James were to do after him, about the "poverty of materials":

> There is scarcely an ore which contributes to the wealth of the author, that is found, here, in veins as rich as in Europe. There are no annals for the historian; no follies (beyond the most vulgar and commonplace) for the satirist; no manners for the dramatist; no obscure fictions for the writer of romance; no gross and hardy offences against decorum for the moralist; nor any of the rich artificial auxiliaries of poetry.

He added that American institutions, contrary to what might be supposed, were not "favorable to novelties and variety." He lamented the fact that all Americans tended to behave like all other Americans and thus to offer little by way of dramatic spectacle or psychological interest to the novelist.

Cooper concluded that it was the business of the American writer to discover new sources of fiction, cut off as he was from so many of those sources that had nourished the European novel. One solution was to do what *Satanstoe* does, concentrate on one of the few places and times in American history which preserved to some extent the settled traditional life of rural England. But *Satanstoe* is rather thin fare compared with any number of English novels of

rural manners. And there seem to be at least two reasons
why this should be so. For one thing, the aristocratic life
in America, even in 1758 (when the action of *Satanstoe*
occurs), had lost some of its color in the clear American
air; and, for another, Cooper had more desire than ability
to render fully even such life as there was in the Littlepage
family. Still, there is in this late novel a new relaxation and
geniality about the author, a new readiness to observe the
way people look, act, and speak. There is a loving sense
of fact that humanizes to some extent Cooper's high sententiousness and modulates his rigid, gentlemanly style (for
Cooper, in the words of D. H. Lawrence, "was a gentleman
in the worst sense"). Cooper's novel does after all recapture
a way of life that sticks in the memory of anyone who has
read the book sympathetically.

*Satanstoe* suggests but does not present fully the fundamental contradiction of Cooper's thought, a contradiction
which becomes the vital paradox at the source of his powers as a romancer. The forest sequences of the novel imply
that the ideal young man of the New World, though his
values will be formed by a traditional society, will also be
at home on the margins of society where all social values
disappear and are replaced by a strict code of the woods,
which entails skill in the lore of the hunt, honor in personal
conduct, piety toward nature, stoic forbearance, a sort of
programmatic masculinity, and celibacy. This is the habitat
and the code of Cooper's most vivid hero, Natty Bumppo
—or, as he is variously called, Leather-Stocking, Deerslayer,
Long Rifle, Pathfinder, and Hawk-Eye. Cooper thus has
two very different heroes in Corny Littlepage and Natty
Bumppo. True, there are formal similarities between the
aristocratic morals of the one and the stoic code of the other
—both involve religion, both insist on hierarchic values. But
one of Cooper's heroes is the product of society and the
other, though he seems to imply a life not apart from society but on its margins, seems ultimately to deny the whole
idea of society.

In short, Cooper found it necessary in America to be both a conservative and an anarchist. The vitality of his romances, the very form in which he sees things, the actions that he is able to make vivid—these stem from the political contradiction at the center of his thought. If some of his most moving passages are elegiac, it is because the very terms in which he conceived the quality of life were becoming, even as he wrote, historically outmoded. The Anti-Rent Laws would of course succeed in breaking up the Westchester estates, leaving little possibility of an hereditary aristocracy. And as the frontier drove west from Albany and Cooperstown across the plains and into California, there would be no more room for Natty Bumppo and his companions. These historical changes, however, did not invalidate, as a source of the American novel, the basic contradiction of Cooper's mind. In different terms the contradiction between the values of a traditional society and those of the lone individual in the marginal hinterland is as much a part of Faulkner's view of things as it was of Cooper's. With some modification the same contradiction lies behind the works of Melville and Mark Twain, among others. It is clear that crotchety as Cooper's thinking sometimes was, he exemplified a dilemma, and explored some of the aesthetic uses to which it might be put, that was not peculiar to him but was at the heart of American culture.

## The Prairie

The five Leather-Stocking novels are *The Pioneers* (1823), *The Last of the Mohicans* (1826), *The Prairie* (1827), *The Pathfinder* (1840), and *The Deerslayer* (1841). They recount the life of the hero (although they do much else besides) from about 1740 to 1806. The chronological order of what takes place in the novels differs from the order in which they were written. In *The Deerslayer*, Natty

Bumppo is a youth winning his spurs; he matures in *The Last of the Mohicans* and *The Pathfinder*, grows old in *The Pioneers*, and dies in *The Prairie*. As James Grossman proposes in his book on Cooper, the reader should proceed through the novels in the order in which they were written. This allows him to share in Cooper's sense of discovery as the aging, unhappy, already anachronistic hunter of *The Pioneers* is imaginatively recreated in the marvelous youth of *The Deerslayer*. Natty Bumppo begins as a real man, and then, by gradual accretion, legendary tales and folklore gather about him until finally he and his adventures and companions are transformed into a general myth.

The word "myth" is not easy to define. But it is a necessary and useful word, and cannot be abandoned. The problem of definition is simplified if we notice that the novel, ever since it began to take its modern form in the seventeenth century, has been pre-eminently a social form of literature and that consequently whenever it has taken on a mythic component, the myth has been of the political, social, or more broadly, the cultural sort. For our purposes, then, the word myth will not include a metaphysical or theological meaning. As it appears in the novel, myth is very seldom a way of ordering transcendent knowledge or belief. It is a way of sanctioning and giving significance to those crises of human experience which are cultural as well as personal: birth, initiation into life, ideal friendship, marriage, war against man or nature, death. It gives significance to these crises of life by an emotive appeal to the past, to the traditions of the culture, or to the superhuman powers of heroes.

In his departures from realism, Cooper is strictly a mythic writer. He does not invent complex poetic symbols, as Henry James or Melville sometimes do. He is never the allegorist, as Hawthorne sometimes is. Cooper banks on the powers of myth to make his narratives vivid and to reaffirm and transmit the values he cherishes.

But are these values really "cultural"? Can we transpose

them into any imaginable social form? Do the mythicized life and opinions of Natty Bumppo affect in any way our idea of culture? The answer to these questions must be radically equivocal, because the significance of the myth of Cooper's hero is itself equivocal, and in fact self-contradictory. In its more conscious and constructive meanings, it is a myth of culture, since the critical episodes in the life of the hero are those which universally involve the life of society, no matter what that society may be. Also Cooper's own ideal social order is imaginatively recaptured and enhanced by the myth—that shared and harmonious social order in which the hereditary aristocracy dwells in its country mansions while on the borders of its lands Natty Bumppo stalks the forests. Such a culture was momentarily possible in eighteenth-century America. But since it had become all but impossible in the time of Cooper, the myth that enhances and justifies it has perforce to be nostalgic, ironic, and self-contradictory. Out of this dilemma come Cooper's most powerful feelings, and the myth of the Leather-Stocking tales, cultural in intent and in its ideology becomes distorted under the pressures of history in such a way that its ultimate meaning is anti-cultural. If, Cooper seems to say, we cannot have the aristocratic agrarian society, in which Cornelius Littlepage and Natty Bumppo are the intuitive coadjutors and twin ideals, then let us have no society at all. Let us depend on the purely solitary and personal virtues of the isolated and the doomed.

Looking over the Leather-Stocking tales from the bird's-eye view, one sees that *The Pioneers* is the realistic origin of Cooper's double-faced myth, the point of departure for the imaginative reconstruction of the hero's life. The scene is Templeton in 1793, a frontier town in New York based on Cooper's recollections of Cooperstown, where he was brought up. Natty Bumppo is shown, in the words of Mr. Grossman, as a "surly quarrelsome garrulous coarse old man" who lives unhappily in a squalid cabin on the outskirts of town, shoots deer out of season, gets arrested, and becomes involved in various sordid ways with the encroaching civilization he hates. Chingachgook, once the great Noble Serpent and immaculate companion of Natty, is now contemptuously known as Indian John, and is a derelict and drunk. *The Last of the Mohicans* begins to shape the myth, celebrating, as it does, the matchless companionship of Hawk-Eye and Chingachgook in their early middle age, celebrating also the death of the young Indian hero, Uncas. *The Prairie* is the *Götterdämmerung* of the series. *The Pathfinder* is about marriage, or rather, since the myth requires celibacy, Natty Bumppo's narrow escape from marriage. Natty's sturdy friend Jasper Western finally marries Mabel Dunham, so that in accordance with Cooper's divided mind on the subject, marriage is sanctioned but the real mythic action is the ritual reassertion of celibacy, the purification and escape from the taint of sex, implied by Natty's stoic withdrawal from the scene. Jasper Western may be a sturdy fellow, but marriage makes him a man of the towns, a lesser being, by the highest standards, than the spotless bachelor of the woods. *Deerslayer* recounts the initiation into life of the young hero as he gradually schools himself in the skills of his calling and receives the accolade of manhood from those who have gone before him—an initiation recapitulated in some ways by Mark Twain's Huckleberry Finn, Melville's Ishmael, Hemingway's Nick Adams (*In Our Time*), and Ike McCaslin in Faulkner's *The Bear* (but cf. Chapter VII).

Thus to isolate the story of Natty Bumppo from the books in which he appears is to emphasize how easily he becomes a mythic figure, existing, like Don Quixote, apart from any and all books. It was certainly Cooper's intention—vaguely as he may at first have conceived it—to create such a mythic figure. That this is so we gather from the prefaces he wrote in 1850 for the Putnam edition of his novels, particularly those to *The Pioneers* and to the Leather-Stocking series as a whole. It is true that Cooper did not set out at the beginning to write a coherent legend of his hero in five volumes. He even says that the Leather-Stocking tales were "written in a very desultory and inartificial manner." Yet he expresses the general intention which, in reading the series of tales and trying to account for their cumulative significance, one supposes him to have had.

Speaking of *The Pioneers,* Cooper notes that he had been correct in calling it a "descriptive tale," because it has an unusually large element of "literal fact." He explains that this is because he had lived as a youth in the town which makes the setting for the book and so had absorbed much of its history and local color. He thinks, however, that so much realism "destroys the charm of fiction." He continues by saying that fiction succeeds better "by delineations of principles, and of characters in their classes, than by a too fastidious attention to originals." In the later tales of the series he undertakes to supply, particularly to the central figure, the generality and ideality missing from *The Pioneers.* In answer to the question whether Natty Bumppo was based on a real man, Cooper says, "in a physical sense, different individuals known to the writer in early life, certainly presented themselves as models; but in the moral sense this man of the forest is purely a creation." Not only is he conceived as a type and an ideal, but, as Cooper says, he is to be accorded whatever significance "can be obtained from a poetical view of the subject." Not intended on the whole to be realistic novels the Leather-Stocking tales "aspire to the elevation of romance." And by way of justification for the manner in which life is viewed in these tales Cooper cites, not a novelist, but Homer.

To read the tales in the order in which they were written is, as D. H. Lawrence says, to experience a *"decrescendo* of reality, and a *crescendo* of beauty"* and to observe the creation of a myth. Thus was the grand scheme of the Leather-Stocking tales realized as the series progressed, whether or not it can be said to have been intended in all its details by the author.

*The Prairie* has more inner coherence and unity of tone

than the other books in the series. The prairie itself lends
unity to this novel. We are always aware of the dark, foreboding panorama that surrounds us. The mood of the book
is autumnal; heavy clouds and dark flights of birds move
through the sky over the somber, empty, majestic plains—
"the final gathering place of the red men," as Cooper remarks in his Preface. The setting encourages an unwonted *cinematic*
and very effective use of the panoramic view alternating
with the close-up scene. So that much of the most arresting
action generated by the book is the action of the eye itself
as it follows the contours and perspectives of enormous
spaces. As usual, the panoramic effects are better than the
close-up scenes, because when we get close to the characters they begin to talk Cooper language to each other. But
*The Prairie* has many beautiful if rather stiffly arranged pictorial compositions. And this is suitable to Cooper's com-
memorative and elegiac tone. The setting is in felicitous contrast to those in which Natty lives his earlier life—the
transparent, virginal Lake Glimmerglass in the idyllic *Deerslayer* or the rugged cliffs, rapids, and forests of *The Last
of the Mohicans*. As always there are passages of vivid action—a buffalo stampede, a prairie fire, and an Indian battle, which alternate with the stately pictorial passages. And
even this elementary narrative structure—the alternation of
the active and the static—takes on a more than usual significance in *The Prairie* because the imminence of the hero's
death, as well as his own reflections upon it, leads us to be
mindful of the mysteries of time and eternity.

The sense of mortality is strongly asserted both by what
we see and by the meditations of Natty Bumppo:

> The heavens were, as usual at the season, covered with
> dark, driving clouds, beneath which interminable flocks
> of aquatic birds were again on the wing, holding their
> toilsome and heavy way towards the distant waters of
> the south. The wind had risen, and was once more sweep-
> ing over the prairie in gusts, which it was often vain to

57

oppose; and then again the blasts would seem to mount into the upper air, as if to sport with the drifting vapor, whirling and rolling vast masses of dusky and ragged volumes over each other, in a terrific and yet grand disorder. Above the little brake, the flocks of birds still held their flight, circling with heavy wings about the spot, struggling at times against the torrent of wind, and then favored by their position and height, making bold swoops upon the thicket, away from which, however, they never failed to sail, screaming in terror, as if apprised, either by sight or instinct, that the hour of their voracious dominion had not yet fully arrived.

Scarcely less powerful is the hero's elegiac oration on the passing of life and the pretentious edifices of man, with its elevated Biblical diction and its touch of Indian forensic style:

It is the fate of all things to ripen and then to decay. The tree blossoms and bears its fruit, which falls, rots, withers, and even the seed is lost! . . . There does the noble tree fill its place in the forest. . . . Then come the winds, that you cannot see, to rive its bark; and the waters from heaven to soften its pores; and the rot, which all can feel and none can understand, to humble its pride and bring it to the ground. From that moment its beauty begins to perish. It lies another hundred years, a mouldering log, and then a mound of moss and 'arth; a sad effigy of a human grave. This is one of your genuine monuments, though made by a very different power than such as belongs to your chiseling masonry! and after all, the cunningest scout of the whole Dahcotah nation might pass his life in searching for the spot where it fell, and be no wiser when his eyes grew dim, than when they were first opened.

The Prairie furnishes several stirring episodes for Natty Bumppo—in this novel always referred to as the old trapper

—to become involved in. And the plot, as Henry Nash Smith points out, allows the author to bring together some of the human types that interest him. As Mr. Smith suggests, it is possible to think of Cooper's characters as ranging between the extremes of social life in the New World. They range, that is, from the pure child of nature represented by Hard-Heart, the young Pawnee Apollo, to Inez and Middleton, the flowers of aristocracy. Mr. Smith notes the contradiction involved in Cooper's view of the advancing frontier, which is good because it reclaims the wilderness in the name of civilization but evil because it entails the extinction of Hard-Heart. Somewhere toward the lower end of the scale we find the old trapper and the remarkable Bush family. And somewhat higher there are the young lovers, Ellen Wade and Paul Hover, solid, healthy, potentially domestic, middle-class types, of the sort who are often young lovers in Cooper's books. We are never to mistake them for the best type of human being, however, since they are neither aristocratic nor marginal. Paul Hover is like Jasper Western in *The Pathfinder*. He does not know the code; he is the kind who would be called "messy" in a Hemingway novel. His boyish, undisciplined extroversion is not to be countenanced, as we see when he naively blunders about an Indian encampment—"straying among the dwellings of the 'Red-skins,'" Cooper coldly reports, "and prying with but little reserve into their domestic economy." And the author adds that "this inquiring and troublesome spirit found no imitators among the Indians. The delicacy and reserve of Hard-Heart were communicated to his people."

Also in *The Prairie* is Dr. Bat, a scientist-pedant who has stepped out of the pages of Smollett or Fielding to investigate the flora and fauna of the plains. In Cooper's hands this stock figure becomes even more tiresome than usual, and the comic passages in which he appears are incredibly bad.

The characters who really matter are (besides the Indians) the trapper and the Bush family, a wild nomadic crew of squatters who have reverted to the legendary pa-triarchal life such as is darkly to be seen in the background of the Old Testament. The Bush family is, as Cooper says, a "fallen race," in the sense that on the frontier they have slid back down the scale of civilization to an archaic condition. And in doing so, Cooper seems correctly to imply, their lawless, colorful, violent ways will remain a part of the American heritage.

The Bush family is the first sign of human life we see moving in the immense landscape Cooper paints at the beginning of the book. Ishmael Bush, the father of the clan, is "a tall, sun-burnt man, past the middle age, of a dull countenance and listless manner. His frame appeared loose and flexible; but it was vast, and in reality of prodigious power." Although clad in "the coarsest vestments of the husbandman," Bush has a touch of barbaric picturesqueness; he wears a gaudy silken sash and a cap of marten's fur; three worthless watches dangle from his clothes. Bush makes a vivid contrast to the large picture in which Cooper carefully frames him—a picture of "long, narrow, barren perspectives," following which "the eye became fatigued with the sameness and chilling dreariness of the landscape."

Traveling westward as evening approaches, the Bush family is suddenly startled by the appearance, against the "flood of fiery light" from the setting sun, of an apparently supernatural figure, colossal, musing, and melancholy. As the figure comes steadily nearer, it is reduced to human size and we behold the old trapper, over eighty now, but still hard and alert, still carrying the famous long rifle, still speaking, too, with an Indian opulence of metaphor—as Ishmael discovers when he has asked how far the old man thinks they have come beyond the Mississippi, and is told that "A hunted deer could not cool his sides in the Mississippi, without travelling a weary five hundred miles."

At the very end of the book we are to be reminded of Natty Bumppo's apparent descent to the earthly scene from the light of the setting sun, in the great death scene in the

Pawnee camp, where Natty, who has been stoically await-
ing the end sitting in a chair at the door of a tepee facing
the setting sun—his dog Hector, now dead and stuffed, at
his feet—rises from the chair at the ultimate moment and
magnificently utters the dutiful word, "Here!"

The story of Natty Bumppo is the most interesting part
of *The Prairie*. He has come to the plains to escape civilization, and he is haunted by the encroachment of the squatters and homesteaders, the sound of whose axes he seems
constantly to hear over the eastern horizon. Squatters like
the Bush family are the real villains, for underneath the
colorful barbarism of their appearance, they are mean-
minded materialists and have no trace of reverence for nature or man. The old trapper sadly watches them with exactly the same feelings aroused in Faulkner's Ike McCaslin
by people like the Snopes family. With McCaslin, Natty
Bumppo ironically reflects on the pride that leads man to
think he can possess the earth. He reflects, too, on the crime
of violating the wilderness and on the expiation the crime
necessitates. But more pessimistic than Faulkner's hero, he
sees no possibility of expiation; there is only death and
forgetfulness.

As always, Natty's relations with others are correct and
ritualistic rather than intimate, and in his advanced age he
is even more hierophantic, certainly more talkative and sententious, than before. Despite the many things we know
about him, he remains a generic being even when he is
most individual, and although his approaching death renders him unwontedly to reminisce about the past, we still
learn very little, for example, about his earliest days, beyond cryptic references to his father and his boyhood
among the Moravian missionaries and Delaware Indians.
His strongest personal feeling in his old age seems to be
his fatherly affection for Hard-Heart, a young brave much
like Chingachgook, but even this human tie is a kind of
atonement—that is, it remains abstract and ideal. This abstractness is intended by the author and is not by any means

61

to be thought of as a failure to render a character concretely.

D. H. Lawrence found *The Prairie* "a strange, splendid book" in which, as in Frank Norris's *The Octopus*, "great wings of vengeful doom seem spread over the west." Lawrence saw in Natty Bumppo the archetypal American and concluded that "the essential American soul is hard, isolate, stoic, and a killer." It is difficult to say what the essential American soul is, but Lawrence is right at least to the extent that many of our writers create idealized characters who have this kind of soul. Hemingway has been the most consistent admirer of the archetype, but Melville, Thoreau, and Faulkner have admired it too. And so have Hawthorne and Poe, although they have customarily observed Lawrence's archetypal American acting on the interior stage of the mind and have shown him making psychological aggressions, coldly rifling the souls of others. It seems a long way from Natty Bumppo to Henry James's cold exploitative characters like Gilbert Osmond in *The Portrait of a Lady*, but Osmond too is hard, isolate, stoic, and, in his way, a killer.

In the emergence of this type, we have an instance of the collaboration of two great influences on American fiction, both of which generated the idea of the isolated individual—namely, Puritanism and the frontier way of life. Writing as a New York aristocrat, Cooper satirizes the Puritans, yet, as he notes at the beginning of Chapter 6 in *The Prairie*, the "American borderer" is as much the product of New England as of the frontier.

The equivocal word in Lawrence's description of Natty Bumppo is "killer." Both Natty and Captain Ahab, or for that matter Ishmael Bush, are killers. But the all-important difference is that Natty kills only out of necessity; and he kills, as it were, lovingly. His code does not allow him to plunder, exploit, or kill in hate. Thus a fundamental moral question in Cooper, and in American fiction generally, is one of piety; characters are judged according to whether they have reverence for life, especially for wild, innocent, untainted life, whether this may appear in a deer on the prairie, a whale in the Pacific, or in an excellent and complicated young American woman on her travels in Europe.

The novelty in the conception of Natty Bumppo and his descendants is the irony of their double personality, and it is this that sets Cooper's hero apart from the softer, less ironic natural piety of the Rousseauistic or Wordsworthian man. The ideal American image is of a man who is a killer but *nevertheless* has natural piety. The "hard, isolate, stoic," or "Indian" quality is what gives the image uniqueness. The romantic individual or solitary hero of nineteenth-century European literature had never been exposed to New England Puritanism or to frontier conditions, and this makes a difference.

In summing up Natty Bumppo's characteristics, Lawrence might have added that he is poetic—not so much in the stiffly florid rhetoric of his speech as in the very quality of his mind. In *The Prairie* the old trapper opposes the scientific views of Dr. Bat with a kind of darkened version of eighteenth-century deism. He subsumes reason, instinct, and "natur'" in one large metaphor which, if it seems as bleak as the prairie, is also as majestic.

Natty Bumppo is, as Walt Whitman said, "from everlasting to everlasting." He is even in the words of Balzac (which nevertheless strike the first note of the modern indiscriminate overenthusiasm with which the French have greeted American fiction), "a magnificent moral hermaphrodite, born between the savage and the civilized worlds." Yet Cooper's hero succeeds in being profound only by being narrow. How, to raise the question again, are we to transfer Natty Bumppo's moral virtues into the context of a possible culture? One thing may be said immediately: we cannot do it without women, and we note that Natty's ideal world, and perhaps Cooper's too, is purely masculine.

No writer can conceive of a fully convincing aristocratic, tragic, or religious culture, or any other culture, unless he can imagine, like Sophocles, Molière, Shakespeare, Dante, or Henry James (to put him for a moment in very great company), a fully developed woman of sexual age. This Cooper cannot do, nor could any other American novelist until the age of James and Edith Wharton. This is a shocking and perhaps unprecedented bias.

Cooper's view of women is not "aristocratic," it is merely cold and patronizing. His rules of female behavior are rigid. No woman, for example, must make the unpardonable mistake of confessing her love for a man before she knows that the man loves her. In *The Spy* a girl makes this mistake and is summarily shot by a bullet which is described as "stray" but is actually fired by the author. The idea of racially mixed marriages is outrageous, as the Indian brave Mahtoree learns in *The Prairie* when he asks the trapper to translate a proposal of marriage to Ellen Wade and receives instead an indignant lecture. In *The Last of the Mohicans* a white girl and the noble Uncas are in love. But Cooper explains this unimaginable situation by saying that the white girl is part Negro. He then kills them both off, thoughtfully giving them a chance of felicity in the happy hunting grounds. It seems clear that Cooper feels that women, to the extent that they materialize out of the pure vapor of which he forms them, are not more real and human but simply more tainted with the original sin of being female. His treatment of women may seem to be determined by the manners of a gentleman. Actually it is determined by age-old folk superstition.

Naturally most of his women, certainly all of his Anglo-Saxon women, are bloodless and dull. Women in Cooper's novels tend, as they do in many of the works of his great descendants, to be seen obliquely and with a rather covert displeasure, or unhappy fascination, or secret vindictiveness; and they fall into mere types and caricatures. No less than Hemingway and Faulkner, Melville and Mark Twain, Cooper is the celebrant of the masculine life.

Cooper's attitude toward women figures prominently

among other causes for the abstractness and generality of his mind. Although only somewhat better than Cooper at portraying women, Hawthorne, like Henry James, had a partly feminine sensibility, if by that is meant a sense of the complexities of the psychological life. And this, together with the dark imagination he inherited from his Puritan forebears and his absorption in his locale, gives his writings the richness of texture conspicuously absent from Cooper's romances. The American imagination needed in the 1830's and 1840's exactly what Hawthorne and, in his different way, Poe brought to it. Although Brockden Brown had made an early beginning, it was left to Hawthorne to introduce into the romance-novel the darker complexities of the imagination. Cooper had firmly established as a source of that poetic quality of the novel we are calling "romance" the nostalgia for the virgin land and the simple life. Hawthorne, no more pastoral than Cooper was Puritan, brings to the novel, as I try to show in the next chapter, the consequential Calvinist drama of the mind in its search for good and evil. It was to be left to Melville (see Chapter V) to join for the first time, on the scale of greatness, the two main sources of American romance: pastoral nostalgia and the moral melodrama.

Hawthorne          Cooper

## Chapter IV

# HAWTHORNE AND
# THE LIMITS OF
# ROMANCE

### The Scarlet Letter

THE SCARLET LETTER has in abundance that "complexity of feeling" often attributed to the American novel. At the same time, the foreground elements of *The Scarlet Letter*—the salient actors and events—have something of the two-dimensionality of actors and events in legend. What baffles our best understanding is how to make the mysterious connections between the rather simple elements of the book and what is thought and felt about them.

Henry James had his eye mostly on the foreground elements when he wrote his pages on *The Scarlet Letter* in his small biography of Hawthorne. Writing in 1879, at the period of *The Portrait of a Lady* and just before his most realistic novels (*The Bostonians* and *The Princess Casamassima*), James judges Hawthorne out of his own preoccupations. He deplores the excess of symbolism and allegory in

Hawthorne's tales and he describes allegory as "quite one of the lighter exercises of the imagination." There is good reason for supposing that *The Wings of the Dove, The Golden Bowl,* and perhaps other late works by James himself have fugitive allegorical elements, and there is the example of Kafka to show that allegory in the novel is not necessarily so light an exercise as James thought in 1879. James made no attempt to read the allegory of *The Scarlet Letter,* contenting himself with pointing out the excessive ingenuity and rather pointless mystification with which Hawthorne tries to endow the scarlet A with transcendent meanings.

The virtue of James's approach is that he starts with the main, the leading fact about *The Scarlet Letter*—namely, that it is primarily *a novel* and not a poem. This is a fact which many modern critics ignore, as they do in speaking of the fictions of Melville, James, Faulkner, and others. After one has accepted and assessed this fact there is time enough to explore some of the poetic dimensions of *The Scarlet Letter* which James felt no impulse to look into.

Although James thought *The Scarlet Letter* a true masterpiece—"beautiful, admirable, extraordinary"—he could not help noting that it was rather "weak" in its "historical coloring" and showed "little elaboration of detail, of the modern realism of research." There was "a certain coldness and exclusiveness of treatment . . . a want of reality and an abuse of the fanciful element . . . The people strike me not as characters," James continues, "but as representatives, very picturesquely arranged, of a single state of mind." James notes the lack of "progression" within the book and the small degree to which the characters, as distinguished from the author's absorption in the meaning of their relationship, contribute to the action.

To extend for a moment the Jamesian approach, one might apply to *The Scarlet Letter* some of the terms worked out by James's disciple Percy Lubbock, in his *The Craft of Fiction* (though Lubbock himself does not mention Haw-

68

thorne). Lubbock saw that in the elusive art of the novel much depends on the placing and use of the point of view, whether this be retained (as it is in *The Scarlet Letter*) by the omniscient author or established in one of the characters. Much depends too on how the point of view is used once it is established in a character—for example, is the observation of events exclusive, partial, biased, and non-dramatic, as it is likely to be when a first-person narrator is used (as in *The Blithedale Romance*)? Lubbock thought correctly that the fuller dramatic effect was achieved by placing the point of view in an observer but setting the mind of the author free when necessary from the confines of the observer's consciousness so that we not only have this consciousness to look through but can stand apart with the author and notice how this consciousness itself becomes a participant in the drama of the novel (Lubbock's example was *The Ambassadors*).

Slighting to some extent, like his master, the power of action and the dramatic articulation of events to give structure to the novel, Lubbock tended to subordinate everything to the portraiture of great characters. Thus he is content to look for structure in the alternation of "picture" and "scene," since it is this alternation that rounds out the portrait. This emphasis will explain why, although Lubbock is a good critic of the "novel," he is impatient with the "romance."

By "picture" Lubbock means "panorama"—all those elements of the novel that explain, round out, and report; the reflection of things from somebody's mind; reminiscence; description; narration; exposition. By "scene" he means the stage effect—dramatic dialogue, action rendered immediately to the reader without foreshortening of time and space. Drama he took to be the great thing; and it was the duty of the novelist to dramatize not only "scene" but, so far as might be possible, "picture" too.

This brief exposition of the Jamesian criticism is perhaps justified because it tends to be ignored by many modern

*New Criticism for review for novel.*

critics. The New Criticism has been interested primarily in poetry and when it has turned to the novel it has too often assumed that the techniques of criticism which are suitable to poetry are sufficient for the novel. Yet clearly the novel has its unique kinds of composition—composition by scene, picture, action, and character as well as composition by metaphor and symbol.

*The Scarlet Letter* is almost all picture. The adultery which sets everything going happens before the book begins, and it is never made believable. There are, to be sure, dramatic scenes—the three scenes on the scaffold; Hester and Pearl at the governor's mansion; Hester, Dimmesdale, and Pearl in the forest; and each of these scenes is exquisite and unforgettable.

Yet compared with the more immediate impact which in different hands they might have made on us, they seem frozen, muted, and remote. There is an abyss between these scenes and the reader, and they are like the events in a pageant or a dream, not like those of a stage drama. They are, in short, little differentiated from the pattern of the whole and they have the effect of being observed by the reader at second hand, of being reported to him, as in "picture." The author's powerfully possessive imagination refuses to relinquish his characters to our immediate perusal or to the logic of their own human destiny. This tight monolithic reticence is what gives *The Scarlet Letter* its unity and its mysterious remoteness. It is at every point the mirror of Hawthorne's mind, and the only one of his longer fictions in which we are not disturbed by the shortcomings of this mind but are content to marvel at its profound beauty.

Inevitably Hawthorne's symbol for the imagination was the mirror. Malcolm Cowley's account of the biographical origin of this idea seems correct. Cowley traces it to Hawthorne's sense of "doubleness," the result of a certain strain of narcissism and the long seclusion of Hawthorne's youth and young manhood. Temperamentally, as Cowley says,

Hawthorne was paradoxically "cold and sensuous, sluggish and active, radical and conservative, and a visionary with a hard sense of money values." From this ingrained doubleness sprang Hawthorne's notion of the imagination. In the Introduction to *The Scarlet Letter*, for example, he uses the mirror to suggest that which gives frame, depth, and otherness to reality. His fictions are mirror-like. They give us a static and pictorial version of reality. They are uncanny and magical, but they capture little of life's drama, its emergent energy and warmth, its conflict, crisis, and catharsis.

James praised Hawthorne because he "cared for the deeper psychology," but he was content to leave the analysis of this psychology to later critics. Many of these have been interested in the way *The Scarlet Letter* plays its apparent meanings off against its submerged meanings. D. H. Lawrence was struck by the "dubiety" and "duplicity" of Hawthorne's imagination. We may wonder if Hawthorne himself was not struck by this, at least as it occurred in one of his characters. For when Hester Prynne stood outside the church listening to Dimmesdale's Election Day sermon she

> listened with such intentness, and sympathized so intimately, that the sermon had throughout a meaning for her entirely apart from its indistinguishable words. These, perhaps, if more distinctly heard might have been only a grosser medium, and have clogged the spiritual sense. Now she caught the low undertone, as of the wind sinking down to repose itself, then ascended with it, as it rose through progressive gradations of sweetness and power, until its volume seemed to envelop her with an atmosphere of awe and solemn grandeur. And yet, majestic as the voice sometimes became, there was forever in it an essential character of plaintiveness. A loud or low expression of anguish—the whisper or the shriek, as it might be conceived, of suffering humanity, that touched a sensibility in every bosom. At times this deep

strain of pathos was all that could be heard, and scarcely heard, sighing amid a desolate silence. But even when the minister's voice grew high and commanding, when it gushed irrepressibly upward, when it assumed its utmost breadth and power, so overfilling the church as to burst its way through the solid walls and diffuse itself in the open air, still, if the auditor listened intently and for the purpose, he could detect the same cry of pain. What was it? The complaint of a human heart, sorrowladen, perchance guilty, telling its secret, whether of guilt or sorrow, to the great heart of mankind, beseeching its sympathy or forgiveness—at every moment, in each accent, and never in vain. It was this profound and continual undertone that gave the clergyman his most appropriate power.

Some early readers of *The Scarlet Letter* believed not only that the subject was sin but that the author condoned sin, at least, the sin of adultery ("Is the French era actually begun in our literature?" cried one outraged reviewer). Certain later critics of Hawthorne have tended to agree that the author does condone sin, not because he was salacious but because, in his skeptical, secularized way, he was following the myth of "the fortunate fall," as Milton may be conceived to have done in *Paradise Lost*. Hawthorne certainly believed that no adulthood, no society, no tragic sense of life could exist without the knowledge of evil—a point he makes clear in the opening sentences of his book. Yet there seems to be no concerted myth of "the fortunate fall" in *The Scarlet Letter*.

What may be called the "grammar-school" idea of Hawthorne's novel supposes it to be a tale of sin and repentance. And this it certainly is, with strong stress on the repentance. More accurately, the subject of the book is the moral and psychological results of sin—the isolation and morbidity, the distortion and thwarting of the emotional life. From another point of view these are shown to be the results not of man's living in sin but of his living in a Puritan society, and thereby, to some extent, in *any* society. And yet it will not do to read *The Scarlet Letter* too closely as a comment on society, which is felt in its pages hardly more pervasively than sin.

To be sure there are elements of social comment in *The Scarlet Letter*. Is it not, for example, a feminist tract? So magically various is the book that one may sometimes think it is, even though a rich sensibility and profound mysteries are not usually associated with feminist literature. But doesn't Hester Prynne turn out to be rather like Hawthorne's sister-in-law Elizabeth Peabody, the emancipated reformer who became the prototype of Miss Birdseye in James's *The Bostonians?* Once a luxurious and passionate woman, Hester takes up a life of renunciation and service. Her life turns "in a great measure from passion and feeling, to thought." In an age when "the human intellect" was "newly emancipated," she assumes "a freedom of speculation, then common enough on the other side of the Atlantic, but which our forefathers, had they known it, would have held to be a deadlier crime than that stigmatized by the scarlet letter." Thus, in her lonely life, Hester becomes a radical. She believes that sometime "a new truth" will be revealed and that "the whole relation between man and woman" will be established "on a surer ground of mutual happiness." She even comes to think in feminist rhetoric, and one can hear not only Hester but Miss Peabody and Margaret Fuller talking firmly about "the whole relation between man and woman."

Undoubtedly, then, *The Scarlet Letter* does have a feminist theme. It is even a tract, yet on the few occasions when it is heard the tractarian tone is tempered by the irony of the author. The book may have other meanings of a social or political kind. Still, one makes a mistake to treat Hawthorne, either in *The Scarlet Letter* or *The Blithedale Romance*, as if he were a political or social writer. He is a very canny observer of political fact, as of all fact, and

73

this is in itself an unusual distinction. But no coherent politics is to be derived from Hawthorne. As Constance Rourke notes, Hawthorne seldom gives any strong impression of a society. *The Scarlet Letter* has, in Miss Rourke's words, "the bold and poetic and legendary outline which may belong to opera." In *The Scarlet Letter* and Hawthorne's other works the people at large are sensed merely as a choric crowd and the few main characters are rather artificially grouped in a village square, an old house, a shop, an isolated farm community, a forest glade, or a garden. The settings do not seem to be permanently related to each other or to the actors who momentarily speak their pieces in them.

In practice Hawthorne was an adherent of the mediocre Pierce wing of the Democratic party. Even less than Henry James had he any command over political theory or, what is more useful to a novelist, the instinct to dramatize politics in action. Hawthorne often gives the illusion of a systematic intellectual prowess, and this has led many readers to find in him an important moralist, political thinker, or theologian. It *is* an illusion, compounded of his hardheaded sagacity and his skepticism, his observance of elemental human truth. But the unities of his conceptions are first of all *aesthetic* unities, and Hawthorne tended to take an art-view of the world in so far as he took any consistent view at all. He stubbornly insisted that one could take such a view even in a democracy which appeared to have little use for aesthetic values.

Two other attitudes toward *The Scarlet Letter* must be noticed. Yvor Winters concludes that it is a "pure allegory" (as opposed to *The Blithedale Romance* and *The Marble Faun,* which Winters calls "novels with unassimilated allegorical elements"). Mr. Winters's discussion of Hawthorne includes a very instructive, if hardly exhaustive, account of the contradictory doctrines of New England Puritanism and of the allegorical sensibility these produced. He points out that the "Manicheistic struggle between Absolute

74

Good and Absolute Evil," as conceived in early New England, was a rigid dualism that provided for a sense of two unalterably opposed and yet related orders of reality and that this dualism encouraged an allegorical habit of mind. He seems broadly correct in remarking that like a Puritan allegory the method of *The Scarlet Letter* is "neither narrative nor dramatic but expository."

If *The Scarlet Letter* is "pure allegory" then the symbols must by definition refer to fairly clear-cut and fixed referents. But of course they don't, and what we have in *The Scarlet Letter* is not pure allegory but a novel with (generally speaking) beautifully assimilated allegorical elements. This Mr. Winters seems indirectly to demonstrate by the unconvincing meanings he assigns to the characters— Hester representing the repentant sinner, Dimmesdale the half-repentant sinner, and Chillingworth the unrepentant sinner.

The view of *The Scarlet Letter* advanced by D. H. Lawrence states a partial truth, as does that of Winters. Lawrence's view, elaborately worked out and restated by Mrs. Q. D. Leavis in her essay "Hawthorne as Poet," holds that consciously or not, Hawthorne was writing a kind of mythic prophecy about the great cultural change involved in the shift from the Old World to the New. Hawthorne, Lawrence seems to think, was depicting in Chillingworth and the young Hester the decline of a richly emotional, patriarchal, aristocratic way of life, and the emergence, in Dimmesdale and the later "social-service" Hester, of a new puritan-democratic consciousness. Lawrence saw this as a profoundly self-contradictory consciousness, as is suggested by little Pearl, who like puritan America, like Hawthorne himself, is mildly genteel on the surface but wild and demonic underneath.

As Mrs. Leavis describes Hawthorne's "myth," it is based on the ritual celebration of the historic transition from the "immemorial culture of the English folk with its Catholic and ultimately pagan roots" to the new Puritan consciousness. With some plausibility she discovers this myth in earlier pieces such as "The Maypole of Merrymount" and "My Kinsman, Major Molineux."

Hawthorne undeniably has the historical sense. And Mrs. Leavis might have gone on to observe that in "Mr. Higginbotham's Catastrophe" and *The House of the Seven Gables* we have in the careers of the rustic jacks-of-all-trade, Dominicus Pike and Holgrave, the succession of a capitalist order to an agrarian one. If she had seen this and other sides of Hawthorne's historical sense, Mrs. Leavis might have been more circumspect. She might have seen that there is no central unifying cultural "myth" in Hawthorne—only a clear perception of historical facts and an ability to endow these with beauty and significance. But the significance arises from the aesthetic harmonies of the composition as we find it from story to story, and although historical facts are observed, no theory or consistent view of history is presented.

Can we not make some kind of synthesis out of all these suggestions? We need some of their complexity. At the same time we have to remember that the simple truth about *The Scarlet Letter* is, as Constance Rourke said, that "Hawthorne was deeply engaged by the consideration of lost or submerged emotion." Let us add to this general formulation of the theme that *The Scarlet Letter* is an allegorical novel and that the allegory both in form and substance derives from Puritanism. Let us add, also, that although no unifying myth is involved, the novel describes the loss or submergence of emotion involved in the abandonment of the Old World cultural heritage which had given human emotions a sanction and a manifold significance.

Neither in *The Scarlet Letter* nor elsewhere did Hawthorne ever make up his mind whether he approved of this loss and submergence. Purely as an artist he often felt dismayed and discouraged by what Cooper called "the poverty of materials" which the workaday, uniform life of democracy had to offer. And on one side of his moral character, Hawthorne had enough passion to make us feel the sadness and chill of the New World—for example, when Hester Prynne lets her rich black hair loose in the forest sunshine but then with her meek masochism hides it again beneath the gray cap. At the same time, the other Hawthorne, the Puritan conventionalist, permits himself a sigh of relief and rationalizes it by reflecting that after all we are disillusioned now, after our passage from the Old World to the New, and if a certain beauty disappears along with licentiousness and sin, that is the price we pay for our stern realism, our rectitude, and our practical sagacity.

If we are to hold to the idea that *The Scarlet Letter* is an allegory, we must assign meanings to the symbols of the story. This is an inviting prospect, but it has often led critics into very tedious speculations. As R. H. Fogle has said, there is generally speaking no special or exclusive symbolism in Hawthorne. His symbols are broadly traditional, coming to him from the Bible, Dante, Shakespeare, Milton, Spenser, and Bunyan—the light and the dark, the forest and the town, the dark woman and the fair woman, the fountain, the mirror, the cavern of the heart, the river, the sea, Eden, the rose, the serpent, fire and so on.

Within the context of these symbols, the allegory proper may be, however, more peculiar to Hawthorne. The allegorical symbols are Puritan categories revised for Hawthorne's own purposes, and they can be assigned provisionally in the following manner.

Hester Prynne, about whom there is something queenly, imperious, and barbaric, as well as fallible and appealing and enduring, represents the eternal woman, perhaps, indeed, the eternal human. When she puts on her gray cap and becomes a kind of social worker, her color and passion, her indeterminate, instinctual being is curbed and controlled. While this is going on Chillingworth and Dimmesdale are destroying each other. They are the two aspects of the will which confused Puritan thought in New England—the active and the inactive. From the beginning,

77

Puritanism generated a strong belief in the efficacy of the will in overcoming all obstacles in the path of the New Israel in America, as in the path of the individual who strove toward Election. But at the same time the doctrine of Predestination denied the possibility of any will except that of God.

Chillingworth unites intellect with will and coldly and with sinister motives analyzes Dimmesdale. This is the truly diabolic act in Hawthorne's opinion. It is what he calls the Unpardonable Sin and it is worse than sins of passions ("He has violated, in cold blood, the sanctity of a human heart," says Dimmesdale. "Thou and I, Hester, never did so!"). Hawthorne is as close a student of those impulses which drive men to plunder and exploit the human heart as Cooper and Faulkner are of the impulses that drive men to plunder and exploit the land that Providence put into the trust of Americans. And for him as for them, violation, or impiety, is the worst of crimes.

Dimmesdale is intellect without will. He is passive; he is all eloquence, sensitivity, refinement, and moral scruple. What violence he has has long since been turned inward. He has preyed on himself as Chillingworth preys on him.

Little Pearl, one should say first, is a vividly real child whom Hawthorne modeled on his own little daughter Una. As a symbol as well as in life she is the offspring of Hester and an extension, as Hawthorne says, of the scarlet A. She represents the intuitive, lawless poetic view of the world. She is the eternal folk imagination, restored in every child, which is the fundamental element of the artist's imagination, and is outlawed by Puritan doctrine. "The spell of life went forth from her ever-creative spirit, and communicated itself to a thousand objects, as a torch kindles a flame wherever it may be applied." Ironically she conspires with everyone else in the tale to recreate the luxurious Hester in the puritan-democratic image. For it is she who insists that Hester shall replace the A and cover her hair with the gray cap.

As will be seen from the above, Chillingworth, Dimmesdale, and Pearl can be conceived as projections of different faculties of the novelist's mind—Chillingworth, the probing intellect; Dimmesdale, the moral sensibility; Pearl, the unconscious or demonic poetic faculty. Hester is the fallible human reality as the novelist sees it—plastic, various, inexhaustible, enduring, morally problematic.

From another point of view, we see that without becoming a myth, *The Scarlet Letter* includes several mythic archetypes. The novel incorporates its own comic-book or folklore version. Chillingworth is the diabolical intellectual, perhaps even the mad scientist. Dimmesdale is the shining hero or to more sophisticated minds the effete New Englander. Hester is the scarlet woman, a radical and nonconformist, partly "Jewish" perhaps (there is at any rate an Old Testament quality about her, and Hawthorne says that her nature is "rich, voluptuous, Oriental." Like many other American writers, Hawthorne is not entirely above the racial folklore of the Anglo-Saxon peoples, which tends to depict tainted women and criminal men as French, Mediterranean, or Jewish—as in Hawthorne's *Marble Faun*, Miriam is Jewish, in Melville's *Pierre* Isabel is French, and in *Billy Budd* Claggart is dimly Mediterranean). Pearl is sometimes reminiscent of Little Red Riding Hood or a forest sprite of some sort who talks with the animals. Later when she inherits a fortune and marries a foreign nobleman, she is the archetypal American girl of the international scene, like the heroines of Howells and James. The subculture from which these discordant archetypes emerge is evidently inchoate and derivative. The symbols do not cohere until they have been made into projections of the faculties of the artist's mind and elements of a quasi-puritan allegory. But to a receptive imagination, they connect *The Scarlet Letter* with universal folklore, as many other novels, good and bad, are connected.

## The A vs. the Whale

One's excuse for trying to define words like "allegory" and "symbol" is that although these words do have fairly stable meanings, one would never gather so from the confusing way people use them in talking about American literature. No wonder the common view persists, both within academic walls and without, that American literature is impenetrably mysterious and that attempts to study it critically are far more suspect than attempts to study other literatures.

The scarlet A is an ordinary symbol (or sign), whereas Melville's white whale, though very much a whale, is a poetic symbol. The usual meaning of the word "symbol" is *something that stands for something else.* Yet as "symbol" is used in technical literary criticism, it means *an autonomous linguistic fusion of meanings.* We can say with relative certainty what the scarlet A stands for. It stands for adultery or, since it is not adultery in itself that interests Hawthorne, it stands for the inevitable taint on all human life, as does the symbol of the hand in the story called "The Birthmark." It is thus a relatively simple sign and not, like the white whale, a complicated cluster of meanings. Hawthorne's half-hearted attempts to make it more mysterious and suggestive, by implying that it glows in the dark, etc., do not succeed. Being an ordinary symbol, the scarlet A is thus suitable to its allegorical context. The whale is much more complex and thus fits well the proliferating implications of *Moby-Dick.*

Melville and Hawthorne often spoke of "allegory" where we would speak of "symbolism." They did not differentiate between the two, and this must be remembered when we find Melville saying in a letter to Mrs. Hawthorne that she had made him newly aware of certain "allegorical" meanings in *Moby-Dick,* or when he mentions with mock horror in *Moby-Dick* itself the possibility that the book might become a "hideous and intolerable allegory." This latter utterance has often been quoted to support the argument that *Moby-Dick* has no symbolic meanings at all but is merely a good sea story. By now, surely, this is not an "argument."

According to modern usage, then, the poetic element of *Moby-Dick,* which enhances the realistic element, is symbolistic, so far as the Whale is concerned. Yvor Winters is misleading when he supposes that *Moby-Dick* is an allegory and that the Whale stands for Evil. The Whale is Evil *for Ahab,* but not for Melville, Ishmael, or the reader. Ahab is, or becomes, a rigid allegorist—that is one of the things wrong with him.

The necessary distinction between allegory and symbolism was made by Coleridge and is related to that between fancy and imagination. With this relation in mind, we recall that despite Hawthorne's reading of English and German romantic literature, his mind was formed pre-eminently by allegorists like Bunyan and Spenser and by the rationalistic mentality of the eighteenth century (his very syntax shows the influence) for which "fancy" was the poetic faculty. On the other hand Melville, more a man of his time, drew his inspiration mostly from Shakespeare and the romantic writers. Hawthorne felt no impulse to transmute his inherited Calvinism into a new view of life; he was content to let it relax into harmony with the dualism and common sense of eighteenth-century thought. Melville felt strongly the impulse to participate in the romantic, Promethean attempt to recreate knowledge and discover undiscovered truth. For him, as for the great romantics of his time, "imagination" was the poetic faculty.

Pure allegory (if it can ever be isolated as such) assumes two fixed discourses—a language of static signs and a set of truths to which they refer. In allegory the signs or symbols have little or no existence apart from their paraphrasable meaning. Allegory flourishes best, of course, when everyone agrees on what truth is, when literature is regarded as exposition, not as discovery. A symbolic or symbolistic literature responds to disagreements about the truth. It purports to discover or create truth, like Coleridge's "Imagination." For the purely symbolistic writer "technique is discovery," to use Mark Schorer's phrase. Thus a poetic symbol not only *means* something, it *is* something—namely, an autonomous truth which has been discovered in the process by which the symbol emerged in the context of the poem. If it still permits us to think of it as an ordinary symbol—as something that stands for something else—we see that it does not point to anything easy to express. Rather, it suggests several meanings.

As has already been observed, the terms we have been investigating are much more suitable to poems than to novels. There are sharp limits to any critique of the novel that regards "technique as discovery." The novel does not often lend itself to linguistic, symbolistic, or epistemological criticism. The language of a great novel may be very bad in detail, as in Dreiser or Balzac, whereas the detailed quality of the language may well make or break a poem. Furthermore, the "poetry" of a novel will probably reside less in the language than in the rhythm and relation of picture, scene, character, and action—although some novels, *Moby-Dick* for example, have, besides this novelistic sort of poetry, metaphoric passages where the particular qualities of the language are all-important.*

## The Blithedale Romance

By 1852 nearly all of Hawthorne's best work was behind him. Coming just after *The Scarlet Letter* and *The House*

* See Appendix I.

*of the Seven Gables,* and just before Hawthorne's life was to be markedly changed by his long sojourn in Europe, *The Blithedale Romance* is the culmination of his most concentrated attempt to write fiction of novel length. Except for *The Scarlet Letter,* Hawthorne's longer fictions never succeed perfectly, despite the many incidental successes which this author could always score. His books falter at various points and then, not knowing how to re-establish the progression, he trots out a traveling puppet show, a masquerade, a symbolic well, an old legend, a mesmerist, as if he were an entertainer on the stage who must improvise in order not to lose his audience. The shorter form of the tale fitted his genius better, and although his work gave him an important place in the history of the novel, he was, strictly speaking, finally unable to master the novel form, without imparting to it a preponderance of romance. This he appears to admit in *The Blithedale Romance.*

Technical questions aside for the moment, this book must always find a place in the affections of readers for being so genuinely original in conception. The Brook Farm experiment, in which Hawthorne himself briefly partook, offered him a various display of manners, attitudes, and odd and salient characters. And if we must suppose that he chose to report only a little of what was to be seen, we have to admit that he did well with that little. As a study of the manners of liberal intellectuals that took a comic view of their advanced ideas, *The Blithedale Romance* had no precedent in America nor, except for the satires of Swift and Peacock, in Europe either. Had any author discovered that the feelings of intellectual women who have to wash dishes and make gruel and who, being modern women, have to form at the same time *ideas about* washing dishes and making gruel was proper material for the novelist?

Zenobia, the tragicomic heroine, is the center of the piece. She is a novelist's success in her faultful and appealing humanity, and sketchy as she is by the strictest standards, Henry James was right in admiring her and in calling her "the nearest approach that Hawthorne has made to the complete creation of a person." The point about Zenobia is the waste and confusion of her inner life, which result from her always living according to this or that literary or political idea rather than according to the natural urgencies of her being. Even in committing suicide, we are told, she "was not quite simple." In actuality the details of her death are repulsive and grotesque; but she had tried to die like "drowned persons" in pictures—"in lithe and graceful attitudes."

As in *The Scarlet Letter*, the general theme is the loss or submergence of emotion. Coverdale, the narrator, is too timid and cold to live the emotional life which his intellect perceives. Hollingsworth, a spiritual cousin of Chillingworth and second-cousin of Melville's Ahab, is a monomaniac, in whom an obsessive goal has compressed and destroyed emotion. Priscilla is a pale New England blossom (like Mrs. Hawthorne), given to psychic experiences which bypass or merely symbolize an emotional life. Zenobia, like Hester Prynne a darkly beautiful and supposedly passionate woman, is a study in the emotional hazards of feminism and transcendentalist utopianism.

By exemplifying this theme in the lives of intellectuals and reformers, Hawthorne launched a small but important group of novels, all of which owe a debt to the original—among them James's *The Bostonians*, Howells's *Vacation of the Kelwyns*, Lionel Trilling's *The Middle of the Journey*, and Mary McCarthy's *The Oasis*. But there is in *The Blithedale Romance* a certain poetic beauty and charm, a finally unnamable Hawthorne magic that is beyond those who follow his lead in subject and theme.

As for the symbols of the piece, they are plain and effective, lending a charm to the story and enhancing its psychology—the veils and masquerades to suggest the falseness of motive and belief; mesmerism to suggest falseness of spirit and emotional confidence tricks; hearth-fire to suggest the genial emotional life which ironically eludes the cold ideology of the Blithedalers. There is also the pastoral setting itself, representing the innocence which these all too civilized utopians cannot recapture. And we note that in a literature rich in pastoral idyls *The Blithedale Romance* is one of the few anti-pastorals—Hawthorne is a partisan of conventional society as he finds it.

Unlike his descendants in the satirical-utopian genre Hawthorne is unable to follow through with his original conception. Blithedale and its interesting people, never very solidly established in the first place, grow dimmer and dimmer, and the story is dissipated into rather weakly related static scenes—a masquerade in the forest (suggestive of comic possibles of which nothing is made), a series of set speeches at "Eliot's pulpit," the suicide of Zenobia.

Part of the trouble is that as the story goes along the author becomes more and more interested in the status of Coverdale as the observer, a problem that for him has literary and moral implications. These reflections in the end lead him to concede that he must make certain fundamental moral objections to what one must think and feel in order to write a novel. In effect he admits that it is not only the poverty of materials in America that has led him, as he says in his prefaces, to write romances rather than novels, but also his puritan scruples—the romance allowing him to treat the physical passions obliquely. And whether it is a separate objection, or merely a rationalization of his scruples, he comes to think, in *The Blithedale Romance,* that the novelist commits the unpardonable sin, that he is a kind of Chillingworth whose probing intellect violates the human heart.

That Hawthorne is deliberately experimenting with the point of view in *The Blithedale Romance* is made clear by the repeated reflections of the narrator, Coverdale, on his own position as observer. Our narrator is a minor poet; he is rather selfish, fastidious, and aloof; he is also mildly ironic and cherishes his ready insight into people and things. There is something illicit about him however. He looks at

85

life furtively; he is a bit of a *voyeur;* he blushes and is a little coy. We are not allowed to see Coverdale directly and the author, having granted him the privileged position of first-person narrator, cannot question his behavior and does not put him on the spot by involving him very deeply in the action.

Thus to his usual method of conducting us through a series of static scenes, Hawthorne adds here a series of positions in the story from which we behold the scenes. And a part of the interest is in the changes of position. We observe the characters at close range in the living room of the farmhouse; we get a more general long-distance view of them from Coverdale's pine-tree eyrie; we see them theatrically framed in the back window of a boardinghouse, as Coverdale watches them from his upstairs room in an opposite building.

We see things differently, too, according to the state of Coverdale's health or mood. When he is sick and feverish, his perceptions are heightened and somewhat morbid. He has been fascinated with the lush Zenobia but now he allows himself to call her an "enchantress" and even wonders if in Zenobia's life "the great event of a woman's existence had been consummated." Convalescing, he reflects that his sickness has been a kind of death and his recovery a rebirth. He has now been reborn to reality and will be able fearlessly and accurately to analyze the community and its inhabitants—as he is really able to do with considerable perspicacity, up to a point.

He sees things clearly if not profoundly. He attempts to look through the eyes of others, in order to compare what he sees with what they see. He rejects the leadership of Hollingsworth when he perceives that what Hollingsworth demands of his friends is precisely that they should surrender their right to see with their own eyes.

At one point Coverdale reflects that his position in the story "resembles that of the Chorus in a classic play, which seems to be set aloof from the possibility of personal concernment." His only relation to the other characters is the sympathy he feels for them as he watches their fate work itself out. Yet, as Coverdale concludes, near the end of the story, there is for the aloof observer an insoluble dilemma in the very nature of story-telling. "It was both sad and dangerous, I whispered to myself, to be in too close affinity with the passions, the errors, and the misfortunes of individuals who stood within a circle of their own, into which, if I stept at all, it must be as an intruder, and at a peril that I could not estimate."

This is sound morality but a bad state of mind for a novelist. The moral question has been interesting Hawthorne all the way through the book. And although we too are interested, we cannot help thinking that he would have written a better novel if only he could have allowed his observer to see what he could see instead of what would test the moral significance of observing. Thus in *The Blithedale Romance* Hawthorne confronts the dilemma his moral views have brought him to. As a novelist, he is more than likely guilty of the Unpardonable Sin. He must perforce pitilessly scrutinize his characters without being able to share with them their imperfect humanity, to acknowledge his kinship with their experience and destiny.

This crisis in Hawthorne's understanding of the limits of his art is retold in Zenobia's legend of "The Silvery Veil" (Chapter 13). This is the story of Theodore (Coverdale) who might have released from thralldom a mysterious Veiled Lady (Priscilla) by kissing her without looking under the veil. Being too cold and skeptical to surrender himself, he insists on raising the veil first. The Veiled Lady remains in thralldom, and Theodore is doomed to regret his cautious scruple for the rest of his life. So, Hawthorne seems to confess, have I failed to release my characters, especially the pallid feminine ones like Priscilla, into life.

It is clear, then, that although Hawthorne was a superb writer of romance and a considerable novelist from any point of view, he was aware that his romances, as he himself insisted on calling them, proceeded in part from his final failure to take a place among the great novelists.

# Chapter V

# MELVILLE AND
# *MOBY-DICK*

MELVILLE's imagination originates in his powerful sense of the irrationality and contradictoriness of experience. His essay on Hawthorne, written in the summer of 1850 while he was composing *Moby-Dick*, gives us a clear impression of this imagination at the high point of its power. We find that what most moves Melville in Hawthorne's tales (for he is reviewing *Mosses from an Old Manse*) is not only their "Shakespearean" profundity, their fine comedy, and power of fantasy but especially their mingling of light and dark. "For in spite of all the Indian-summer sunlight on the hitherside of Hawthorne's soul," Melville writes, "the other side—like the dark half of the physical sphere—is shrouded in a blackness, ten times black." Melville speculates that "this great power of blackness" derives from "that Calvinistic sense of Innate Depravity and Original Sin, from whose visitations, in some shape or other, no deeply thinking mind is always and wholly free." Reading Hawthorne's tales, Melville writes, "You may be witched by his sunlight—transported by the bright gildings in the skies he builds over you; but there is the blackness of darkness beyond."

As everyone notices, Melville's essay has as much to do with the qualities of his own imagination as with Hawthorne's. They share many perceptions, to be sure. But Hawthorne put his finger on the essential difference when, after briefly renewing his acquaintance with Melville in Liverpool in 1856, he remarked that although Melville talked endlessly and eloquently of the ultimate dilemmas of truth and belief, he could neither believe "nor be comfortable in his disbelief." Having very little of the aloof, contemplative skepticism of Hawthorne, and being unable to discover any philosophical or religious synthesis he could believe in, Melville became a kind of alien wanderer in the world of the imagination, seeking a truth that should be at once a truth of reason and a truth of art. As a thinker, Melville was an inspired amateur, with an agonized and troublesome yen (as Hawthorne seems to have felt) for posing insoluble problems. As an artist, Melville was again the inspired amateur, who despite his great native gifts (perhaps the greatest ever given to an American) never developed a firm novelistic or poetic sense of things. He had little patience with the quotidian demands of the art of the novel or the poem; he had little power of invention; he showed none of Hawthorne's understanding of the quality and scope of his own imagination. His goal was the highest; no one short of Shakespeare would do as the ideal. His career as a writer was bound to be precarious and desperate, the results fragmentary and uneven.

It seems generally agreed that the voyages of Melville's heroes in his early books—*Typee* (1846), *Omoo* (1847), *Mardi* (1849), *Redburn* (1849), *White-Jacket* (1850), and *Moby-Dick* (1851)—are, in one sense, quests for truth. That the quest is conceived as both rational and aesthetic is suggested by *Mardi*, where the voyage to sea expands, is arbitrarily transformed rather, into an allegorical-symbolic fantasy in which the truth-seeking philosopher Babbalanja asserts the view that ideally the poet and the philosopher have the same mission. The vision of truth Taji, the questing hero of the book, longs for will be one that is gained simultaneously, as it were, by rational and aesthetic means. Unfortunately, Taji does not succeed, and at the end he is shown sailing further into the problematical seas, having left a world which strikes him as being the abode of unreason and ambiguity, a world symbolized by the wraith-like creature called Yillah (the princess of light) and by the sinister Hautia (the queen of darkness).

Although Melville never, even in his last years, ceased to protest and resist the necessity of remaining skeptical, he had got hold of such truth as was to come to him, by the time he had finished *Mardi* and *White-Jacket*. This truth is that man lives in an insolubly dualistic world, that his profoundest awareness does not transcend the perception of his paradoxical situation, caught as he is between apparently eternal and autonomous opposites such as good and evil, heaven and hell, God and Satan, head and heart, spirit and matter. Only in *Moby-Dick* (among his longer works) does Melville's imagination provide a metaphor adequate to his darkly skeptical view. In the white whale, and the tremendous actions he sets off, the polarities that preoccupy Melville are for once magnificently expressed. And although this fortunate conjunction of the philosophic and the poetic does not produce a truth that transcends Melville's radical skepticism, it does produce a work of art which is so far the grandest expression of the American imagination.

But even as Melville's imagination achieved its great feat the spectacle of disaster is powerfully before us. In Ahab the reason and the aesthetic sense pull apart. Ahab has had his humanities, as we are told. He is still drawn to the aesthetic, the intuitive, the poetic experience. He still has some of the "low enjoying power" as well as the "high

91

perception," and he still has fellow feeling and natural piety (the phrases I have quoted here are from Chapter 37, "The Sunset," which contains an important soliloquy by Ahab). But gradually his intellect is drawn apart from whatever might nourish, harmonize, and symbolize it, and in its isolation, it grows willful, obsessive, and finally suicidal. Except for the narcissism that makes a mad allegorist of Ahab, he is blind to all the imaginative versions of reality that his own mind or that of others may offer to him.

There is, unhappily, a good deal of Ahab in Melville, and, on the evidence of *Pierre* and *The Confidence Man,* we conclude that Melville, after *Moby-Dick,* faced a deeply stultifying dilemma. He saw that to write at all one had to assume that reason and the aesthetic sense, the high perception and the low enjoying power, must lead at some point to the same synthesis. Yet for Pierre the provisional syntheses offered by the aesthetic sense fail to satisfy the intellect's thirst for absolute truth or to modify its perception of irreconcilables. Thus the rational and the aesthetic are at once incompatible and mutually indispensable. This is of course a paralyzing dilemma, if you allow it to become one, and Melville did. In a more highly organized mind, or a more serenely contemplative mind, or a mind richer in its aesthetic sense, this dilemma is not an impasse, but merely one of the large facts of experience, to be treated like any other fact. But for Melville the dilemma was almost fatal; it suggested to him, as to his Pierre, that aesthetic perception was mere illusion and that rational perception was an alien activity, doomed to monomania and nihilism.

Thus both *Pierre* (1852) and *The Confidence Man* (1857) are studies of man caught among "the ambiguities" (as the subtitle of *Pierre* says). *Pierre* is a melodrama of incest and suicide, showing man crushed by the contradictions involved in his attempt to live a moral and creative life, whereas *The Confidence Man* is a comedy of appearance and reality, showing the absurdity of man's attempts to attribute meaning and value to a world in which these can have no ground or status.

Not until *Billy Budd* (except in some of his poems) does Melville seem to give us a sense of ambiguities resolved and irreconcilables reconciled—for in *Billy Budd,* Melville finds some comfort in the idea that, beyond the special illusion of unity a work of art provides, irreconcilables may perhaps be absorbed in history or in legend. But this is a matter that may be better discussed at the end of the present chapter.

## How *Moby-Dick* Was Written

The scope and tone of *Moby-Dick* appear to have changed while Melville was writing it. Just what the changes were, and what induced them, is the subject of much interesting scholarship. For our purposes, certain plausible speculations by George R. Stewart, in an essay called "The Two Moby-Dicks," will suffice.

With the exception of the fanciful *Mardi,* Melville's first five books had been based partly on personal experience. The first book, *Typee,* told a somewhat romanticized story of the author's actual sojourn in the Marquesas Islands after he deserted the whaling ship Acushnet, on which he had sailed some months previous. Mr. Stewart conjectures that in its original conception *Moby-Dick* was to be another of Melville's quasi-autobiographical travelogues, this time recounting his adventures on the Acushnet up to the time of his leaving the ship in the Marquesas. As he wrote, however, the story took on ever new possibilities for him, and these possibilities finally crystallized into a whole new conception of the book. Having already substantially completed the writing of the story as he first conceived it, however, the author did not start entirely afresh but included

93

all or most of the original version, with varying degrees of revision, in the book as we now have it.

Thus we may suppose that Chapters 1–15, in which after various adventures Ishmael and Queequeg arrive in Nantucket, are substantially as they were in the original version. Chapters 16–22, concerning the preliminaries to sailing, belong to the original version, but with considerable rewriting. Chapters 23 to the end constitute the new version of the book, with the exception of certain passages which appear to have been salvaged and interpolated from the original version.

Something like this undoubtedly happened, and it accounts for certain inconsistencies in the book. For example, the fact that the Pequod appears to head for Cape Horn but actually, without sufficient reason for the change, rounds the Cape of Good Hope, that the Pequod is said sometimes to have a wheel and other times a whale-bone tiller, that Stubb is called both third and second mate (although Melville settles on the latter), and so on. More remarkable is the virtual disappearance of some of the characters who figure largely in the opening chapters. Queequeg, to whom we have been introduced in much detail, becomes merely one of the harpooners. Bulkington, although apparently destined for some heroic role, is dismissed with a poetic epitaph. Ishmael himself all but disappears as a character and as the observer becomes hardly more than the voice of the omniscient author. Ahab, perhaps originally conceived as one more portrait in Melville's gallery of tyrannical and irritable captains, becomes a great, doomed hero. The language itself, rather jocose and colloquial at first, becomes opulent with metaphor, simile, and oratorical flourishes.

What caused this flowering of Melville's genius cannot, of course, be known. But figuring prominently in the miracle must be his rereading of Shakespeare during the time he was working on the book. The influence of *Lear* and *Macbeth* is felt as one beholds Ahab and listens to his speeches and soliloquies. The language and metaphor of Shakespeare make themselves strongly felt in *Moby-Dick*, though not, we observe, in the earlier chapters. Probably it occurred to Melville, as he paused in the process of writing, that two factual narratives about whaling which he had read might be woven into his narrative—one concerning the ramming and sinking by a whale of the Nantucket ship Essex, another concerning a monstrous white whale called Mocha Dick. It is probable too that he discovered that the legends, tall tales, and folklore of whaling could be more than embellishments to his narrative; they could be for him what other bodies of folklore had been for Homer, Virgil, or Camoens (an author of whom Melville was fond)—the materials of an epic. Finally, one may suppose that partly under the influence of Hawthorne he saw that Ahab might be not only a quasi-Shakespearean hero, doomed by an inordinate pride or tragic ignorance, but also the protagonist in a kind of Puritan inner drama, a drama of the mind in its isolation and obsession. For if Ahab is akin to Shakespeare's heroes, he is more so to such Hawthorne characters as Chillingworth, the pattern of whose life also became, in Hawthorne's phrase, "a dark necessity."

The reason one is interested in the process by which *Moby-Dick* evolved from a travelogue to the complex book it is is that as readers we often seem to share Melville's excitement as he and we make new discoveries—as we push farther into the unknown and find metaphors and formulations that make the unknown knowable. Melville thought of art as a process, as an emergent, ever creative, but never completed metaphor. Thus he makes his imaginary poet in *Mardi* triumphantly exclaim, in reference to the epic he has written, "I have created the creative!" In taking the view that a work of art is not a completed object but is an imperfect form which should be left only potentially complete, Melville is much closer to Whitman than to Hawthorne.

And what he says about the technical whaling sections of *Moby-Dick* applies as well to the whole book.

> It was stated at the outset, that this system would not be here, and at once, perfected. You cannot but plainly see that I have kept my word. But I now leave my Cetological System standing thus unfinished, even as the great Cathedral of Cologne was left, with the crane still standing upon the top of the uncompleted tower. For small erections may be finished by their first architects; grand ones, true ones, ever leave the copestone to posterity. God keep me from ever completing anything. This whole book is but a draught—nay, but the draught of a draught. Oh, Time, Strength, Cash, and Patience!

*Moby-Dick*, like the cathedral with the crane on its tower, allows us to see—in fact insists that we shall see—some of the machinery by which it was built, some of the processes of construction. Two passages may be quoted in this connection. The first was presumably interpolated in Chapter 16 and sounds, as Mr. Stewart suggests, like something one might as soon expect to find in a novelist's notebook as in his novel. Melville seems almost to be arguing himself into believing that a tragic hero might be made out of a Nantucket whaleman, especially if he spoke in the Quaker manner:

> So that there are instances among [the Nantucketers] of men, who, named with Scripture names—a singularly common fashion on the island—and in childhood naturally imbibing the stately dramatic thee and thou of the Quaker idiom; still, from the audacious, daring, and boundless adventure of their subsequent lives, strangely blend with these unoutgrown peculiarities, a thousand bold dashes of character, not unworthy of a Scandinavian sea-king, or a poetical Pagan Roman. And when these things unite in a man of greatly superior natural force, with a globular brain and a ponderous heart; who has

also by the stillness and seclusion of many long night-watches in the remotest waters, and beneath constellations never seen here at the north, been led to think untraditionally and independently; receiving all nature's sweet or savage impressions fresh from her own virgin voluntary and confiding breast, and thereby chiefly, but with some help from accidental advantages, to learn a bold and nervous lofty language—that man makes one in a whole nation's census—a mighty pageant creature, formed for noble tragedies. Nor will it at all detract from him, dramatically regarded, if either by birth or other circumstances, he have what seems a half wilful over-ruling morbidness at the bottom of his nature. For all men tragically great are made so through a certain morbidness. Be sure of this, O young ambition, all mortal greatness is but disease.

In this passage we join in the discovery of ideas that were to produce Ahab. In Chapter 14, "Nantucket," we participate in the process by which an epic emerges—namely, by the transmutation of the central facts about the life of a culture into poetry by means of the accretion of folklore, legend, and myth. The wave-like amplification and building-up, followed by the lyric subsidence at the end, is characteristic of Melville's imagination and is similar to the action of the book as a whole, as well as to various sections of it. One may be pardoned, then, for including here a long quotation:

Nantucket! Take out your map and look at it. See what a real corner of the world it occupies; how it stands there, away off shore, more lonely than the Eddystone lighthouse. Look at it—a mere hillock, and elbow of sand; all beach, without a background. There is more sand there than you would use in twenty years as a substitute for blotting paper. Some gamesome wights will tell you that they have to plant weeds there, they don't grow naturally; that they import Canada thistles; that they have to send beyond seas for a spile to stop a leak in an oil cask; that pieces of wood in Nantucket are carried about like bits of the true cross in Rome; that people there plant toadstools before their houses, to get under the shade in summer time; that one blade of grass makes an oasis, three blades in a day's walk a prairie; that they wear quicksand shoes, something like Laplander snowshoes; that they are so shut up, belted about, every way inclosed, surrounded, and made an utter island of by the ocean, that to their very chairs and tables small clams will sometimes be found adhering, as to the backs of sea turtles. But these extravaganzas only show that Nantucket is no Illinois.

Look now at the wondrous traditional story of how this island was settled by the red-men. Thus goes the legend. In olden times an eagle swooped down upon the New England coast, and carried off an infant Indian in his talons. With loud lament the parents saw their child borne out of sight over the wide waters. They resolved to follow in the same direction. Setting out in their canoes, after a perilous passage they discovered the island, and there they found an empty ivory casket,—the poor little Indian's skeleton.

What wonder, then, that these Nantucketers, born on a beach, should take to the sea for a livelihood! They first caught crabs and quohogs in the sand; grown bolder, they waded out with nets for mackerel; more experienced, they pushed off in boats and captured cod; and at last, launching a navy of great ships on the sea, explored this watery world; put an incessant belt of circumnavigations round it; peeped in at Behring's Straits; and in all seasons and all oceans declared everlasting war with the mightiest animated mass that has survived the flood; most monstrous and most mountainous! That Himmalehan, salt-sea Mastodon, clothed with such portentousness of unconscious power, that his very panics are more to be dreaded than his most fearless and malicious assaults!

And thus have these naked Nantucketers, these sea hermits, issuing from their ant-hill in the sea, overrun and conquered the watery world like so many Alexanders; parcelling out among them the Atlantic, Pacific, and Indian oceans, as the three pirate powers did Poland. Let America add Mexico to Texas, and pile Cuba upon Canada; let the English overswarm all India, and hang out their blazing banner from the sun; two thirds of this terraqueous globe are the Nantucketer's. For the sea is his; he owns it, as Emperors own empires; other seamen having but a right of way through it. Merchant ships are but extension bridges; armed ones but floating forts; even pirates and privateers, though following the sea as highwaymen the road, they but plunder other ships, other fragments of the land like themselves, without seeking to draw their living from the bottomless deep itself. The Nantucketer, he alone resides and riots on the sea; he alone, in Bible language, goes down to it in ships; to and fro ploughing it as his own special plantation. *There* is his home; *there* lies his business which a Noah's flood would not interrupt, though it overwhelmed all the millions in China. He lives on the sea, as prairie cocks in the prairie; he hides among the waves, he climbs them as chamois hunters climb the Alps. For years he knows not the land; so that when he comes to it at last, it smells like another world, more strangely than the moon would to an Earthman. With the landless gull, that at sunset folds her wings and is rocked to sleep between billows; so at nightfall, the Nantucketer, out of sight of land, furls his sails, and lays him to his rest, while under his very pillow rush herds of walruses and whales.

## An Epic Romance

This term is perhaps the inevitable one for Melville's great book. But *Moby-Dick* is extremely impure art; it is a hybrid, one of the most audacious, surely, that have ever been conceived. As Melville himself exclaims at one point, "I try everything. I achieve what I can."

The partly romanticized travelogue-novel which the book was apparently first intended to be still contributes its considerable realism and wealth of detail to the whole. And of course those admonitory critics who are always telling us that *Moby-Dick* is just a good whaling yarn and should be discussed only as such seem at first to have their point. But the realistic sea-going novel as practiced by Melville and by Cooper, Smollett, Marryat, and Dana, whose example Melville followed, is not a particularly interesting form, exciting as it is to read. Although *Moby-Dick* contains many novelistic elements—of character, panorama, scene, and action—it has fewer that repay study than, for example, *The Scarlet Letter*. If we are to follow Melville's imagination, we have to go afield from the sea-novel, although we always come back to it as we read.

As was suggested earlier, in discussing allegory and symbol, *Moby-Dick* is in one sense a symbolist poem. It contains also strong melodramatic, if not fully tragic elements. It is certainly in one sense a comic work. And some passages, such as appear in the inconceivably beautiful chapters called "The Funeral," "The Pacific," "The Dying Whale," and "The Symphony," are sheer lyric.

One does not detract from the book in saying that it has a "made-up" quality, that it is a good deal "put together," and is very much a piece of literary fabrication. In view of this one has trouble associating it quite so readily with the epic imagination of the Bronze Age and the Age of the

Vikings as Newton Arvin does in his book on Melville (which is, however, at least through the chapter on *Moby-Dick*, much the best book).

As an epic, *Moby-Dick* follows in some ways the universal convention to which it belongs. It celebrates, that is, customs, techniques, occupations, ideals, and types of heroic humanity which are characteristic of the culture in which they appear. Given the culture Melville is expressing, what would we expect him to include in his epic? We must have heroes, nobility, and these will be the heroes of the American nineteenth century—hunters, exploiters, captains of industry (for Ahab *is* one of these, and the Pequod is a beautifully efficient factory for the production of whale oil). What skills and preoccupations will be stressed? Not the martial skills of the *Iliad*, nor the political and moral skills of the *Aeneid*, nor the theological and political prowess of *Paradise Lost*, but the techniques of subduing nature—and thus the descriptions, as loving and detailed as that of Achilles's shield in the *Iliad*, of the ship, the whale boats, and all their intricate apparatus. But although superficially resembling the *Odyssey*, *Moby-Dick* lacks, among other things, the rich observation of *ethos*, of ways of life, real and fabulous, which we find in Homer's poem. The *Odyssey* is extremely sophisticated about manners and morals and is actually more novelistic than *Moby-Dick*.

In a democratic epic such as *Moby-Dick* avowedly is we would expect a celebration of the ideals of equality and brotherhood, on the one hand, and individualism, on the other. The ideal masculine attachment here is not the hierarchic relation of Achilles and Patroclus, tender as that is, but the perfect fraternal equality of persons of different race. Thus Ishmael and Queequeg join the much discussed company of Natty Bumppo and Chingachgook, Huck Finn and Jim. The different ideal of individualism is expressed in the ready derring-do and self-respecting unconventionality of all the main figures. And Ahab becomes, as the "dark necessity" of the story sets in, a heightened example of independent man, as if Melville were out to test some of the extreme implications of the dominant Emersonian creed of self-reliance.

As is suggested by the passage about Nantucket, quoted above, the raw material for the great metaphors of Melville's epic is "American humor"—that is, the body of folk sayings, jokes, and tall tales that had formed by Melville's time a reservoir of legendary materials on which he could draw. The story of the white whale is of course in itself a very tall tale and, in the manner of the tale teller, Melville adduces a considerable number of fancies and rumors about Moby-Dick's almost supernatural powers. One finds frequent references to semilegendary early heros, like George Washington, Andrew Jackson, Franklin. The main characters, even Ahab, behave and speak sometimes like the humorous, boastful frontiersmen and canny, canting, mystical Yankee peddlers who figured in the oral legend and on the popular stage of Melville's time.

The native legends, which Melville was the first important writer to use with any fullness, are unusual in the history of the world by being predominantly humorous. The humor, as Constance Rourke has shown, oscillates rather wildly between extremes, being on the one hand boasting, oratorical, even megalomaniac and on the other meditative, soliloquizing, oddly indirect, covert, and sad. It is characteristically oral, even after being incorporated into so literary, so *written* a book as *Moby-Dick.* For Melville presents his story to us as if he felt the necessity of talking us, and himself, into accepting it. He does not accredit it by saying that the Muse told it to him. He assumes, rather, the guise of the salesman and the showman. In the very first chapter we find that whereas a hero of another epic might attribute his turn of fortune to Hera or Zeus, Ishmael regards himself as a sort of bit player in an extravaganza produced by "those stage managers, the Fates"—showmen who, as we may think more than once in reading *Moby-Dick*, resemble P. T. Barnum, rather than Zeus.

And, doubtless, my going on this whaling voyage, formed part of the grand programme of Providence that was drawn up a long time ago. It came in as a sort of brief interlude and solo between more extensive performances. I take it that this part of the bill must have run something like this:

*"Grand Contested Election for the Presidency of the United States.*

"WHALING VOYAGE BY ONE ISHMAEL.
*"BLOODY BATTLE IN AFGHANISTAN."*

Though I cannot tell why it was exactly that those stage managers, the Fates, put me down for this shabby part of a whaling voyage, when others were set down for magnificent parts in high tragedies, and short and easy parts in genteel comedies, and jolly parts in farces—though I cannot tell why this was exactly; yet, now I recall all the circumstances, I think I can see a little into the springs and motives which being cunningly presented to me under various disguises, induced me to set about performing the part I did, besides cajoling me into the delusion that it was a choice resulting from my own unbiased freewill and discriminating judgment.

The brash, vaunting tone of "American humor" is heard throughout *Moby-Dick,* as in the episode (to take but one example out of a hundred) in which Stubb bedevils and hoodwinks the master of the French ship Rosebud. (*ambergris* )

Yet the most beautiful pages in *Moby-Dick* are those in which the insistent, though often disembodied voice of Ishmael takes on the flowing, meditative tone of introspection and revery. Thus at the end of Chapter 35 we have Ishmael on the masthead. He is so engrossed in his own thoughts that he forgets to watch for whales, meriting the reproach that "Whales are scarce as hen's teeth whenever thou art up there." But then with an abrupt but not disconcerting change from this jocose beginning we follow

Ishmael's flow of consciousness as he "takes the mystic ocean at his feet for the visible magic of that deep, blue, bottomless soul, pervading mankind and nature; and every strange, half-seen, beautiful thing that eludes him; every dimly-discovered, uprising fin of some undiscernible form, seems to him the embodiment of those elusive thoughts that only people the soul by continually flitting through it." Then nearly losing consciousness under the spell of the fantasy, he imagines himself in a moment of panic dropping with a shriek into the sea. And Melville winds up the chapter, as he often does, with a moral based on an elaborate analogy: "Heed it well, ye Pantheists!" "American humor," with its sense of violence and the precariousness of life, is aware of ranges of reality unsuspected by "pantheists"—or by the Emersonian transcendentalists Melville may have in mind when in describing the "mystic ocean" into which Ishmael gazes he makes it resemble the Oversoul.

To pursue the method suggested in Constance Rourke's *American Humor* (for that is what I have been doing in the above paragraphs) is to discover the legendary materials of Melville's epic of whaling. It gives us some insight into the origins of the great images, persons, and actions of the book. It is even a way of understanding some of the author's leading attitudes about life. It gives us, above all, the sense of the genial, the humane, and the creative. And if it does not show us all that is apprehended by what Ahab calls the "high perception," it does make us feel the natural, the aesthetic texture of life that appeals to the "low enjoying power." Perhaps only Mark Twain and Faulkner have known as well as Melville how to capture in their stories the variegated musings of the folk humor, and how to play these off against actions whose meaning is abstract and universal.

# The Meaning of *Moby-Dick*

If we think of the dramatic action involving Ahab and the pursuit of the whale, isolating this in our minds from the almost encyclopedic context in which it occurs, we are conscious of a meaning, even of a didactic purpose. Just what the meaning is has been the subject of much speculation. Undoubtedly the first step towards understanding *Moby-Dick* is to observe what is really very obvious: it is a book about the alienation from life that results from an excessive or neurotic self-dependence. Melville has conceived of his moral fable in a way which makes *Moby-Dick* distinctly a book of its time and place and allies it intimately with the work of other American writers. As Newton Arvin demonstrates, there is some reason to think of Ahab as guilty of *hybris,* in the Greek sense, or of excessive pride, in the Christian sense; but there is more reason to think of him as guilty of or victimized by a distorted "self-reliance." An alternative to Ahab's suicidal course is proposed by the author. But since Mr. Arvin explains this in a way which seems generally to confirm the view of the American imagination as we are attempting to understand it in the present book, let us listen to him. Mr. Arvin begins by saying that "the alternative to Ahab's egotism" is not the Greek "ideal of 'nothing too much'" nor the Christian ideal of "a broken and contrite heart." Rather, he says,

> On one level it is an intuition that carries us beyond morality, in the usual sense, into the realm of cosmic piety; on the usual ethical level, however, it is a strong intuition of human solidarity as a priceless good. Behind Melville's expression of this, one is conscious of the gravity and the tenderness of religious feeling, if not of religious belief; it came to him in part from the Christian tradition in

which he had been nurtured. The form it took in him, however, is no longer specifically Christian; as with Hawthorne and Whitman, it was the natural recoil of a sensitive imagination, enriched by the humanities of romantic idealism, against the ruinous individualism of the age. It is Melville's version of Hawthorne's "magnetic chain of humanity," of Whitman's "manly attachment": so far, it is an essentially humanistic and secular principle.

The only caveat that needs to be added to these words is that the "intuition of human solidarity as a priceless good" is stronger in Melville and Whitman than in Hawthorne and that for all of them "human solidarity" means not a settled social order but a more or less unstable idyllic relationship, a personal and ideal sharing of the human fate among people temporarily brought together by chance or by a common purpose. The intuition of solidarity tends to come to American writers only when the solidarity is precarious and doomed by the passing of time or by the mere anarchic instinct of the individual. And so the American novel is full of idealized momentary associations—Natty Bumppo and his companions, Hawthorne's Blithedalers, Ishmael, Queequeg and the crew of the Pequod, Huck Finn and Nigger Jim on their raft, or—that classic example of the instability and mixed motives that characterize united action among Americans—the Bundren family in Faulkner's *As I Lay Dying*. Even such relatively stable social orders as that of the Bostonians described in James's *The Europeans* or that of the New Yorkers in Edith Wharton's *Age of Innocence* have to regroup themselves and suffer a good deal of agony in order to put up a united front against the foreigner who, in each novel, threatens invasion.

But to take up Mr. Arvin's argument again, one notes, in carrying it a step further, that the moral action of *Moby-Dick* is not strictly tragic or Christian. It is an action conceived as taking place in a universe of extreme contradictions. There is death and there is life. Death—spiritual, emotional, physical—is the price of self-reliance when it is pushed to the point of solipsism, where the world has no existence apart from the all-sufficient self. Life is to be clung to, if only precariously and for the moment, by natural piety and the ability to share with others the common vicissitudes of the human situation. These are the clear alternatives.

What must be remembered is that this is a melodramatic view of things. Strictly speaking, both Greek and Christian tragedy offer an ideal of catharsis or redemption—forms of harmonious life that come about *through* death. It is this life through death that Ishmael seems to have been given in the Epilogue, when he alone is saved by the coffin-life-buoy. But is this really a catharsis, a redemption, a rebirth? The momentary sense of harmony and joy is all too easily dispelled by the chilly gloom, the final despair, of the last words. "On the second day, a sail drew near, nearer, and picked me up at last. It was the devious-cruising Rachel, that in her retracing search after her missing children, only found another orphan."

For Melville there is little promise of renewal and reward after suffering. There is no transcendent ground where the painful contradictions of the human dilemma are reconciled. There is no life *through* death. There is only life *and* death, and for any individual a momentary choice between them. What moves Melville most powerfully is the horror that is the violent result of making the wrong choice. He is moved too by the comic aspect of the spectacle, the absurdity of such a creature as man, endowed with desires and an imagination so various, complex, and procreative yet so much the prisoner of the cruel contradictions with which, in his very being, he is inexorably involved. Finally, he is moved by the blissful, idyllic, erotic attachment to life and to one's ideal comrades, which is the only promise of happiness.

Solipsism, hypnotic self-regard, imprisonment within the self—these themes have absorbed American novelists. The Concord transcendentalism, of which Melville was very much aware and whose sensibility he in many ways shared, was a philosophy—or rather an ethical poetry—of the self. The idea of the image reflected in the mirror or in the water appeals as strongly to Melville as to Hawthorne, and like Hawthorne he uses this literary convention to point up the dangers of an exaggerated self-regard, rather than, as Whitman and Emerson loved to do, to suggest the vital possibilities of the self. At the very beginning of *Moby-Dick* we are shown "crowds of water-gazers" who are "posted like silent sentinels" around the shores of Manhattan and are "fixed in ocean reveries." And then, says Melville, amplifying his effect with his usual semi-humorous parody of learning, there is the still deeper "meaning of that story of Narcissus, who because he could not grasp the tormenting, mild image he saw in the fountain, plunged into it and was drowned. But that same image, we ourselves see in all rivers and oceans. It is the image of the ungraspable phantom of life; and this is the key to it all."

This last statement is tantalizing and although it sounds a little offhand, like a too facile way to end a paragraph, it also sounds and *is* important. For the book is to offer the alternative of Narcissus. One may, like Ahab, look into the water, or into the profound and ultimately unknowable abyss of nature, and see only one's own image or an ungraspable phantom, a white whale which is only a projection of self. Or, like Ishmael or Starbuck, one may see one's own image but in a context of life and reality which is *not* one's self. To be Ahab is to be unable to resist the hypnotic attraction of the self with its impulse to envelop and control the universe. To be Ishmael is to be able at the last minute to resist the plunge from the masthead into the sea one has with rapt fascination been gazing at, to assert at the critical moment the difference between the self and the not-self. To be Starbuck is to understand what the white whale might mean to a man like Ahab but to insist "with the stubbornness of life" that the whale is merely "a dumb brute" to seek vengeance on which is "blasphemous" and "madness."

Chapter 99, "The Doubloon," tells us much about the meaning of *Moby-Dick*. The doubloon is a gold coin Ahab has nailed to the main mast. It is to be won by whoever first sights the white whale. Ishmael describes the coin in detail (if indeed Ishmael can be called the narrator at this point; he is always ostensibly the narrator but in much of the latter part of the novel he is not *felt* as such). The coin is from Ecuador. "So this bright coin came from a country planted in the middle of the world, and beneath the great equator, and named after it; and it had been cast midway up the Andes, in the unwaning climate that knows no autumn." In the ambiguous symbolism of the coin, involving three mountains crowned respectively with a flame, a tower, and a crowing cock, we see "the keystone sun entering the equinoctial point at Libra" (the Scales). Without worrying over the rather labored symbolism, we note that for author-Ishmael the coin represents the equator, the dividing line in a dualistic world. From the point of view of the equator, there are in human destiny two grand alternatives: the self-absorption which leads to isolation, madness, and suicide, or the imperfect but more or less objective perceptions of the world which allow one to cling to life. All this is shown in the procession of the main figures of the drama as each in turn meditates momentarily on the coin. Ahab soliloquizes thus:

> the firm tower, that is Ahab; the volcano, that is Ahab; the courageous, the undaunted, and victorious fowl, that, too, is Ahab; all are Ahab; and this round gold is but the image of the rounder globe, which, like a magician's glass, to each and every man in turn but mirrors back his own mysterious self.

The others respond to the symbolism of the coin in their different ways, but each is free of Ahab's imprisonment. Starbuck sees the symbolism of the ordinary pious Christian life. Stubb is reminded of his *carpe diem* philosophy, his jolly acceptance of life and death. Flask, even less imaginative, sees simply a gold coin that, as he pauses to calculate, would buy nine hundred and sixty cigars. The Manxman, a primitive soothsayer, sees merely a vague doom. Fedallah, the Parsee harpooner Ahab has smuggled aboard, sees the fire worshiped in his religion. Pip, rather reminiscent of King Lear's fool, expresses with a theological despair, one may think, the impossibility of seeing anything, the impossibility of knowledge. To him it is not only Ahab who is imprisoned within the self; it is in the nature of man to seek but not to find, to look but not to see. Thus he mutters: "I look, you look, he looks; we look, ye look, they look." Little Pip is Melville's Christian caveat. As we are told in "The Castaway" (Chapter 93), Pip "saw God's foot upon the treadle of the loom, and spoke it; and therefore his shipmates called him mad. So man's insanity is heaven's sense. . . ." Heaven's sense may be glimpsed by visionaries, Melville concedes, but it cannot be brought to bear on such actions as are reported in *Moby-Dick*.

As a symbol the whale is endlessly suggestive of meanings. It is as significant and manifold as Nature herself, and, of course, that is the point. Like nature the whale is paradoxically benign and malevolent, nourishing and destructive. It is massive, brutal, monolithic, but at the same time protean, erotically beautiful, infinitely variable. It appears to be unpredictable and mindless; yet it is controlled by certain laws. The chapter on "The Whiteness of the Whale" is a *tour de force* of learning and ingenuity such as Melville liked to get off. It remains, however, rather inert, and like some of the excessively extended chapters on cetology, or the interpolated story of the Town-Ho, it forces us to step outside the action of the book in order to take in a sort of sideshow at a moment when we are all for getting on with the main event. Still the idea of the whale's whiteness is indispensable. Whiteness is the paradoxical color, the color that involves all the contradictions Melville attributes to nature. It signifies death and corruption as readily as virginal purity, innocence, and youth. It has the advantage of being, from one point of view, the color that contains all colors, whereas from another point of view, it suggests a *tabula rasa* which may be imaginatively endowed with significance according to the desire or obsession of him who beholds it. It also readily suggests the sense of the uncanny or the preternatural out of which mythic and religious ideas are formed.

As Melville writes:

> Is it that by its indefiniteness it shadows forth the heartless voids and immensities of the universe, and thus stabs us from behind with the thought of annihilation, when beholding the white depths of the milky way? Or is it, that as in essence whiteness is not so much a color as the visible absence of color, and at the same time the concrete of all colors; is it for these reasons that there is such a dumb blankness, full of meaning, in a wide landscape of snows—a colorless, all-color of atheism from which we shrink?

These rhetorical questions help us to understand what Melville has in mind. Yet the most memorable passages about the whiteness of the whale are in other chapters where Melville the unsurpassable poet lays aside the rather awkward philosophizings that encumber portions of his book. The essential voice of Melville is to be heard in the half humorous, subtly erotic lyric tone which is peculiar to *Moby-Dick:*

> A gentle joyousness—a mighty mildness of repose in swiftness, invested the gliding whale. Not the white bull Jupiter swimming away with ravished Europa clinging to his graceful horns; his lovely, leering eyes sideways intent upon the maid; with smooth bewitching fleetness, rippling straight for the nuptial bower in Crete; not Jove,

not that great majesty Supreme! did surpass the glorified
White Whale as he so divinely swam.

But we should not think Melville a very great poet if he had
not written passages like the following (from "The Funeral," Chapter 69):

> The vast tackles have now done their duty. The peeled
> white body of the beheaded whale flashes like a marble
> sepulchre; though changed in hue, it has not perceptibly
> lost anything in bulk. It is still colossal. Slowly it floats
> more and more away, the water round it torn and
> splashed by the insatiate sharks, and the air above vexed
> with rapacious flights of screaming fowls, whose beaks
> are like so many insulting poniards in the whale. The
> vast white headless phantom floats further and further
> from the ship, and every rod that it so floats, what seem
> square roods of sharks and cubic roods of fowls, augment
> the murderous din. For hours and hours from the almost
> stationary ship that hideous sight is seen. Beneath the
> unclouded and mild azure sky, upon the fair face of the
> pleasant sea, wafted by the joyous breezes, that great
> mass of death floats on and on, till lost in infinite per-
> spectives.

The point of these remarks on "the meaning of *Moby-
Dick*" will have been missed unless it is seen that they
attribute a less manifold meaning to the book than is sometimes attributed to it. The symbols are manifold and suggestive; the epic scope is opulent; the rhetoric is full and
various; the incidental actions and metaphors are richly absorbing. The meaning is profound. But at the same time
it is narrow. The issues, as opposed to the states of mind
and feeling they generate, are all simplified; they are abstracted and compressed to a degree incompatible with the
broader reach, the more comprehensive concreted significance of greater poems like *King Lear, The Divine Comedy,*
or *The Iliad*. These poems bring to the given facts of human

112

destiny a universal tragic conception of their meaning. Melville's mind, no less profound in its intuitive sense of life, is nevertheless comparatively narrow and abstract. In this as in its incomparable discoveries of language, its appropriation of new subject matters, and its opening out of new aesthetic experience, *Moby-Dick* is at once the most startling and the most characteristic product of the American imagination.

## A Note on *Billy Budd*

Melville's last novel has enjoyed a well-deserved popularity in recent years. The mood is of reminiscence and profundity. There is much reflection, somewhat Conradian, on the problems that are raised by the plight of a serious, well-meaning individual, Captain Vere, as he faces some of the insoluble dilemmas involved in man's life in society and in history— dilemmas made specially urgent for him because he is in a position of command and responsibility. There is the vivid parable-like drama of Billy himself, who is destined innocently to kill Claggart and to die for the deed. There is also an implied lesson: that the appropriate virtues, as we contemplate the fate of man in history, are resignation and stoic forbearance; that the appropriate moods are elegy and pathos; and that there is perhaps the glimmering possibility of grace or spiritual rebirth manifesting itself in history.

These qualities, however, are not the ones commonly pointed out by the critics who have written on Melville in the last fifteen years (for example, they hardly ever mention Captain Vere, who is at the moral center of the book). Most of these critics have followed the lead of F. O. Matthiessen in *The American Renaissance* and have viewed Melville's novel as a drama of religious revelation. An extreme instance of this reading of *Billy Budd* is found in R. W. B. Lewis's *The American Adam*. Mr. Lewis seems to place *Billy Budd* virtually at the top of the American literary accomplishment. He thinks of it as a kind of New Testament, which corrects the errors and completes what was left unfinished and unsaid in *Moby-Dick*, a kind of Old Testament. For Mr. Lewis, *Billy Budd* is a form of revelation or dramatic "comment" moving dialectically towards divine truth. In *Billy Budd*, that is, fallen humanity is reborn in the Christ-like hero, and for the first time an American fiction has "entered, once and for all, into the dimension of myth," by which Mr. Lewis means the myth of the death and rebirth of the divine hero, since for him this single mythic motif constitutes "myth" in general.

Yet surely *Moby-Dick* is closer to the grand archetypes of the American imagination than is *Billy Budd*. And one's reason for thinking that this is so is Mr. Lewis's reason for thinking that it isn't. For as he correctly writes, "*Moby-Dick* is an elaborate pattern of countercommentaries, the supreme instance of the dialectical novel—a novel of tension without resolution." Exactly so. The imagination that created *Moby-Dick*, and other great American works from *The Scarlet Letter* to *Light in August*, is, then, not specifically tragic and Christian, but melodramatic and Manichaean. It does not settle ultimate questions; it leaves them open.

*Billy Budd*, as its opening pages strongly insist, is more political than theological or mythic. Its spirit is closer to Edmund Burke than to Kenneth Burke, a critic who has influenced Mr. Lewis. It dramatizes the conservative idea that society must follow a middle way of expediency and compromise. Society cannot be based on the contrary absolutes of good and evil represented by Billy Budd and his traducer Claggart. If these absolute extremes enter the arena of society, they assume a revolutionary form and so from the point of view of political realism, it is proper that they should destroy each other. But this is hardly a "resolution" of any sort, except perhaps as showing that contradictions are absorbed in history. The Biblical metaphors

Melville uses suggest a quasi-Augustinian idea of grace revealed in history. But still the final impression we get from Melville's story is less the mystery of incarnation than the mystery entailed in the eternal contradiction of good and evil, the kingdom of light and the kingdom of darkness. The political structure of society cannot countenance this extreme polarity. But this polarity may, nevertheless, be the very substance of the aesthetic imagination, as indeed, in *Billy Budd*, it is. And in this sense Melville's last novel appeals to us on the same grounds as does *Moby-Dick*.

# Chapter VI

# THE LESSON OF THE
# MASTER

## *The Portrait of a Lady*

HENRY JAMES's *Portrait of a Lady* (1880) was the first novel by an American that made, within the limits of its subject, full use of the novel form. By comparison, no previous American novel, even those of James, can claim to be fully "done." From James's point of view the older American romance-novelists had many faults. Some of these he singles out explicitly in his biography of Hawthorne, others, as was noted in Chapter I, he directly or indirectly deals with in his prefaces and critical writings. Cooper, Hawthorne, and Melville (actually James seems to know next to nothing of the last) relied too readily on extravagant events and startling characters. They failed to render experience fully. They failed to illustrate and dramatize connections and relations. They did not see (in the words of the Preface to *Roderick Hudson*) that for the true novelist "the continuity of things is the whole matter . . . of comedy and tragedy."

To read the first page of *The Portrait of a Lady* is to step into a world unfrequented by the earlier American novelists. A handsome pictorial representation, a fine old house, beautiful lawns and gardens, a group of people being set in motion—all these may be found in Cooper's *Satanstoe* or Hawthorne's *House of the Seven Gables*. But James's procedure is different from that of the earlier writers. The effect he seeks is more organic and self-contained. At the same time, there is more detail, more careful observation, for he has "researched" his subject—something which Hawthorne, as James said, tended to leave undone. We encounter at the very beginning the author's reference to his book as a "history" and we are perhaps reminded that in his essay "The Art of Fiction" (1884) he was to say that the novel should give the same impression of veracity as does history itself.

On the broad, sloping lawn of the mansion James calls Gardencourt we discover people taking tea, and they are finding it agreeable, not only because it tastes good but because drinking it is a mild ritual by which they show themselves to be a part of a way of life, a social order which we understand is to figure strongly in the book, as strongly as does the life of the Westchester aristocracy in *Satanstoe*. Yet the life of James's characters will be illustrated and dramatized with a far more exact and also a more poetic art than one can find in Cooper's novel.

To admit, as most readers would, that there is an element of poetry in *The Portrait of a Lady* is to admit that though it has all of the novelistic virtues, it has others too. There is a sense in which one might speak of the "poetry" of *Pride and Prejudice* or *Middlemarch*—a poetry of picture and scene, a poetry felt to belong to the organized effect of character, action, and setting. But this is, so to speak, novelistic poetry, of the kind every interesting novel has. *The Portrait* has it too, but it also has a further dimension of poetry, to understand which one must perceive that James's novel is akin to romance as the others are not.

It is an important fact about James's art that he gave up

what he considered the claptrap of romance without giving up its mystery and beauty. Mr. Leavis in *The Great Tradition* is not interested in James as a romancer, but he nevertheless notes that James is a "poet-novelist" and says that he combines Jane Austen's skill of observing and dramatizing manners with Hawthorne's "profoundly moral and psychological . . . poetic art of fiction." This is very well put, and it supports the supposition of this chapter that a part of James's great program for improving the novel consisted of the reconstitution, on new grounds, of romance. Often one has difficulty in pinning down any one element of a James novel as belonging to romance because the author has so completely subdued and transmuted it to suit his exacting novelistic purposes. The element of romance becomes generally subverted and assimilated; yet in turn it imparts the glow of poetry to the realistic substance of the novel. Which is to say in a different way what Mr. Leavis says in the following: "James's own constant and profound concern with spiritual facts expresses itself not only in what obviously demands to be called symbolism, but in the handling of character, episode, and dialogue, and in the totality of the plot, so that when he seems to offer a novel of manners, he gives us more than that and the 'poetry' is major."

The conscious assimilation of romance into the novelistic substance of *The Portrait* took place in two different ways. It was assimilated into the language of the book and produced a general enrichment of metaphor. It was also (1) brought in in the character of Isabel Archer, the heroine, (2) who is to a considerable extent our point of view as we read. Isabel tends to see things as a romancer does, whereas the author sees things with the firmer, more comprehensive, and more disillusioned vision of the novelist. Thus James brings the element of romance into the novel in such a way that he can both share in the romantic point of view of his heroine and separate himself from it by taking an objective view of it.

119

The metaphors of *The Portrait of a Lady* do not often rival the amazingly elaborate figures one encounters in James's later works, but by contrast with the usual practice of the novel at the time James wrote they are notably daring—so much so that sometimes they seem to lead a life of their own within the spacious world of the book, although in each case we are led to see the relevance of the metaphor to the course of events and to the pattern of unfolding significance. There is a paradox, says James in his Preface to *The Portrait,* in trying to write a fiction at once so complex and so ambitious. The paradox is that a novel so conceived must "positively . . . appear more true to its character in proportion as it strains, or tends to burst, with a latent extravagance, its mould." Metaphor offered to James a kind of repository or annex in which the latent extravagance of his imagination might take form. As has often been noticed the main figures of speech in James's novel—although the variety is rich—have to do with the house and the garden.

The metaphors are sometimes extravagant. For example we read of Isabel that "her imagination was by habit ridiculously active; when the door was not open it jumped out of the window." But that is a mere piece of fancy and reminds us less of the characteristic practice of James than of the quaint wit of Hawthorne. Ordinarily, James's metaphors, in *The Portrait* as elsewhere, are not quaint and concise. They are suggestively imaginative and they are likely to be given a tone of elevated levity which at once enjoys what is being said and takes note of its extravagance. As often as not the Jamesian metaphor shows that mixture of serious poetic imagination with humor which we find in other American writers, notably Melville, Mark Twain, and Faulkner. Although one would hardly mistake the style of any one of these writers for that of any other, all of them are fond of the serious, intricately sustained joke. Here is James speaking of Ralph Touchett's pose of facetious irony, which Isabel, in her earnest sincerity, finds baffling and also reprehensible. Sensing his inner despair and sorry that he is sickly, she wants to come directly to the "real" Ralph Touchett, but he himself explains the value of his pose:

"I keep a band of music in my ante-room. It has orders to play without stopping; it renders me two excellent services. It keeps the sounds of the world from reaching the private apartments, and it makes the world think that dancing's going on within." It was dance music indeed that you usually heard when you came within earshot of Ralph's band; the liveliest waltzes seemed to float upon the air. Isabel often found herself irritated by this perpetual fiddling; she would have liked to pass—

James finds the metaphor, once launched, too good to drop—

through the ante-room, as her cousin called it, and enter the private apartments. It mattered little that he had assured her they were a very dismal place; she would have been glad to undertake to sweep them and set them in order. It was but half-hospitality to let her remain outside.

The idea of leaving and entering a house, the contrast of different kinds of houses, the question of whether a house is a prison or the scene of liberation and fulfillment—these are the substance of the metaphors in *The Portrait of a Lady*. Figuratively speaking, the story told in the novel is of Isabel's leaving an American house—a way of life, that is— for a European house. Ostensibly she conceives of this as an escape from frustrating and cramping confinement to a fuller, freer, more resonant and significant life. Actually, it is not hard to see that although James has much admiration and tenderness of feeling for his heroine, he gives her an element of perverse Yankee idealism of the sort that he was shortly to portray in the more exacerbated form of positively per*verted* idealism in Olive Chancellor in *The Bostonians*. So that for all her dark-haired, gray-eyed beauty, her delightful young enthusiasm, and her zest for life, there is in Isabel a fatal susceptibility to a form of imprisonment worse than that she has escaped. Figuratively, the house in which she lives as the wife of Gilbert Osmond confines her in a hopeless imprisonment she could not consciously have imagined.

Our first sight of Isabel occurs when with her abrupt charm and her disarming candor she walks across the lawn at Gardencourt, the Touchetts' English estate, and presents herself to her cousin Ralph, his father, and Lord Warburton. But then in the form of a flash-back we are speedily acquainted with the general circumstances of Isabel's childhood and girlhood. We find her in the old family house at Albany talking with Mrs. Touchett and greeting with joy Mrs. Touchett's offer to take her to Europe. "To go to Florence," says Isabel, "I'd promise almost anything!" She sees in this offer an escape from the loneliness of the life she has known in the great, empty, dismal house. Yet now that escape is in view, Isabel admits that she does not hate the house or the circumstances of her early life, even though Mrs. Touchett dismisses the place as "very bourgeois." "I like places in which things have happened," says Isabel, "—even if they're sad things. A great many people have died here; the place has been full of life." And to Mrs. Touchett's query "Is that what you call being full of life?" she replies, "I mean full of experience—of people's feelings and sorrows. And not of their sorrows only, for I've been happy here as a child."

Still, the possibility of living a full life in Albany seems remote to Isabel. And the only considerable picture of her as a young girl that James gives us suggests that she had found the Albany house not so much the scene of human sufferings and joys as the somewhat bleak abode of a life of fantasy and reading, a life isolated from reality. Isabel had been accustomed to read and daydream in a room known as "the office" that lay beyond the library.

The place owed much of its mysterious melancholy to the fact that it was properly entered from the second door of the house, the door that had been condemned, and that it was secured by bolts which a particularly slender little girl found it impossible to slide. She knew that this silent, motionless portal opened into the street; if the sidelights had not been filled with green paper she might have looked out upon the little brown stoop and the well-worn brick pavement. But she had no wish to look out, for this would have interfered with her theory that there was a strange, unseen place on the other side —a place which became to the child's imagination, according to its different moods, a region of delight or terror.

She is sitting in this room when Mrs. Touchett comes to see her, except that being now a young woman with undefined but strong purposes she is, on this fateful afternoon, not engaging in childish fantasy but, having given her mind "marching orders," she has sent it "trudging over the sandy plains of a history of German thought."

Despite her disorganized and tenuous education and the puritanism of her native Yankee temperament, Isabel is now ostensibly ready to pursue an enriched life of the emotions and of thought. A way of life characterized by its intricate amenity, its depth of emotion, and its richness of traditionally ordered experience cannot be symbolized by the house at Albany. But it can by the Tudor mansion of the Touchetts, to which Isabel is introduced when she arrives in England.

Her uncle's house seemed a picture made real; no refinement of the agreeable was lost on Isabel: the rich perfection of Gardencourt at once revealed a world and gratified a need. The deep embrasures and curious casements, the quiet light on dark polished panels, the deep greenness outside, that seemed always peeping in, the sense of a well-ordered privacy in the centre of a "property"—a place where sounds were felicitously accidental, where the tread was muffled by the earth itself and in the thick mild air all friction dropped out of contact and all shrillness out of talk . . .

There is no paper in the windows of this house, no need to isolate oneself from the world outside. On the contrary the "greenness outside" seems "always peeping in" and the garden, where at important points in the novel Isabel will receive and reject proposals of marriage from Lord Warburton and Caspar Goodwood, seems as much a part of the house as does its own interior. Consequently, the garden makes an inevitable part of the general metaphor which represents the enriched sensibility of the heroine.

> She was always planning out her development, desiring her perfection, observing her progress. Her nature had, in her conceit, a certain garden-like quality, a suggestion of perfume and murmuring boughs, of shady bowers and lengthening vistas, which made her feel that introspection was, after all, an exercise in the open air, and that a visit to the recesses of one's spirit was harmless when one returned from it with a lapful of roses.

In a novel which describes a fall from innocence, it is suitable that the tragic action should be metaphorically mirrored in the heroine's mind by this imaginative conjunction of the garden and the ancient house, in which the garden stands for Isabel's Eve-like innocence and the house for a civilization that has lost its innocence but has acquired—along with its corruption—wisdom, maturity, and the whole involved and valuable accretion of culture. Thus Isabel is akin not only to the heroines of George Eliot, such as Hetty Sorrel, Maggie Tulliver, Rosamond Vincy, and Gwendolen Harleth, with whom James compares her in his Preface; nor is she akin only to Shakespeare's Portia, with whom James also compares Isabel, calling Portia "the very type and model of the young person intelligent and presumptuous."

Isabel also resembles the strong-minded Rosalind in *As You Like It* and the innocent and expectant Miranda in *The Tempest*. And the particular charm of these girls is that they are "real," that they make positive demands on life, but that they are at the same time figures of romance. James is also thinking of the Miltonic archetype of all feminine innocence, as is suggested by his using, as Leon Edel points out, the language of *Paradise Lost* to describe Isabel as she sets out on her adventures: "The world lay before her—she could do whatever she chose."

Chapter 42 of *The Portrait* brings to its fullest realization, though not to its last refinement, the characteristic art of James, that art which I am attempting to define as an assimilation of romance into the substance of the novel. James describes this chapter by saying that, "It is obviously the best thing in the book, but it is only a supreme illustration of the general plan." In this chapter James was able to achieve supremely the "circuit" of the real and the ideal, of action and fantasy, and thus to capture along with the realistic substance of the story the wonder and beauty of romance while at the same time rejecting the conventional devices of romance.

Isabel, now the wife of Osmond, sits one evening by the fire in the drawing room of Osmond's house, and with a combination of disillusioned insight and darkly working imagination she recognizes for the first time the true character of her husband and the true nature of her predicament. The problem, as James sees it, is how to present an episode in which nothing happens except an "extraordinary meditative vigil" but which will have all the excitement of action and high adventure. The problem is how to make the "mystic conversion" of Isabel's adventures, which have actually been "mild," into "the stuff of drama," how, as he goes on to say, to produce "the maximum of intensity with the minimum of strain." The "circuit" of the real and the fantasied, the "mystic conversion" of which James speaks, is to be established not, certainly, through a

mere retelling or summing-up of Isabel's "mild adventures,"
but by giving us her sense of them. "Without her sense of
them, her sense *for* them, as one may say, they are next to
nothing at all." Although there are no overt happenings in
this chapter, it nevertheless, as James says, "throws the action further forward than twenty 'incidents' might have
done. It was designed to have all the vivacity of incident
and all the economy of picture. Isabel sits up, by her
dying fire, far into the night, under the spell of recogni-
tions on which she finds the last sharpness suddenly wait.
It is a representation simply of her motionlessly *seeing*, and
an attempt withal to make the mere still lucidity of her
act as 'interesting' as the surprise of a caravan or the
identification of a pirate."

What occurs in Isabel's mind is the kind of disillusioned
and profoundly realistic perception of truth about oneself
and one's situation that is called "tragic recognition." Yet it
comes to her in images that belong as much to melodrama
as to tragedy. "Her soul was haunted by terrors," says
James, "which crowded to the foreground of thought as
quickly as a place was made for them." One of these terrors is the new image she has formed of her husband, an
image which distinctly reminds us of one of the cold, selfish
villains of Hawthorne, a Rappiccini or a Chillingworth. She
thinks of Osmond's "faculty for making everything wither
that he touched, spoiling everything for her that he looked
at. . . . It was as if he had had the evil eye; as if his
presence were a blight and his favor a misfortune."

She reflects that she had set out with her husband for
"the high places of happiness." She had taken "all the first
steps in the purest confidence," but now "she had suddenly
found the infinite vista of a multiplied life to be a dark
narrow alley with a dead wall at the end." The man who
had so narrowed and enclosed her life, a creature of darkness, now steps forth into the light—"she had seen only half
his nature then, as one saw the disk of the moon when it

was partly masked by the shadow of the earth. She saw the full moon now—she saw the whole man."

But the full force of Isabel's recognition is appropriately conveyed by the metaphor of the house and the garden. She has escaped, to be sure, the isolation and girlish ignorance she had known at Albany, but she has lost the felicitous synthesis of innocence and experience symbolized as a possibility for her by Gardencourt. Her marriage, as she now sees, had made her the inhabitant of a different house.

> She could live it over again, the incredulous terror with which she had taken the measure of her dwelling. Between these four walls she had lived ever since; they were to surround her for the rest of her life. It was the house of darkness, the house of dumbness, the house of suffocation. Osmond's beautiful mind gave it neither light nor air; Osmond's beautiful mind indeed seemed to peep down from a small high window and mock at her.

And so Isabel comes to see that

> under all his culture, his cleverness, his amenity, under his good-nature, his facility, his knowledge of life, his egotism lay hidden like a serpent in a bank of flowers.

Her youthful innocence and good-will have been foully traduced, she has been the victim of an elegantly sordid conspiracy, the possibility of a full life she had envisioned has been spoiled. And we are left to recall, with a sense of its tragic irony, her early declaration to Lord Warburton that "I can't escape my fate"—that fate which Isabel had thought would consist of some rewarding involvement in life. For although she has rather grand aspirations, an essential stipulation of her fate, as she understands it, is that she shall never be exempt "from the usual chances and dangers, from what most people know and suffer." She has found knowledge and suffering no doubt, but of the grimmest sort. In her plight there can be no such clarion awakening and engagement of her human faculties as she had supposed might be the result of knowledge and suffering. Indeed there seems nothing left for her but a life of duty and abnegation. As we leave her at the end of the book she seems veritably to belong to the sisterhood of Hester Prynne.

But we know why Hester Prynne is made to suffer; conventional morality imposes on her its punishment for a sin of passion. For better or for worse, Isabel remains scrupulously virginal. She has been guilty of no misconduct in which we find any real justification for suffering. And we do, of course, want to find some measure of justification; otherwise we shall have to convict James of palming off on us under the guise of moral complexity what is morally speaking a mere melodrama of victimized innocence, a tale of merely senseless cruelty and pathos.

Is James himself subtly vindictive in his attitude toward Isabel? He clearly admires her for her almost redemptive American probity and moral spontaneity, and yet he just as clearly thinks her guilty of presumption, and of bad manners that are only just barely made tolerable by her ingenuous charm. Nor does James approve of her upbringing or of her father, one of those somewhat disorderly, nomadic Americans for whom he always shows a dislike. Isabel has been taught to "affront her destiny," as James says in his Preface; and this, one supposes, is less correct than *con*fronting it. Even supposing, as there is some speculative ground for doing, that James has a neurotic involvement with his heroine which leads him to fear her female aggressiveness and thus to take satisfaction and to derive a feeling of security in showing her, though possessed of animal spirits, to be sexually cold, and in leading her, finally, to her cruel fate—even supposing on these or other grounds a genuine animosity on the part of James toward his heroine, the fact remains that this is surmounted by his admiration of her and his profound sympathy with her. And in any case Isabel is so completely created a character that she lives her life independently of the approval or disapproval the author may feel toward her, whether we deduce his feeling from the novel itself or from our knowledge of his life and temperament.

Sometimes moved, as one must be, by a desire for a more earthly and simple morality than James's usually is, one wishes that Isabel Archer were more like Kate Croy of *The Wings of the Dove* or even the unpleasantly named Fleda Vetch in *The Spoils of Poynton,* girls in whom the general quality of self-assertion has a sexual component. But despite her deeply repressed sexuality, Isabel remains among the most complex, the most fully realized, and the most humanly fascinating of James's characters. Consequently we cannot think her a mere case of victimized innocence. She has so many powers, imperfect though they are, of knowledge, of feeling, of imagination that her fate must surely issue in some crucial way from her being the sort of person she is. If she is disqualified for triumph, it is not in the obvious way of James's other victimized innocents, like Catherine Sloper in *Washington Square,* who is homely and timid, like Maisie in *What Maisie Knew* or little Miles and Flora in *The Turn of the Screw,* who are children, or like Milly Theale in *The Wings of the Dove,* who is dying of tuberculosis. Isabel's disqualification is that of heroines and heroes throughout tragic literature—a blindness to reality, a distortion of awareness, that puts her at the mercy of the perverse and self-destructive inner motives struggling in her for the upper hand.

Without attempting any sort of full discussion of Isabel and her troubles, one may note that she sees reality as the romancer sees it. This is obvious as a general proposition, since Isabel is patently romantic in the sense that she has highly imaginative dreams which prove to be beyond the possibility of fulfillment. A realistic young woman, or, for that matter, a conventionally romantic one, would have accepted Lord Warburton as a good catch, for he is, after all, an excellent man as well as a rich and noble lord. But

Isabel has higher ideals than any she thinks can be realized by a life with Lord Warburton. Her personal romance includes strenuous abstractions that lead her to aspire to far more than the conventional romance of marrying an English nobleman. She therefore perversely and no doubt quite mistakenly decides that to marry Lord Warburton would be to "escape" her "fate." "I can't escape unhappiness," she says. "In marrying you I shall be trying to." And she continues by saying that by marrying Lord Warburton she would be "turning away," "separating" herself from life, "from the usual chances and dangers, from what most people know and suffer." Lord Warburton's answer is one that would in the main turn out to be true: "I don't offer you any exoneration from life or from any chances or dangers whatever." He is brought by Isabel's behavior to a true understanding of her, and he exclaims, "I never saw a person judge things on such theoretic grounds." Her theory is that he is merely "a collection of attributes and powers," but this is clearly a false theory. Despite his being a hereditary nobleman and so, bound to the formalities and duties of his station in life, he presents himself to her with perfect candor as a man, and not a lord, who needs and desires her. Thus Isabel's vague democratic objections to English aristocracy, which in any case she seems generally to admire, are not the real reason why she rejects Lord Warburton. Nor when she does marry does she choose a man notable for democracy. She rejects Lord Warburton at the behest of her puritan spirituality, which leads her to flee from the mere physical and social realities of life as these would be should she marry him. Perversely and mistakenly, her argument is that marriage to Lord Warburton would exempt her from life. Better a collection of attributes and powers (which in any case Lord Warburton is not) than a collection of sterile tastes and appetites, which Gilbert Osmond certainly is. But Isabel does not see Osmond for what he is until too late. (I am assuming here as elsewhere that Isabel's choice is, for all practical purposes, between Warburton and Osmond. Ralph is in love with her, but his illness disqualifies him. The persistent Caspar Goodwood presents himself at intervals, but Isabel does not see him as an actual possibility. She seems to conceive of him as worthy but as rather stodgy in his conventional Massachusetts way. She scarcely thinks of him as being momentously on the scene until at the very end of the novel when he proposes to rescue her from Osmond and, in his vehemence, frightens her with his masculine aggressiveness by giving her, so far as the reader knows, her only kiss.)

How is it that the image Osmond presents to the world so easily commands Isabel's assent? This is a hard problem, but the answer may be suggested by observing that although Isabel's vision of things is neither that of self-interested common sense nor that of worldly romance in which poor girls marry great lords, it emphatically is that of the romance associated with the American tradition of puritanism and transcendentalism. Isabel subscribes to the American romance of the self. She believes that the self finds fulfillment either in its own isolated integrity or on a more or less transcendent ground where the contending forces of good and evil are symbolized abstractions. She sees her fate as a spiritual melodrama. Her grasp of reality, though manifold in its presumptions, is unstable, and her desire for experience is ambivalent. She rejects Lord Warburton ostensibly because she fears that marrying him will exempt her from life. But Ralph Touchett, who often speaks with the wisdom of the author, has no trouble in securing a contradictory admission from his amusing and perplexing cousin. At the end of a lengthy dialogue about her rejection of Lord Warburton, Ralph conjectures, "You want to drain the cup of experience," and gets out of Isabel this surprising answer, "No, I don't wish to touch the cup of experience. It's a poisoned drink! I only want to see for myself." To which Ralph adds a comment in the partial truth of which we may see a link between Isabel and Osmond: "You want to see, but not to feel."

*cf Fleda
Vetch*

Ralph has hit upon a truth about his cousin. The kind
of cold, amoral aloofness, the possibly morbid passion for
observing life at a distance—these are real traits of Isabel's
character. True, they are no more than strong strands in
her fabric. But they are strong enough so that she responds
to Osmond's talk about how "one ought to make one's life
a work of art," without being aware of the inhumanity and
the withering aestheticism such an idea may imply. Only
when it is too late does she discover the cold malignancy
of her husband. Only too late does she see that, apart from
his need of the money she has inherited from her uncle,
she is cherished by Osmond only to the extent that he can
consider her another art object in his collection. Only too
late does she understand the subtle corruption that leads
Osmond to try to arrange his daughter's education so as to
make her life "a work of art." Listening to Osmond's plans
for Pansy's schooling, Isabel seems to see at last "how far
her husband's desire to be effective was capable of going
—to the point of playing theoretic tricks on the delicate or-
ganism of his daughter." In this way Isabel, who is herself
every bit the theorist Lord Warburton accused her of being, comes to understand the perverse puritan impulse
which Hawthorne called "the Unpardonable Sin." The sin
is the same whether one's cold, theoretical manipulation of
others has an aesthetic motive or as with Hawthorne's Chillingworth or Ethan Brand a quasi-scientific one.

*cf
Charlotte*

Isabel's romance of the self, as was suggested above, requires that self-fulfillment shall take place only at a high
level of abstraction, where the disinterested pursuit of perfection may be carried on. And although Ralph Touchett
warns his cousin that Osmond is a "sterile aesthete," she
sees in him at once the high priest, the devoted custodian,
and martyr of the life of perfection. She is very far from
believing that the ordinary vulgar circumstances of one's
life have anything to do with one's self. She finds it incon-
ceivable and rather degrading that anyone should suppose
the self to be in any sort of dialectic with the mere things

one is surrounded by. In Chapter 19 there occurs an important exchange between Madame Merle and Isabel on this point. They have been talking about the inevitable "young man with a mustache" who must figure in some way in every young woman's life. Madame Merle speculatively inquires whether Isabel's "young man with a mustache" has a "castle in the Apennines" or "an ugly brick house in Fortieth Street." And when Isabel says characteristically, "I don't care anything about his house," Madame Merle replies, "That's very crude of you." And she continues by saying,

> There's no such thing as an isolated man or woman; we're each of us made up of some cluster of appurtenances. What shall we call our "self"? Where does it begin? Where does it end? It overflows into everything that belongs to us—and then it flows back again. I know a large part of myself is in the clothes I choose to wear. I've a great respect for *things!* One's self—for other people—is one's expression of one's self; and one's house, one's furniture, one's garments, the books one reads, the company one keeps—these things are all expressive.

This bit of worldly wisdom strikes Isabel as being worldly, all too worldly, but not as being wisdom. "I don't agree with you," she says. "I think just the other way. I don't know whether I succeed in expressing myself, but I know that nothing else expresses me. Nothing that belongs to me is any measure of me; everything's on the contrary a limit, a barrier, and a perfectly arbitrary one." To find the fulfillment of self through superiority to mere things and without attention to what others may think about what one does —this is the feat Isabel supposes Osmond to have accomplished. Actually as she comes tragically to see, Osmond is above all men enslaved by things and by what he supposes others to be thinking of him. "She had thought it a grand indifference, an exquisite independence. But indifference was really the last of his qualities; she had never seen anyone who thought so much of others."

The moral world shared by Isabel and Osmond—a world in which Lord Warburton has no place—is that of the high Emersonian self-culture. In the sordid elegance of Osmond's implacably willed hedonism we discover the final possibilities of corruption in this culture, which is of course no less subject to corruption than any other moral idealism. In Isabel's unhappy career we estimate the tragic implications of an idealism that in effect directs one to seek the rewards of the fully "lived life" without descending from one's high pedestal into its actual conditions. In Isabel's sincere presentation of her essentially spiritual quest as a quest for a real involvement in "the usual chances and dangers" of life lies the tragic irony of the story. And it has, furthermore, the advantage of verisimilitude since that is how an ambitious young woman in the latter part of the nineteenth century—spiritual puritan though she might be—would conceive of her quest, knowing it to be no longer inevitably the part of woman to isolate herself from the world either because of religious conviction or in acquiescence to the conventions about woman's place.

Isabel Archer may be said to have the imagination of romance most notably in the sense that she responds to character intensely only when it conceives of itself at a high level of abstraction and when its acts are symbolic of ideal values. When this imagination is confronted by an appealingly complex human being, such as Lord Warburton, it sees only "a collection of attributes and powers." Like the romancer, Isabel refuses to impute significance to human actions unless they are conceived as being exempt from the ordinary circumstances of life, whereas the genuine novelist sees in ordinary circumstances the inescapable root condition of significant actions.

So, to carry the analogy only one step along, James in the end brings Isabel's point of view around from that of the romancer to that of the novelist. Like *The Blithedale*

*Romance, The Portrait of a Lady* explores the limits of romance. But whereas Hawthorne seems to admit that he cannot be the true novelist and thus surrenders the imagination of the novelist to that of the romancer, James does the opposite, affirming the primacy of the novelist's imagination. But though he rejects romance as a moral view of the world, he assimilates into the very substance of the novel, by means of metaphor and the charm of the heroine herself, the appeal of romance. Thus he is able to meet superabundantly the requirement for the novel which he calls in the Preface to *The American* satisfying "our general sense of the ways things happen" and at the same time he is able to provide the novel with the poetry of romance.

So much, and as it would seem, no more is to be done with *The Portrait of a Lady* as a romance. In James's books one catches hold of the romance only just as it is disappearing into the thicket of the novel. Thus it is a thankless task to pursue too long and arduously something that is always being assimilated into something else. James is not a romancer like Hawthorne or Melville; he is a novelist to the finger tips.

It is true that, compared with any English novelist one might mention, James shows a strikingly varied interest in the literary forms associated with romance. He is not interested in pastoral idyls, to be sure. But many of his novels, as Jacques Barzun has pointed out, have a strong element of melodrama, from the early *Washington Square* to the late *Wings of the Dove*. Yet none of his fictions end in the sheer horror produced by the unresolved tensions of melodrama. This is true, for example, of the late short novel *The Other House*. In the first two thirds of the book we have the conflict of a "good" woman and a "bad" woman, a tale of frustrated love and revenge, and the drowning by the bad woman of a little girl. But even this thriller runs afoul of Jamesian complications before we are through with it. It turns out that the villainous woman is not, after all, guilty of unalloyed villainy. It is shown that she has attractive qualities, and it is shown that although she committed a particularly repulsive murder, the moral question finally involves the conscious or unconscious complicity in the crime by several of the people around her. The conclusion of the book is rather feeble and unsatisfactory, but the crime is made to seem that of a social class and a particular way of life, a crime that is compounded by everyone's agreeing to hush it up. By this time the tale has become quasi-tragic and our minds are directed as in the plays of Ibsen, which influence *The Other House*, to a social problem, the corruption of the bourgeoisie. The abstract actions, the stirring contradictions, the relative freedom from social and moral perplexities that we look for in melodrama—all these are excitingly present in *The Other House*, but they do not see James through to the end. Instead he characteristically makes the attempt to assimilate the purely melodramatic elements of the story into a novelistic conception. *The Other House* is an instructive investigation, from the Jamesian point of view, of the limits of melodrama.

A more striking departure from the practice of the English novelists (for, after all, Dickens and Conrad, among others, make use of melodrama) is James's use of a symbolistic or allegorical poetry in the late novels—notably *The Wings of the Dove* and *The Golden Bowl.* That these novels are akin to poetry has long been recognized. For example, Stephen Spender once compared *The Golden Bowl* illuminatingly with Eliot's poems. And many people have noted a certain ritualistic poetry of sacrifice and elegy in *The Wings of the Dove* and have seen in this story of the betrayal and death of a blameless young woman a resemblance to Racine's *Iphigenia* and Shakespeare's *Othello*. And Quentin Anderson's argument that *The Ambassadors, The Wings of the Dove,* and *The Golden Bowl* constitute in their cumulative significance a "divine novel" allegorically presenting James's version of his father's Swedenborgian theology is an important discovery.

Nevertheless, it seems to me that the foregoing discussion

of *The Portrait of a Lady* marks out in a general way the borders beyond which an examination of James's more poetic dimension cannot go without becoming irrelevant to the question of James as a master of the craft of the novel. Even in reading a book which has so beautiful a central conception as *The Wings of the Dove* one is not recompensed by the allegory for the vexation of finding a novel which is so attenuated and prolix. One reads it, that is, stubbornly *as a novel*. One sets out with high hope and is immediately gratified by the unsurpassable rendering, at the beginning, of Kate Croy and her incomparable father; one is impressed and interested by Mrs. Lowder and her household; one gives a slightly baffled assent to Merton Densher; one finds the diaphanous Milly Theale beautiful and touching. But then the *longueurs* set in, along with the infinitely syntactical language which seems to engross no recognizable experience, and we are forced to settle for two fine scenes: Milly confronting the Bronzino portrait at Lord Mark's country house and Densher standing in the rain outside the Venetian café recognizing through the window Lord Mark. In short the metaphorical effects of *The Wings of the Dove*, which contain a sort of half-rendered allegory, do not strike one, like those in *The Portrait of a Lady*, as forming a positively valuable component of the whole. They strike one, rather, as negative facts—attenuations of the naturalistic substance of the novel. It is not possible for James, given his characteristic genius, to render an allegory in the form of a novel. But it is possible for him to weaken a novel by giving it an elusive aura of allegory. This at least is what one feels in actually reading the book. The allegory assumes substance and significance when it is considered as a part of the history of ideas, but that is another matter.

# Chapter VII

# MARK TWAIN AND THE
# NOVEL

## Huckleberry Finn

APART from any and all of its meanings *The Adventures of Huckleberry Finn* (1885) delights the reader first and last by its language. The book makes a music of words which is beautifully sustained and modulated to the very end. The language is original and it has proved to be one of the most important discoveries—for it was discovered and adapted rather than being created out of the whole cloth—that have occurred in American literature. Hemingway's well-known pronouncement that "all modern American literature comes from one book by Mark Twain called *Huckleberry Finn*" states a large truth, even though literally it is untrue. Wherever we find, in writers such as Stephen Crane, Sherwood Anderson, Sinclair Lewis, Faulkner, or Hemingway himself, a style that flows with the easy grace of colloquial speech and gets its directness and simplicity by leaving out subordinate words and clauses, we will be right in thinking that this is the language of Mark Twain.

In the works of these writers we are not asked to accustom ourselves to a version of traditional "literary" English, as we are in reading Cooper, Hawthorne, Melville, or James, writers whose versions of English are sometimes highly idiosyncratic and imprisoned in their own special conventions. And yet, close as it is to the spoken English of rural Southwest America, the language of *Huckleberry Finn* is itself a new literary style which, as the works of Hemingway show, is capable of extreme conventionalization. It is literary because it is sustained beyond the span of spoken language to meet the requirements of a long story and because it is consciously adapted to the purposes of a novel which even those critics who object to the concluding part of the book, where Tom Sawyer takes over, on the ground that this makes a disunity, admit to be in the main a masterpiece of literary form. But it is also literary because, unlike ordinary spoken language, it is always conscious of the traditional English—notably of the Bible and Shakespeare—from which it is departing. The language of *Huckleberry Finn* is a kind of joyous exorcism of traditional literary English, but this ritual act allies it irrevocably with what it exorcises. And half the pleasure of reading the book comes from the alternation of tension and release as the language modulates or, as often happens, shifts with wonderful abruptness from traditional literary English to colloquial American.

This running relation between styles is most easily observed in the passages of burlesque and parody, as when the Widow Douglas tries unsuccessfully to "learn" Huck about Moses and the Bulrushers or in the scene where the Duke is working up to a delivery of Hamlet's soliloquy—

> Hamlet's soliloquy, you know; the most celebrated thing in Shakespeare. Ah, it's sublime, sublime! Always fetches the house. I haven't got it in the book—I've only got one volume—but I reckon I can piece it out from memory. I'll just walk up and down a minute, and see if I can call it back from recollection's vaults.

So he went marching up and down, thinking, and frowning horrible every now and then; then he would hoist up his eyebrows; next he would squeeze his hand on his forehead and stagger back and kind of moan; next he would sigh, and next he'd let on to drop a tear. It was beautiful to see him. By and by he got it. He told us to give attention. Then he strikes a most noble attitude, with one leg shoved forwards, and his arms stretched away up, and his head tilted back, looking up at the sky; and then he begins to rip and rave and grit his teeth; and after that, all through his speech, he howled, and spread around, and swelled up his chest, and just knocked the spots out of any acting ever *I* see before.

But a more subtly amalgamated language than that of burlesque is what makes the style of *Huckleberry Finn*. Among innumerable examples, there is Huck's version of the parting words of the woman who befriends him when, dressed as a girl, he stops by at her house: "If you get into trouble you send word to Mrs. Judith Loftus, which is me, and I'll do what I can to get you out." It is a perfect sentence considered either as "correct" English or ordinary speech, except for the incorrectness of "which is me." But the "which is me" is of the essence of Huck's style, the only graceful way of saying what it says. Any of the other possibilities would be awkward or preposterous—such as "which am I" or "who am I" or "who is me" or "that's my name" or "which is my name." The last alternative would be the least false; but it would be too formal and the natural tone of the sentence would have been thrown out of key. Huck's language flows with the effortlessness of the river itself, filling its mold to perfection, and in fact making in its restless energy its own ever new mold as it goes along. "We said there warn't no home like a raft, after all. Other places do seem so cramped up and smothery, but a raft don't. You feel mighty free and easy and comfortable on a raft."

The language of *Huckleberry Finn* is a perfect vehicle for the hard, common-sense realism for which the book is famous and which, as much as the language itself, gives the book its important place as a precursor of modern literature. The author always seems to know when a detailed inventory of objects will be effective, and he sometimes makes these very detailed indeed. He knows too when to suppress detail, as in his descriptions of the raft. He gives a fairly factual account of the raft—how it was built, how it was steered, how Huck and Jim built the tepee on a raised platform, how they cooked fish and coffee. And yet the raft is rather vague in detail, perhaps because it is most important for what people feel about it and what they do and say on it. Pap's cabin in the woods, the "house of death" that floats down the river, the Gangerford house, these are described, particularly their contents, with more factual precision than the raft.

The greatness of *Huckleberry Finn* is in the simple clairvoyance of the truth it tells. Huck Finn, our observer and narrator, sees *everything* with the same impassive clarity and the same total lack of distortion with which he sees the most ordinary stick, stone, or fishhook. Unspeakable violence and cruelty, fraudulence and pretense, sordidness and glory, the sublime and ridiculous, pride and humility—all these are to be seen in the strong, representative episodes that epitomize so much of American civilization as they unfold before Huck on the trip down the river. This realism would not be a triumph if behind the impassive mask Huck remained unfeeling. But his feelings are strong, his reticences sensitive, and his sympathies and resentments plain. Nor do these feelings affect the cool steadfastness with which he sees and reports fact. In later writers such as Stephen Crane and Hemingway we encounter the same impassive clairvoyance, yet at no time do these authors succeed in reporting so much of the essential reality of a civilization. Doubtless this is what Lionel Trilling has in mind when he says that the greatness of *Huckleberry Finn* lies

142

in "its power of telling the truth" and what T. S. Eliot means when he praises Huck's "vision" of the real world.

But to see truth clearly is to see that it is not always simple or predictable. So Mark Twain himself recognizes in one of the witticisms of Pudd'nhead Wilson's Calendar (in *Following the Equator*): "Truth is stranger than Fiction, but it is because Fiction is obliged to stick to the possibilities; Truth isn't." This aphorism, applied to *Huckleberry Finn*, leads us to see, what is in any case obvious, that Mark Twain's greatest book is poetic as well as realistic, for a part of the truth it encompasses is of the sort we cannot even conceive without the intervening illusion of poetry.

Bernard De Voto, a dedicated Mark Twain critic and scholar, had no more than the most elementary understanding of poetic fictions and indeed he seemed not to believe in the virtue and substance of literature at all. He often put himself in the vanguard of those who automatically reject all talk of the "myth," "symbols," and "levels of meaning" literature may contain. Yet, with a rough accuracy, he says this of *Huckleberry Finn:* "Like *Tom* and in much greater measure it has a mythic quality. This is in part the river itself, the Mississippi which had dominion over Mark's imagination and here becomes a truly great symbol. Thus realism, fantasy, satire, mythology, and the tragic knowledge of man, all of them a good many layers deep, united in Mark Twain's masterpiece."

The river is a "symbol" all right, a symbol of nature and of God in nature. Both Mr. Trilling and Mr. Eliot say that in *Huck Finn* the river is "a god" and Mr. Trilling quotes from *The Dry Salvages*, a poem by Mark Twain's fellow Missourian, the lines about the river: "I do not know much about gods; but I think that the river / Is a strong brown god." The river throws off in the mind of Huck Finn an abundance of poetic forms and feelings. It is a poetic symbol, of the sort described above in Chapter IV, and it is analogous, as a symbol, to the whale in *Moby-Dick*. Like

So many critics
seem to stress only
the positive, genial,
poetic
nature of the
whale.

good
**

the white whale it has the complex and contradictory qualities of nature as well as of deity, being not only genial,
sustaining, and nourishing but also sinister and dangerous.

As for the mythic quality alluded to by Mr. De Voto,
this need not concern us at any length. It is present in at
least two forms—in the theme of initiation and in what may
be called the ritual of exorcism. The departures from and
returns to the river as Huck goes through his adventures
approximate the *rite de passage* which in religious cult introduces a boy into manhood, so that in this respect one
thinks of *Huckleberry Finn* in relation to the book of Cooper's Mark Twain most disliked—*Deerslayer,* as well as in
relation to *The Red Badge of Courage,* Hemingway's *In
Our Time,* and Faulkner's *The Bear.* Actually, however, this
myth is present in *Huckleberry Finn* only dimly, as a kind
of abstract framework or unrealized possibility. This is typical of American literature. Generally speaking, it is not a
literature in which the classic actions of the soul as traditionally depicted in myth, religion, and tragedy are carried
through. Only in *Deerslayer* and *The Bear* is the drama of
initiation rendered with any fullness. Characters in American fiction who seem to be, because of their situation and
prospects, candidates for initiation do not usually change
much under the pressure of what happens to them and
when the author ascribes to his character, as in *The Red
Badge of Courage,* a new manhood, new courage, new
tragic awareness of life, it sounds unmistakably like "the
moral"—in short, an afterthought—and we do not feel that
the theme of initiation has been dramatically realized. In
looking for the typical American candidates for initiation,
one finds either that, sensitive, suffering, and intelligent as
they may be, they turn out like Christopher Newman in
James's *The American* to be impervious to transformation
and tragic awareness or, like Huck Finn himself (or Frederic Henry in *A Farewell to Arms*), they are already initi-
ated, they already know the real world with a tragic awareness. There is no real change in Huck Finn during the

144

course of the book, except that he comes to adopt, as he reflects on his duty to Jim, a morality based on New Testament ethic rather than the convention of his time and place.
This is a great achievement but it doesn't make a myth of
initiation. What we have is only some of the abstract framework of this myth and some of its poetic awareness of the
presence of deity in nature.

*Huckleberry Finn* is full of exorcism, and exorcism being a kind of magic, it arouses the emotions of awe and
of wonder out of which myth grows. Jim teaches Huck a
great deal about the magic of hair balls and other objects
useful in banishing witches and placating the malign powers of the universe, and his tales and incantations are fertile
ground for the sensibility of myth.

Analogous to this superstitious magic, but having nothing ostensibly to do with myth, is what one might call the
intellectual exorcism of false forms by the sympathetic
magic of parody and burlesque. Huck Finn frees himself
of the romance imagination of Tom Sawyer, more or less
as Sancho Panza does that of Don Quixote, by saying in
various contexts: I don't take no stock in it. He ironically
detects and parodies the graveyard romanticism of Emme-
line Grangerford. Describing the pictures on the walls of the
Grangerford house, Huck says:

> There was some that they called crayons, which one of
> the daughters which was dead made her own self when
> she was only fifteen years old. They was different from
> any pictures I ever see before—blacker, mostly, than is
> common. One was a woman in a slim black dress, belted
> small under the armpits, with bulges like a cabbage in
> the middle of the sleeves, and a large black scoop-shovel
> bonnet with a black veil, and white slim ankles crossed
> about with black tape, and very wee black slippers, like
> a chisel, and she was leaning pensive on a tombstone on
> her right elbow, under a weeping willow, and her other
> hand hanging down her side holding a white handker-

chief and a reticule, and underneath the picture it said "Shall I Never See Thee More Alas."

The falseness of conventional religion is burlesqued in a thousand ways, but not often with the irony of the passage that describes the church service just before the ancient feud of the Shepherdsons and Grangerfords breaks out again with bloody cruelty:

> Next Sunday we all went to church, about three mile, everybody a-horseback. The men took their guns along, so did Buck, and kept them between their knees or stood them handy against the wall. The Shepherdsons done the same. It was pretty ornery preaching—all about brotherly love, and suchlike tiresomeness; but everybody said it was a good sermon, and they all talked it over going home, and had such a powerful lot to say about faith and good works and free grace and preforeordestination, and I don't know what all, that it did seem to me to be one of the roughest Sundays I had run across yet.

Had D. H. Lawrence concerned himself with *Huckleberry Finn,* he would doubtless have pointed out, with a measure of plausibility, the book's profoundest, more hidden and most ambivalent exorcism—that of European culture itself.

Mark Twain made himself famous for his enmity to Scott, Cooper, and the Gothic and sentimental novelists. His thrusts at these writers and their imitators are often hilarious. In *Roughing It* he ironically contrasts Cooper's "scholarly savages" with the tribe of mangy and disconsolate Indians which, as he learns on his trip West, are called the Goshoots. In Chapter 51 of *Roughing It* there is a farcical account of the communal composition of a novel, which turns out to be a farrago of Gothic horrors and tear-soaked domestic scenes. And everyone remembers the accusations against Scott in *Life on the Mississippi,* where the author of *Ivanhoe* is accused not only of infecting the Southern mind with "romantic juvenilities" and "windy humbuggeries" but also with having caused the Civil War. Contrasting *Don Quixote* with *Ivanhoe*, Mark Twain accounts for the superiority of the first by saying that it "swept the world's admiration for the medieval chivalry silliness out of existence; and the other restored it." *Huckleberry Finn* is also a book one of whose functions it is to sweep silliness out of existence.

But Mark Twain's most famous diatribe against the false forms of romance is "Fenimore Cooper's Literary Offenses." One never reads *Deerslayer* quite as one had, after hearing the suggestion that the name of the noble chieftain—Chingachgook—should be pronounced "Chicago." Mark Twain's general indictment of *Deerslayer* is a serious criticism, even though a rebuttal to most of the particulars suggests itself as one reads:

> It has no invention; it has no order, system, sequence, or result; it has no lifelikeness, no thrill, no stir, no seeming of reality; its characters are confusedly drawn and by their acts and words they prove that they are not the sort of people the author claims that they are; its humor is pathetic; its pathos is funny; its conversations are—oh! indescribable; its love-scenes odious; its English a crime against the language.

A writer of fiction, says Mark Twain, should "eschew surplusage. . . . use the right word, not its second cousin. . . . employ a simple, straightforward style." His characters should not behave like "windy melodramatic actors," their actions should be consistent with the personality attributed to them by the author, and their speech should be consistent and not, like that of Natty Bumppo, elevated and rhetorical at one moment and then, for no observable reason, colloquial at the next.

Still, all this is not an attempt to demolish romance and substitute realism. On the contrary, despite its negative approach, Mark Twain's essay is intended to show how romance must be written. He is lecturing Cooper on the "rules

147

governing literary art in the domain of romantic fiction."
He is pleading not for realism as such but for realism as
the only way of effectively assimilating the miraculous. A
leading rule of fiction is that "the personages of a tale shall
confine themselves to possibilities and let miracles alone;
or, if they venture a miracle, the author must so plausibly
set it forth as to make it look plausible and reasonable."

Huck Finn shares Mark Twain's view of the imagination
of romance, as we see whenever Tom Sawyer is present.
Tom's head is full of the claptrap of romance, and for him
it would be unthinkable to set Jim free from the cabin where
in the late chapters of the book he is imprisoned, without
doing it as such things are done in "the books," even though
this entails an elaborate paraphernalia of moats, coats of
arms, mysterious letters, and various impractical instru-
ments of liberation. Tom's insistence on doing it the "right"
way, the "regular" way, as specified by the authoritative
books, makes the whole procedure, Huck has to admit,
"mixed-up and splendid." Still, he can't help finally exclaiming, "I don't give a dead rat what the authorities thinks
about it."

In *Huckleberry Finn* Mark Twain's imagination, when it
is poetic, is the imagination of idyl and of melodrama. That
life on the raft is idyllic and that *Huckleberry Finn* is a
pastoral fiction that looks back nostalgically to an earlier
and simpler America—this does not need arguing. It is only
somewhat less obvious that the book banks heavily on melodrama—and burlesque and farce, which are to comedy what
melodrama is to tragedy. T. S. Eliot is correct in saying
that neither a tragic nor a happy conclusion would be appropriate for Huck himself. His life simply continues its pattern of unresolved contradictions; he will go on as the impassive observer and participant in abruptly alternating
experiences of contentment and horror.

The melodrama in *Huckleberry Finn* is to be seen not
only in stagey episodes like that involving the villains
aboard the wrecked "Walter Scott" but in the sheer sensa-

tional violence of the Shepherdson-Grangerford feud and the murder of Boggs and in episodes like Pap's wrestle with the angel of death. The dramatic lights and darks of the Calvinism on which Mark Twain was brought up seem mirrored in the very thunderstorms that roll spectacularly through the vast sky above the tranquil river. On aesthetic grounds at least, Jim seems right when he makes the oracular pronouncement that Huck is watched over by two angels, one of them light and the other dark.

There is no doubt that Mark Twain's imagination was profoundly affected by the doubleness of his personality and the contradictoriness of his feelings and opinions. He was a gay *farceur* and a saddened cynic, a romancer and a pessimistic determinist, a raffish westerner and a "candidate for gentility," a radical democrat and a hobnobber with Standard Oil executives, a disinterested genius and a commercial opportunist, an author who liked to project his own divided character by portraying twins and dealing in mistaken identities. All of his critics and biographers seem agreed on Mark Twain's doubleness, whether they go on to say, with Van Wyck Brooks, that his inner contradictions thwarted and ruined a literary genius or to say, with Mr. De Voto, that they did not. Probably all his critics agree too that Mark Twain's habit of mind was originally derived from the small-town life on the river that he knew as a boy and from his later feelings about it. When Mark Twain invoked Hannibal, Mr. De Voto says, "he found there not only the idyl of boyhood but anxiety, violence, supernatural horror, and an uncrystallized but enveloping dread." To know experience in this form is to prepare oneself for the imagination of *Huckleberry Finn*.

## Pudd'nhead Wilson

*Huckleberry Finn* is, as everyone says, "one of the great books of the world." Yet aside from the first part of *Life on the Mississippi* there is nothing anywhere else in Mark Twain's writing that is really first-rate, especially if one is thinking of his contribution to the progress of the novel. There has been a tendency in recent years to overestimate Mark Twain, particularly among those readers who are quick to object to any semblance of difficulty or obscurity in literature. One often senses that this kind of reader exalts Mark Twain less out of a genuine pleasure in his writing than out of a desire to protest what is thought to be the unnecessarily elaborate language and imaginative conceptions of Melville, James, and Faulkner. Aside from the question as to whether these writers deserve the chastisement, it is unfortunate that so large an emotional investment should, for such mixed reasons, have been made in Mark Twain. (A similarly disproportionate emotional [and financial!] investment has been made in recent years, for similar reasons, in Boswell and Boswell's Dr. Johnson.) For many Americans it is especially difficult to be objective about American writers, and even more difficult to be objective about Mark Twain, of whom it is said more insistently than of any of our other great prose writers that he is the "most American."

Two recent essays on *Pudd'nhead Wilson,* one by F. R. Leavis and the other by Leslie Fiedler, make, in their different ways, strong cases for the book. And if neither essay seems quite restrained enough in its praise, they nevertheless make a valuable point of departure. Mr. Leavis, whose passion is generally for the moral quality of literature, is interested in "the complexity of ethical background" which he finds in *Pudd'nhead Wilson.* His essay is eloquent and in many ways exact, but his eloquence rides the impetus of his having discovered a complexity of ethical background to an overestimation of the book. It will probably be a long time before another critic calls Pudd'nhead "the poised and pre-eminently civilized moral center of the drama." This would seem to be high praise for a man who, though undeniably civilized, is only Tom Sawyer grown up and become a conventional and respected citizen of small-town America, after enduring a period of scorn while he was regarded as the village atheist and crank.

Fiedler speaks of *Pudd'nhead Wilson* as barely failing to be "the most extraordinary book in American literature." He sees in *Pudd'nhead Wilson* a book that might have been, but for Mark Twain's revisions, his technical botches, and his indecision about how to dramatize the ultimate ironies he had in mind, "a rollicking, atrocious melange of bad taste and half understood intentions and nearly intolerable insights into evil, translated into a nightmare worthy of America"—the language, obviously, of commendation. In contrast to Fiedler's view that Mark Twain's book lights up the most profound of American moral dilemmas, Mr. Leavis finds the book somehow "English," and oddly remarks (though only parenthetically) that Mark Twain, considered in relation to Hawthorne and James, "in some ways strikes an English reader as being less foreign, less positively un-English, than either of them." All the novels considered in the present study have in one way or another "complexity of ethical background." What is unusual, however, and what interests Leavis, as it must interest us, is that in *Pudd'nhead Wilson* the ethical background is brought into the foreground—that is, it is shown to operate in the observable manners and morals of a certain place at a certain time and thus is rendered in more concrete particularity than is usual in great American novels, of which, one must add, *Pudd'nhead Wilson* is not quite one.

Pudd'nhead is Mark Twain, on the Tom Sawyer but not the Huck Finn side of his personality. He stands at the head of the procession of small-town intellectuals, cranks, and nonconformists that we find in American fiction, especially of the 1920's, although the type continues to be represented—for example, the Gavin Stevens of Faulkner. The village intellectual is common in Sherwood Anderson and Sinclair Lewis, and Lewis, one might say, *was* this type. It is of the essence that Pudd'nhead Wilson is scorned by the citizenry as a crank, a complainer, and an ironist, that he stubbornly takes up a position of aloofness and non-conformity, but that ultimately he shows that he is in no way radically alienated from the conventional ways and in fact dreams of being one of the boys. Pudd'nhead Wilson is finally able to vindicate his Tom Sawyer-like fantasies and crotchets by putting them to direct, socially approved use. His ingenious mind, his eye for paradox and irony, and his contemned collection of fingerprints reveal in the end that the supposedly aristocratic Tom Driscoll is the son of the mulatto slave girl Roxana and that Chambers, Roxana's supposed son, is actually the legitimate heir of the Driscolls. This mix-up of identities, the effect of which is both en-hanced and confused by the improbable arrival of the Italian twins, leads us into the moral complexities of the book and into that nightmare of racial contradiction and paradox which Mark Twain looks at with a tremendous clairvoyance and candor, although it cannot be said that Pudd'nhead himself is much aware of the depths of the racial dilemma in American life.

The most important meanings of *Pudd'nhead Wilson* are suggested by comparing it with *Huckleberry Finn* (which was published nine years before *Pudd'nhead*). Fiedler rightly calls it a prosy book, in which we have "fallen" from the more poetic *Huck* and in which the social realities ob-served in *Huck* strike us in a different way. Our feelings about justice and injustice are strongly aroused in the ear-lier book, but they are relatively abstract and universal feelings. In *Pudd'nhead,* we remain through nearly all the book in one small town. Moral issues are ostensibly illus-trated in the actions of people in whom we have become interested and in whose fate we feel that we should have a stake. It is not possible "to light out" down the river, if things get hot in Dawson's Landing. Indeed, what happens "down the river" is that there slaves are sold into a far worse servitude than they know in Dawson's Landing, so that throughout the book we think of the Deep South as a kind of mythic but ever-present Hell. The Deep South gives a sinister implication to the small-town treacheries, minor felonies, and social deceptions which more or less sustainedly engage our moral feelings as we read the book. And it comes unmistakably to symbolize that irredeemable slavery—social, psychic, cosmic—to which every human being is in his own way subject. The effect on Mark Twain of the paradox of freedom and slavery is expressed by Mr. Fiedler as follows:

> The Civil War is the watershed in Twain's life between innocence and experience, childhood and manhood, joy and pain; but it is politically, of course, the dividing line between slavery and freedom. And Twain, who cannot deny either aspect, endures the contradiction of searching for a lost happiness he knows was sustained by an institution he is forced to recognize as his country's greatest shame. It was the best he could dream: to be free as a boy in a world of slavery!
>
> In *Tom Sawyer*, this contradiction is hushed up for the sake of nostalgia and in the name of writing a child's book; in *Huck* it is preserved with all the power of its tensions; in the last book it falls apart into horror.

Because the contradiction has indeed fallen apart in *Pudd'nhead Wilson* and also because it is shown to be of the essence of American social life, which consequently has its own fearful capacity to fall apart, Mark Twain's book gives in retrospect a new sense of some of the meanings of *Huckleberry Finn*. The apparently free and open world of the earlier book seems more precarious and more wistfully elusive because, in *Pudd'nhead Wilson,* we have seen its fluid moral life fixed and intensified in power by being expressed in social conventions and institutions.

It is difficult to think of the fluid moral world of *Huckleberry Finn* without recalling how directly it reflects the folkways of Mark Twain's prewar time and place. And indeed *Huck* draws heavily upon folklore for its materials, for the quality of its humor, and for its language. Yet Bernard De Voto was telling only half the story in his general insistence that Mark Twain's art and his intelligence were no more than this folklore organized in book form. Mr. Leavis is correct, of course, in admitting the presence of what he calls the "folk mind" in Mark Twain, and in going on to insist that this must not keep us from seeing also the presence of the mind of Western civilization.

Leavis says that Mark Twain's best writing is the product of "a life's experience brooded on by an earnest spirit and a fine intelligence." And he goes on to say that outside of his best writing Mark Twain still appeals to us as a man of intelligence and inner stress. For he "was no simple being, and the complexity of his make-up was ordinarily manifested in strains, disharmonies, and tormenting failures of integration and self-knowledge."

Yet the folk imagination is always pertinent in considering Mark Twain. In *Pudd'nhead Wilson* there is nothing like the rich store of folk motifs one finds in *Huck*. But there is, as in *Huck*, an imaginative conception at the symbolic heart of the book which before drawing on Mr. Fiedler to define it one may call a universal "Manichaean" dualism which has been given a special quality, in Mark Twain, by the Calvinism of his early environment and by the racial conflict. Fiedler writes that an important dimension of *Pudd'nhead Wilson* is to be found in

> the symbolic meanings inevitably associated with the colors white and black, meanings which go back through literature . . . and popular religion . . . to the last depths of the folk mind. No matter how enlightened our conscious and rational convictions may be in these matters, we are beset by a buried ambivalence based on this archetypal symbolism of light and dark. Twain himself in this very novel speaks unguardedly of the rain trying vainly to wash soot-blackened St. Louis white; and the implication is clear: black is the outward sign of inward

evil. In this sense, the Negro puzzlingly wears the livery of the guilt we had thought the white man's. But *why?* It is a question which rings through the white man's literature in America; and the answer returns in an ambiguity endlessly compounded.

A book that does as much as *Pudd'nhead Wilson* to objectify and illustrate the "buried ambivalence," "the archetypal symbolism of light and dark" that characterize the American imagination cannot be called a failure either artistically or morally. There is always a sense in which the artistic and the moral elements of a literary work, especially a not quite perfect one, are separable. And *Pudd'nhead Wilson* is a book which forces us, more than it can afford to do, to be conscious of the separation. In considering Mark Twain's book as an example of the art of the novel, one observes that the moral truth it asserts is not adequately attached to the characters, or dramatized by them. In the history of ideas and of American civilization Mark Twain's demonstration of what kind of institutions those are which objectify in social power the poetic dualism in "the last depths of the folk mind" is of the first importance. To Mr. Leavis the fact that this has been done attests to an accomplished art work—so he appears to affirm when he says that "*Pudd'nhead Wilson* should be recognized as a classic of the use of popular modes—of the sensational and the melodramatic—for the purpose of significant art." Mr. Fiedler finds an artistic success in Mark Twain's nightmare of racial contradiction. And indeed Mark Twain's astonishing clairvoyance and honesty have given *Pudd'nhead Wilson* a strong moral action, an action one can describe as a radical dilemma turned into a stirring dialogue of traditions, attitudes, and social forces.

But what keeps this book from being a great novel is that the characters and their relationships are not adequate to the moral action; the split between action and actors runs through the book. And although this would not nec-

essarily be a flaw in a romance, even less in a Platonic dialogue, it is in a novel—in a fiction, that is, where the attempt
is made to bring forth the ethical background and embody
it in the foreground.

Except as something we can ourselves imagine, the pu-
tatively tragic action of the book fails, finally, to take on
rhythm and form. It is never fully articulated and the book
coheres only by its almost geometric demonstration, its true
and false equations, its revelation and redistribution of opposites. There are no characters who are capable, either by
themselves or in relation to each other, of giving the book
a sustained organic life—not even Roxy, who is as vibrantly
alive and human as anyone in Mark Twain's books. She is
not allowed, by what she says, does, feels, and thinks, to
command or permeate the novel, although there are certain scenes—notably the one in the old barn where she contemptuously tells Tom the truth about his parentage—to
which she gives dramatic effectiveness. Wilson himself is
an original type—but a type still, for we never understand
much of what he feels or why he does what he does. We
are not told out of what complex of experience and feeling
issued his aphorisms in the Calendar, and except for the
ones that are mere easy cynicism we do not believe them
to have come from him. The fable of overreaching and disaster Mr. Fiedler dimly perceives in the career of Tom Driscoll remains a shadow, a distant imputation of tragedy.
And to the mere receptive sense of the reader Mark Twain's
novel seems finally, as a work of near-art, to exist as a stiffly
dialectic moral action, together with a considerable presentation of manners and morals, into which the breath of life
has entered only here and there. Mark Twain's real fictional
province is not the novel proper, but the borderland between novel and romance. *Huckleberry Finn* is his one complete triumph, even though the tragic dialogue to which
*Pudd'nhead Wilson* almost gives shape will always haunt
our minds.

# Chapter VIII

# THREE NOVELS OF
# MANNERS

In a sense, the novel, as defined above in Chapter I, *is* the novel of manners. In other words, all novels, committed as they are to "render reality closely and in comprehensive detail," must report the manners of the characters, must report, that is, all the special attitudes, gestures, and conventional responses people make because they belong to a certain class, a certain time, or a certain school of thought or conduct. This will always be a large part of the reality the novelist renders, whether he writes like Jane Austen or Theodore Dreiser.

But we do not call Dreiser a novelist of manners. The author of *Emma* and *Pride and Prejudice* is perhaps not the greatest novelist of manners, but she is the purest, and we can take her kind of novel as the archetype of the form. It is distinguished from the novel in general because it concentrates so calculatedly on manners, because it focuses on a particular social class or group of classes above the lower economic levels, and because it has an affinity in tone and method with the high comedy of the stage. Most important of all, such moral standards as are advanced by the author are those of society (probably not those of any one class) or have, at least, a concrete social sanction and utility. According to these standards, aberrations and distortions of conduct in individuals will be corrected (as in *Pride and Prejudice* or Howells's *Vacation of the Kelwyns* or James's *The Ambassadors*) or if these aberrations are incorrigible in any individual, he may be destroyed or expelled by society (as in *The Great Gatsby* or James's *The Europeans* or Edith Wharton's *The Age of Innocence*). And very often, of course, the standard of judgment invoked will not be any particular social convention but the socially shared sagacity known as "common sense." Very often too we find common sense being brought into play to correct ideals which are fanatical or absurdly impractical and are at odds, therefore, with the necessary compromises and imperfections of any social order.

In Europe some of the greatest novelists have been expert practitioners in this genre: Cervantes, Fielding, Stendhal, Balzac, Tolstoy, Miss Austen herself. But in America, with the exception of Henry James, the novelists of manners are among the writers of second or third rank: Edith Wharton, Ellen Glasgow, Howells, John O'Hara, J. P. Marquand, Sinclair Lewis, Scott Fitzgerald. The great writers, such as Melville, Hawthorne, or Faulkner, sometimes approach the novel of manners—as in *Pierre, The House of the Seven Gables, The Blithedale Romance,* or *The Sound and the Fury.* But it is not their natural style, they seldom sustain the tone, and there is always something else in these books more arresting than the observation of manners.

The reasons for this contrast are not obscure. For one thing, as Cooper complained, there are no manners in America to observe, compared, that is, with Europe. And what manners there are are nearly uniform among all Americans. This is of course not literally true, either of

Cooper's time or ours. But the novelist needs a more vivid variety of manners than, so far, he has discovered in this country. Also, there is the persistent distrust of or simple lack of interest in the idea of society itself, so that it seems unnatural to most American writers to suppose that social conventions and laws are beneficial to the individual. Even in Henry James, great novelist of manners though he is, moral value is likely to be personal and intuitive, and to rest less in convention than in the possible native excellence of human nature, and although some of its ends are social, it is not derived from any social order. True, James's interests and commitments lead him to advance a large and perhaps rather vague ideal of social honor and benignity. But he appeals, as surely as Cooper, Melville, Mark Twain, Faulkner, and Hemingway, to a personal sense of rightness as the source and warrant of moral value.

The European novel of manners has always achieved its effect by bringing people of different social class into conflict. But in America nearly everyone a novelist of manners might be interested in has been middle-class, and has very likely prided himself on manners indistinguishable from a lower class which is always incipiently middle-class itself. Only in Cooper's New York and Westchester, in old New England, in the old South, in Mrs. Wharton's New York, in Ellen Glasgow's Richmond, and perhaps one or two other places, like G. W. Cable's New Orleans, have there been momentarily settled social conditions involving contrasting classes with contrasting manners.

On the whole our novelists have not been interested in social manners but in "personalities of transcendent value," as Van Wyck Brooks called Henry James's characters, personalities who transcend among other things the amenities and discipline of social intercourse. It does not matter very much on board the Pequod that Ahab is a bourgeois entrepreneur, Starbuck a petty bourgeois, and Ishmael an aristocrat. Such social differences matter scarcely more at a table in a Paris café described by Hemingway in *The Sun*

159

*Also Rises*. We understand characters in Melville and Hemingway, as we do in most American writers, by what they are at heart. And this is not shown to us, except superficially, by their differences in manners, because the decorum they display is their personal way of living what they believe in or doing what they are fated to do. We are asked by these novelists to judge characters, not by measuring them against socially derived values, but by their adherence to an idea of conduct which is personal, intuitive, and stoic, and which, though it may come round to the universal values of Christianity and democracy, does so without much social mediation.

So far, then, the American novelist of manners has been more at the mercy of his environment than has the European—in the sense that the American social scene has not been so interesting, various, and colorful as the European. The novelist who undertakes to reflect our social scene, or some segment of it, in literal detail, as Sinclair Lewis did in *Babbitt* or Howells in *A Modern Instance* or Mrs. Wharton in *The Age of Innocence*, finds that not all his wit and perspicuity can save his novel from reflecting too strongly the comparative social dullness of America.

Whenever it turns out to be a brilliant and memorable book, the American novel of manners will also be a romance; more than likely the observation of manners and the painting of the social scene will be a by-product of the romance that really engages the author's mind. There may thus be some utility in considering from this point of view, as I do in the ensuing pages, three novels of manners: *The Great Gatsby*, G. W. Cable's *The Grandissimes*, and Howells's *The Vacation of the Kelwyns*. So apparently odd a conjunction of books may call for explanation. The reader might well expect to encounter in any discussion of the novel of manners Mrs. Wharton's *Age of Innocence*, Ellen Glasgow's *Romantic Comedians* or *The Sheltered Life*, any one of several of James's books, and so on. My reason for considering the three books I do is first of all my special

160

affection for them, which I hope the reader will indulge. But more important they are original novels, which advanced, each in its way, the art of the novel in America—despite the fact that two of them have exerted no observable influence and have remained virtually unknown. *The Age of Innocence* is an excellent novel of manners but there is nothing original in its conception, except the peculiarly bleak pessimism of Mrs. Wharton's temperament, just as there is nothing really original in Miss Glasgow's work, fine as some of it is, beyond the feminine narcissism that almost ruined her as an artist. To embark on a discussion of James as a novelist of manners would be to embark on a complete book about James. Finally, I have wanted to resurrect, if possible, Cable's *Grandissimes* and Howells's *Vacation of the Kelwyns.*

I have arranged the three novels in what seems to be a decreasing order of inner tension and dramatic power. *Gatsby* is one of those serious comedies that are finally indistinguishable from tragedy. *The Grandissimes* does not achieve the tragic effect—its darker tones are those of melodrama. *The Vacation of the Kelwyns* is one of those rarities in American fiction—a novel that celebrates, without becoming vapid, the relaxation of the will and what Lionel Trilling, after Wordsworth, calls the "sentiment of Being," and in itself exemplifies these amiable and vital qualities.

By thus arranging these three books I have hoped to suggest anew that the American literary mind is not necessarily *fated* to move always toward high tensions, extreme situations, and unresolved contradictions, even though it usually has done so when it has been at its best. Luckily it moves also toward the kind of easy native connection with life which is celebrated, by all three novelists discussed in this chapter, but most fully by Howells. It remains only to say that I have written about *Gatsby* on the assumption that the reader is fairly familiar with it. My assumption that most readers do not know *The Grandissimes* and *The Vacation of the Kelwyns* is based on the fact that neither has been reprinted in recent times.

## The Great Gatsby

Lionel Trilling speaks of *Gatsby* as follows: "To the world it is anomalous in America, as in the novel it is anomalous in Gatsby, that so much raw power should be haunted by envisioned romance. Yet in that anomaly lies, for good and bad, much of the truth of our national life, as, at the present moment, we think about it." The special charm of *Gatsby* rests in its odd combination of romance with a realistic picture of raw power—the raw power of the money that has made a plutocracy and the raw power the self-protective conventions of this plutocracy assume when they close in a united front against an intruder.

*Gatsby* gives us an unforgettable, even though rather sketchy, sense of the 1920's and what the people were like who lived in them. We know what the people were like because we are shown the publicly recognized gestures and attitudes by which they declare themselves as belonging to a certain ambiance at a certain time. Their manners (perhaps one should say their mannered lack of manners) are a clearly minted currency as readily negotiable as the money they all have such a lot of. At the same time the hero who comes to his spectacular grief is not only a man of the 1920's but a figure of legend. No one can doubt that the legend engaged the imagination of the author more deeply than the society in which the legend is played out.

Mr. Trilling attributes the continuing freshness and significance of *Gatsby* to "Fitzgerald's grasp—both in the sense of awareness and appropriation—of the traditional resources available to him." And this will apply whether we are thinking of the book as a romance or as a novel of manners. The story of Jay Gatsby is in origin an archetype of European legend and it is fascinating to observe how, in Fitzgerald's hands, this legend is modified and in some ways fundamentally changed in accordance with American ideas.

The European (perhaps universal) archetype has been memorably described, in relation to the novel, by Mr. Trilling himself. In his Introduction to *The Princess Casamassima,* Mr. Trilling refers to the legend of "the Young Man from the Provinces" which finds expression in certain great novels, such as Stendhal's *The Red and the Black,* Dickens's *Great Expectations,* and Balzac's *Père Goriot.* The young hero of the legend is likely to come from obscure or mean beginnings. There is some mystery about his birth; perhaps he is really a foundling prince. He is "equipped with poverty, pride and intelligence" and he passes through a series of adventures which resemble the "tests" that confront the would-be knight in Arthurian legend. He has an enormous sense of his own destiny. The purpose of his quest is to "enter life," which he does by launching a campaign to conquer and subdue to his own purposes the great world that regards him as an insignificant outsider. "He is concerned to know how the political and social world are run and enjoyed," as Mr. Trilling writes; "he wants a share of power and pleasure and in consequence he takes real risks, often of his life."

At this point one begins to see how much and how little Gatsby belongs to the tradition of the Young Man from the Provinces. He has the necessary obscure beginning, born Gatz somewhere in the Middle West. He has come to the more socially advanced East and made his way to a position of wealth and influence. He is more or less a mythic figure; he seems to have sprung from "a Platonic conception of himself" rather than from any real place; he is rumored to be the nephew of the Kaiser; he pretends to be an Oxford man and to have lived like a young rajah in all the capitals of Europe; he has committed himself "to the following of a grail." A good deal of this legendary build-up is comic in tone and satiric in intent. But Arthur Mizener, Fitzgerald's biographer, is correct in saying that the ironies

of *The Great Gatsby* are never allowed to destroy the credence and respect given by the author to the legend of
his hero. The life and death of Gatsby inevitably call to
the mind of Nick Carroway, the narrator, the ideal meaning of America itself. Gatsby somehow invokes the poetic
appeal of the frontier and his pursuit of the ideal recalls
once again the "transitory enchanted moment when man
must first have held his breath in the presence of this con-
tinent, compelled into an aesthetic contemplation he neither understood nor desired, face to face for the last time
in history with something commensurate to his capacity
for wonder."

These concluding lines are so impassioned and impressive, even if a little overopulent in the Conradian manner,
that we feel the whole book has been driving toward this
moment of ecstatic contemplation, toward this final moment
of transcendence. What, at the end, has been affirmed? Apparently it is not the "power and pleasure" derived from
knowing and mastering "the political and social world." At
the end of *Père Goriot* what is affirmed by Eugene Rastignac's challenge to Paris *is* this "power and pleasure." And
whereas it is true that Julien Sorel in *The Red and the
Black* seeks an ideal transcendence, in the manner of many
French heroes, from those of Racine to those of Malraux,
his field of operations is social to a far greater degree than
Gatsby's is ever shown to be.

Gatsby does not seek to understand and master society
as an end; and we have to take it on faith that he has
understood and mastered it at all—was he *really* a bootleg-
ger and a dealer in dubious stocks? Of course he was, but
neither he nor his author nor his author's narrator, himself
a bond salesman, shows any interest in these activities. Nor
has Gatsby's shadowy battle with the world been, as it is
for his European counterparts, a process of education and
disillusion. He does not pass from innocence to experience
—if anything it is the other way around, the youth who
climbed aboard the millionaire's yacht being more worldly

164

*interesting twist*

*experience → innocence*

than the man who gazes longingly at the green light across the bay. In *The Great Gatsby* society and its ways, so far as the hero knows them, are not ends but means to a transcendent ideal. Finally, as Nick Carroway thinks, the ideal is so little connected with reality that it consists merely in *having* an ideal. Ideality, the longing for transcendence, these are good in themselves. So Nick Carroway implies when he shouts across the lawn to Gatsby, "They're a rotten crowd. You're worth the whole damn bunch put together." For even though Carroway "disapproved of him from beginning to end," he is forced thus to pay tribute to Gatsby's "incorruptible dream." Nor is the abstractness of Gatsby's dream modified by the fact that it centers around Daisy Buchanan, whom he has loved and lost. He does not see her as she is; he does not seem to have a sexual passion for her. He sees her merely as beauty and innocence —a flower, indeed, growing natively on the "fresh green breast of the new world."

Fitzgerald suggests near the end of the book that Gatsby is in the legendary line of Benjamin Franklin or Poor Richard. So we see from the self-disciplinary schedule Gatsby had written down as a boy and had always kept with him:

Rise from bed . . . . . . . . . . . . . . . . . 6:00      A.M.
Dumbbell exercise and wall scaling . . 6:15–6:30    "
Study electricity, etc. . . . . . . . . . . . . . 7:15–8:15   "

and so on down to:

Study needed inventions . . . . . . . . 7:00–9:00 P.M.

But he is also of the company of Natty Bumppo, Huck Finn, and Melville's Ishmael. For although he is treated with more irony than they, as befits a later worldliness, he shares their ideal of innocence, escape, and the purely personal code of conduct. Like them he derives his values not from the way of the world but from an earlier pastoral ideal.

But Gatsby lived too late. He is made to die sordidly in

his swimming pool, shot by a garage proprietor. He cannot, like Huck Finn, light out for the territory. He cannot achieve even the dubious rebirth of Ishmael in the far Pacific. He cannot die full of years, facing the setting sun and attended by the primeval prairie gods, like Natty Bumppo.

None of these earlier heroes makes an assault on a plutocracy that has settled into a position of power and prestige. That was not an option in their time and place. When Gatsby does this he becomes what his predecessors never were: a tragicomic figure in a social comedy. He does not know how to conform to the class to which Daisy belongs and to this class he seems ridiculous, with his "gorgeous pink rag of a suit," his preposterous mansion, and his chaotic parties—parties at which ordinary people seem somehow to become themselves fantastic and to assume names like Miss Claudia Hip and the Dancies (I refer here to the inspired list of names, itself a great comic achievement, at the beginning of Chapter 4—there is an only somewhat less brilliant collection of comic names in the description of the masquerade at the beginning of Cable's *Grandissimes*). In Gatsby, that is, we have a figure who is from one point of view a hero of romance but from another is related to the gulls and fops of high comedy.

No one seems to know what T. S. Eliot meant when he wrote Fitzgerald that *Gatsby* was the first step forward the American novel had made since Henry James. The statement seems meaningful, however, if we compare *Gatsby* with James's only novel of similar theme, *The American*. Christopher Newman is a more relaxed, less willful, and less self-destined figure than Gatsby, but he comes of a similarly legendary America, makes a great deal of money, and vainly pursues a woman who is the flower of a high world forever closed to him. James, however, is content with his pleasure in the odd angularities of the legend of the successful American. And he sends Newman home, baffled and saddened by his rejection but not mortally hurt. It is a part of the fate of both Newman and Gatsby that they

166

have information with which they could avenge themselves on their highly placed antagonists and that out of magnanimity they both refuse to do so.

But Fitzgerald has made more of the legend. For whereas Newman remains an odd though appealing stick of a man Gatsby has a tragic recklessness about him, an inescapably vivid and memorable destiny. He has something of that almost divine insanity we find in Hamlet or Julien Sorel or Don Quixote. Fitzgerald's great feat was to have opened out this possibility and to have made his American hero act in a drama where none had acted before. For although there had been reckless and doomed semilegendary heroes in American fiction, none had been made to play his part in a realistically presented *social* situation. Fitzgerald opened out the possibility, but scarcely more. It was not in him to emulate except for a brilliant moment the greatest art.

## Cable's *Grandissimes*

George Washington Cable is remembered, if at all, as a local colorist who wrote quaint, pathetic, and humorous tales about Creole life in Louisiana, and who sometimes gave his characters a dialect speech too irksome to read. People who have gone beyond the tales and sketches in *Old Creole Days* to Cable's novels remember them as being rather incoherent, charming perhaps, but marred by sentimentality and a facetious humor. On the whole these notions about Cable are true. Up to a point, they are even true about *The Grandissimes* (1880). But in this novel about life in New Orleans in 1803 Cable transcended his usual limitations and wrote a minor masterpiece.

Reading this novel today one can see that there were good reasons why in the early 1880's Cable was regarded as the peer of Henry James, Howells, and Mark Twain, why in 1883 Matthew Arnold—an unlikely reader of Cable, it would seem—proclaimed himself "perfectly delighted" with Cable's books. And the fact is that there are things in *The Grandissimes* that are beyond the reach of any of Cable's contemporaries. James could never have presented the story of the slave woman Clemence who, being suspected of sorcery, is caught in a bear trap by the Creole aristocrats, hanged, cut down, told to run, and, as she runs, shot, so that she "leaped into the air and fell at full length to the ground, stone dead." As a novel of political analysis that sees society both in ideological terms and as having "an atmosphere of hints, allusions, faint unspoken admissions, ill-concealed antipathies, unfinished speeches, mistaken identities, and whisperings of hidden strife," *The Grandissimes* makes Howells's most ambitious social novel, *A Hazard of New Fortunes,* seem like child's play. Cable's powers of intellectual analysis as well as his power of presenting manners and morals dramatically and symbolically are not matched in Mark Twain, with the possible exception of *Pudd'nhead Wilson.* And if he shares with Mark Twain a taste for American humor, he also has the more intellectual comic sense of the novelist of manners.

Nor does this exhaust the list of Cable's remarkable, though unfulfilled, talents. There is in *The Grandissimes* a truly Faulknerian strain of dark melodrama. The best example of this is the story of Bras Coupé, a heroic Negro prince brought from Africa in the slave ship *Egalité.* He refuses to work and there follow scenes of violence, of flight and pursuit, and of torture which are presented with tremendous effect. The story is made to serve as a kind of archetypal image which gives meaning and resonance to the book. It is referred to at various points and is told in the middle of the novel by three different persons on the same day.

As a novel of ideas which describes an intricate society full of both demarcations and ambiguities of class, caste, and race, *The Grandissimes* is something of a rarity in

American fiction. In the life of New Orleans at the moment in 1803 when the American government was trying to placate and absorb the resisting Louisianans, Cable had an ideal subject. He had made extensive studies of New Orleans as a newspaperman and during the writing of *The Grandissimes* he was making an investigation for the Census Bureau of "The History and Present Condition of New Orleans." He was thus able to give his novel the solid sociological foundation for which Edmund Wilson praises it in an essay of some years ago. He had also one of the classic situations of the novel of manners—the dissolution of one class (the Creole aristocracy) and its replacement by another (the bourgeois "Américains").

*Old Creole Days* and *Mme. Delphine,* among Cable's early writings, are well worth reading. Despite their realism, however, Cable put into them a rather gratuitous mystification about who is who and who is doing what, and it was only in *The Grandissimes* that he made mystification into mystery, that he dealt, in other words, with some of the inscrutable facts at the foundations of modern society and did his best to articulate these facts dramatically and ideologically. Only one other nineteenth-century American novel does this as well—James's *Princess Casamassima,* and if Cable has the less piercing intuition and the more parochial subject he in part makes up for it by being more at home among general political ideas than James.

Appropriate to the mood of mystery, foreboding, subdued violence, and confused identities, the novel begins with a masquerade. As we go on, it takes us some time to straighten out the characters. Two heroes, however, soon emerge, Honoré Grandissime and Joseph Frowenfeld. Honoré is the scion of his family. In his ancestors the Creole pride has been very strong—their "preposterous" pride, as Cable says, "apathetic, fantastic, suicidal, lethargic and ferocious as an alligator." In the well-known manner of American aristocracies, this one has grown far more reactionary than its European counterparts. Educated in Paris,

Honoré has discovered how isolated from the modern world his family has become and he is determined to liberalize its ways.

Frowenfeld is a young pharmacist fresh from Philadelphia. He is full of reforming zeal and progressive principles, a fierce democrat. In the person of Frowenfeld, Cable finds a way to make capital out of the Jamesian theme of the innocent Yankee whose views are enlarged and humanized by contact with an old, rich, corrupt social order.

The rather preachy Frowenfeld and the contemplative Honoré Grandissime learn a good deal from each other because of their differences. But they have something in common too—namely they are both in quest of reality. Frowenfeld is "as fond of the abstract" as the Creoles are "ignorant of the concrete." And much of the moral action of the novel is concerned with the successful attempt of the two friends to come, in their different ways, into contact with social reality as well as with their own deeper emotional natures. Cable himself feared that he had failed to make a memorable character in Frowenfeld because of the difficulty of making plausible a hero who is too "goody-goody." He was perhaps unnecessarily concessive here, although of the two, Honoré Grandissime is the more substantial and significant figure.

Cable himself did not descend from the Creole caste. Although he was born in New Orleans, his mother was of Puritan New England stock and his father came from a Virginian family. He clearly admired the amenity of Creole life and treated it with a good deal of sympathy. As a young man he had fought in the Confederate cavalry (although he was only five feet six and never weighed much over 110 pounds). Yet he had formed liberal political ideals and deplored the injustices upon which Creole society had been based. His knowledge of the world made him contemptuous of the helplessness and ignorance of the Creoles, who seemed never to touch in any creative way either reality or passion except as these were mediated by their slaves. The fastidious and neurotic isolation of the Creoles Cable suggests by his description of the Grandissime mansion which is raised above the ground on fifteen-foot pillars and by his picture of the family here in their self-congratulatory, ritual reminiscences while beyond the river the slaves toil in "a land hung in mourning, darkened by gigantic cypresses, submerged; a land of reptiles, silence, shadow, decay." No wonder such a family should fear reality and that Honoré should lament that "I am but a *dilettante,* whether in politics, in philosophy, morals, or religion. I am afraid to go deeply into anything, lest it should make ruin in my name, my family, and my property."

Yet despite his fear of going deeply, Honoré's aristocratic background and contemplative nature have made him aware of political realities unknown to less disillusioned minds. The difficulties involved in adjusting New Orleans to free institutions are the topic of the densely meaningful chapter called "That Night." Here the new Yankee governor and Honoré Grandissime discuss the problem of making a government "freer than the people wish it." And when the governor utters the conventional idea that no community will sacrifice itself for mere ideas, Honoré says, "You speak like a true Anglo-Saxon" and assures him that New Orleans is just the kind of community to do so. As the discussion goes on, the dark tangle of passions and interest that underlie politics is suggested by the ritual chant and Calinda dance in a slave-yard, the purport of which is a satire of the ruling classes, the point being that the pride of the Grandissimes must now humble itself before the Yankees.

There is a good deal of highly effective symbolism in Cable's novel, mostly having to do with light and dark and the ambiguity not only of racial strains but of reality itself. This symbolism (used with equal effectiveness in American literature perhaps only in *Light in August* and in Melville's *Benito Cereno*) stems from the dread and guilt which remain unconscious in most of the characters but is articulated by Honoré when to Frowenfeld he professes himself amazed at "the shadow of the Ethiopian—the length, the blackness of that shadow." We sit, he says, "in a horrible darkness."

Nevertheless the novel should not be regarded as "symbolistic"; it is not a drama of meaning. We do not have in *The Grandissimes* an epistemological symbolism. The book does not ask the intelligence to concern itself with meaning but rather to grasp and cleave to the concrete conditions of life. We have, as in so many American fictions, a realistic novel tending away from strict realism toward the romance by way of melodrama.

The symbols are involved in the intricacies of experience but (as in Cable's ancestral Calvinism) they move, not toward ambiguity and multiple meaning, as in symbolistic art, but toward ideology and dialectic. The structure of the book is melodramatic. That is, it conceives of life as a hazardous action between very marked, perhaps irreconcilable extremes which, appropriate to the subject, are racial, social, and political extremes. As in so many of the novels we are considering, alternative fates are offered to the actors —they can transcend the contradictions of their experience by an act of horror, violence, or suicide, or they can momentarily escape the contradictions by a loving connection with the ordinary realities of nature and the humanities of men.

The two heroines of the story, the young widow Aurore Nancanou and her daughter Clothilde, are members of the De Grapion family, which has had an ancient feud with the Grandissimes. Aurore's husband has been killed and her property lost in a duel with Agricola Fusilier, a relative of the Grandissimes and the patriarch of the clan. The ladies are endowed by Cable with perhaps a little too much fine, ineffable femininity. They are creatures of the age of Howells, and, as women (*white* women, that is) they will not be questioned too far, nor set too firmly in the world. Yet a sufficient reason for their child-like fragility is supplied by their having in their own way the Creole unworldliness.

They are at least appealing and amusing, with their Creole version of English, as when they say things like "Oo dad is, 'Sieur Frowenfel'?" "fo' wad you cryne?" or "doze Creole is *lezzy!*" And they are human enough to lend much more than a formal interest to the healing of old family differences which is symbolized by the marriage of Honoré to Aurore and the union of North and South symbolized by the marriage of Frowenfeld and Clothilde.

In the background of the Nancanou ladies there is the sinister figure of the soothsayer Palmyre Philosophe and the voodoo world she inhabits. A quadroon, Palmyre has in "the clear yellow skin of her cheek" a faint flush that suggests "cold passion." She has "a barbaric and magnetic beauty that startled the beholder like an unexpected drawing out of a jewelled sword." Although we are thoughtfully reassured by the author that Palmyre has "that rarest of gifts in one of her tincture, the purity of true womanhood," he leaves us to adjust this pious idea to the obvious fact that Palmyre's murderous vendetta with Agricola Fusilier and her feline hatred of men, her "femininity without humanity," are the results of the radical distortions of her strongly passional nature that have been produced by social injustice.

The violence of Palmyre finds its counterpart in the paralyzed will, the deeply stricken silence and passivity of another quadroon, Honoré Grandissime's half brother who bears the same name and haunts him throughout the novel, as the dark, invisible side of the moon haunts the light. Yet before his inevitable suicide, there is enough latent violence in him to stab Agricola Fusilier after he has been hit in the face with a cane for refusing to take his hat off.

Cable supplies Agricola Fusilier with a detailed genealogy. He is the descendant of an Indian princess dressed in "swan skins" and the plumes of flamingoes whom an impetuous Creole ancestor had snatched out of the Louisiana canebrake. He has the traits of the Fusiliers, who are like dark hawks among the "lily white" Grandissimes. But, an old man now, he has grown seedy; his beard wags wildly, his clothes are rather dirty and they show the styles of three decades.

Like some dimly remembered ancestor of the Compson or Sartoris families in the novels of Faulkner, Agricola Fusilier is the master of a high rhetoric. Buffoon and savage though he is, there is something moving in his taking up the cause of Frowenfeld after Frowenfeld's pharmacy has been wrecked by resentful Louisianans who consider him a meddling Yankee and lover of Negroes—"You are under the wing of Agricola Fusilier, the old eagle—you are one of my brood—Professor, listen to your old father." And he rescues the young man "from the laughs and finger-points of the vulgar mass," calling him, out of sheer *noblesse oblige*, "my friend—my vicar—my coadjutor—my son." We remember this moment of atonement later when Agricola Fusilier dies of his knife wounds and pronounces his benediction, "I forgive everyone. A man must die—I forgive—even the enemies of Louisiana."

This is a moment of pathos and surrender perhaps matched only in the episode where Charlie Keene, the consumptive doctor, walks on the levee at night and looking out over New Orleans muses on the "beautified corruption" of the scene and sighs "dissolution, dissolution." Dr. Keene, one might add, is involved in a web of hopeless loves that give a lyric quality to Cable's book. He is in love with Clothilde, as Palmyre is with Honoré (white) and as Honoré (the quadroon) is with Palmyre.

In trying to suggest the quality of *The Grandissimes* I have inevitably made it sound more compact, intense, and rapid than it actually is. Despite the political intelligence, comic acuity, social passion, and ideological poetry which Cable marshaled in this novel, a good deal of it is written in the rather loose manner of the Howells age. There is some facetiousness, some sentimentality, and too much genteel maundering. One has to be ready to put up with this:

that petted rowdy, the mocking bird, dropped down into the path to offer fight to the horse, and failing in that, flew up again and drove a crow into ignominious retirement

in order to arrive at perfection like this:

from a place of flags and reeds a white crane shot upward, turned, and then, with the slow and stately beat peculiar to her wing, sped away until, against the tallest cypress of the distant forest, she became a tiny white speck on its black, and suddenly disappeared, like one flake of snow.

The most unkind trick time has played on Cable is the decline of the vogue of dialect speech. The vogue was flourishing when Cable wrote and he uses more dialect than a modern novelist would do. He had a rich linguistic store to draw on and a highly developed ear for language, so that we hear at one time or another not only Creole English but Creole French and Negro French and English. The Creole English also varies according to the speaker. Most difficult of all are the few interpolated songs that combine French and African dialects and whose rhythmic pattern and refrains seem to suggest New Orleans jazz.

But perhaps a generation somewhat receptive to the verbal facility of Joyce and Faulkner can rediscover a certain pleasure in the language of a minor virtuoso like Cable. His Creole English is not hard to fathom, and it is impossible not to be delighted by things like, "You know my cousin, Honoré Grandissime, w'at give two hund' fifty dolla' to de 'ospill laz mont?" or Raoul Innerarity's allegorical painting of "Louisiana rif-using to hanter de h-Union."

In the following it is hard to know which is better, the French song or the paraphrase furnished by the Negro singer:

Dé 'tit zozos—yé té assis—
Dé 'tit zozos—si la barrier.

Dé 'tit zozos, qui zabotté;
Qui ça ye di' mo pas conné.

Manzeur-poulet vini simin,
Croupé si yé et croqué yé;
Personn' pli' tend' yé zabotté—
Dé 'tit zozos si la barrier.

Dat mean—two lill birds; dey was sittin' on de fence an'
gabbin' togeddah, you know lak you see two young gals
sometime', an' you can't mek out w'at dey sayin', even ef
dey know demself? H—ya! Chicken hawk come 'long dat
road an' jes' set down an' munch 'em, an' nobody can't no
mo' hea' deir lill gabbin' on de fence, you know.

Modern literature has taught us again that language is full
of comic possibilities. And *The Grandissimes* has many incidental linguistic *contretemps,* as when one character says,
"Ah lag to teg you apar' " and another asks, "See me alone?"

*The Grandissimes* is a more complex hybrid than *The
Great Gatsby;* it is richer and more various, but also more
cluttered and more loosely written. It possesses in greater
volume the standard novelistic devices. There are many
characters, and the leading ones are well established in the
circumstances of their lives; we watch them, too, as their
opinions and feelings change under the pressure of circumstance and of what they come to perceive about themselves
and their relation to other people, as well as to ideas and
to history itself. No single legendary hero steps to the center
of the stage to impose the quality of his life on the whole,
as in *Gatsby.* What happens rather is that a strongly realistic
social novel becomes at the same time a poetic melodrama.
The charm of *The Grandissimes* is that like *Gatsby,* in its
different way, it is a peculiarly successful union of the novel
of manners with romance.

## The Vacation of the Kelwyns

The subtitle of Howells's novel is "An Idyl of the Middle Eighteen-Seventies." Published in 1920, it is one of Howells's last novels and quite possibly his best (it was first written in 1910).

The trouble with Howells in general is first of all that he never tried hard enough. There is a real laziness, as well as a prudishness, about his mind, and in his novels he is always making great refusals. He had a furtive, cunning intelligence which perhaps knew more about ordinary American life than any novelist has ever known. But he had little imagination, little power of making a fable, of launching an exciting action, little power even of establishing an atmosphere that could be sustained through a novel. He lacked, as James said, that "grasping imagination" which an American novelist would need if he were to deal fully with American life. What little imagination he had was incapable either of grasping, as imagination, the facts his intelligence perceived or of imparting to his novels a coherent form. His stories are full of unbridged gaps, and he is seldom able to give that indispensable impression, as James always does even in his inferior work, of a coherent action that includes and relates all the elements of the fiction. There is no *voice* which we can recognize as Howells. There is only the long shelf of thirty-odd novels, which, though they are estimable documents for the critic and historian, contain very few fictional triumphs which are not brought off better by someone else.

It is a pleasure, then, to read this late book. Here, the aged Howells makes a virtue out of not trying very hard, and *The Vacation of the Kelwyns* is not only charming for its pervasive quality of reminiscence, calm wisdom, and idyllic pleasure in life; it is given a unity of effect by this pervasive quality and by the hard, gritty, comic sense of reality and of human limitation that goes along with it.

The story has to do with Elmer Kelwyn, a professor of historical sociology at Harvard, Mrs. Kelwyn, and their two boys. The Kelwyns are in their forties. They are liberal, genteel, middle-class people, and they have the moral earnestness of their kind, as well as the uncertainty how to face life as they find it outside of their circle of experience. They are more overtly and admittedly jealous of their genteel social position than their more modern counterparts would be. But they live frugally, having only a little money beyond the professor's salary (which means that even at best they can keep only two maids). In the summer they usually board with a farmer or at a hotel, it not being quite suitable to their position to prepare their own meals—indeed Kelwyn remembers positively as larks those few periods in their lives when they did their own cooking. Mrs. Kelwyn is not as intellectual as her husband but is predictably sharper in her social insistences and moral opinions.

As the story opens we find that the Kelwyns have taken a house for the summer in New Hampshire. The house is owned by a neighboring Shaker community, and they take on as tenants a farmer and his wife—the Kites—on the understanding that Mrs. Kite will cook and keep house and that her husband will not only work the farm for his own profit but perform such services for the Kelwyns as saddling the horse. The moral dilemmas of the story appear when it becomes clear that the Kites are, by the Kelwyns's standards, hopelessly unenlightened; they are backward, slovenly, and inefficient. Mr. Kite is morose, profane, suspicious, brutal; and his wife, though pleasant enough, is incapable of planning anything in advance or of improving her primitive methods of housekeeping. The first meal is a minor tragedy: the milk is spotted with dirt from the cellar rafters, the butter is rancid, the bread uneatable, the tea is like tar.

Much of the story has to do with the struggle of the Kelwyns to improve the Kites. They try reason and sympathy; they try threats, though being sensitive people, they are ashamed of having done this. They suffer from the moral ambiguities of the situation. Are the Kites really guilty of malfeasance? Or are they to be regarded as merely the victims of their own ignorance and of the narrow horizons of their degenerate, post-Calvinist provincialism? It is, of course, a veritable dilemma of modern liberalism. Are the Kites to be treated as criminals or unfortunate victims of their environment? And if they are to be treated as both, are they more criminal than victimized or vice versa? And in the matter of practical action, should the Kelwyns fire the Kites or respond to the moral impulse to try to improve them? Meanwhile, the Kelwyns feel more and more degraded by living with such people—as well as with the other local types they come in contact with, all of whom Howells shows in an unfavorable light: the pusillanimous Shaker ladies, the local farmer with his obscene humor about death, the drunken Allson down the road, with his suffering wife and brood of children.

There are two other important characters in the novel. Parthenope Brook, aged twenty-seven, is the Kelwyns's cousin. Elihu Emerance, who seems to be vaguely modeled on Howells himself, is an itinerant schoolteacher, farm hand, playwright, and jack-of-all-trades. Parthenope is the orphaned daughter of two expatriates who have gone to Italy to paint. A product not only of foreign education but very distinctly of the highest Emersonian culture, she is intensely romantic and idealistic. She is one of the tense, beautiful, willful, aspiring American girls, like Imogen Graham in Howells's *Indian Summer,* whom we meet so often in the fiction of the period. She had been brought up, says Howells, in a culture where "Womanhood stood high in the temple of the cult." Howells had himself contributed much to the cult of ineffable womanhood which he shared with James, though with markedly less ambiguity than James showed. But here his point is that Parthenope Brook is too good to be true. Her ideals are too abstract and rigid, her will is too tense. She must be chastened, relaxed, and humanized; and this takes place through her love for Emerance. Like Howells himself, Emerance is socially between the Kites and the Kelwyns. He is the son of humble parents, but he has acquired culture and such manners of the gentleman as are needed in America. His apparently disorganized and aimless life and his being, as he says, "an experimenter" at first disgust Parthenope, who believes that a man should have a single ideal fanatically pursued, as do the heroes of the novels she admires. She is baffled, fascinated, and repelled by the variousness of Emerance's personality and interests, as well as by the touch of raffishness and untidiness that clings to him. "Doesn't Emerson say, 'Be true to the dream of thy youth?'" she asks. To which Emerance irritatingly replies, "Ah, but to which one?"

The process by which Parthenope is at last brought round to accept Emerance as her fiancé is the familiar educative one by which pride is relaxed, prejudice dispelled, and ignorance enlightened as to the limited utility of the Ideal. It is a lesson, too, in the necessity of deriving the Ideal from the reality of circumstance, a lesson in the conditioning of the will by the actualities of one's life.

Meanwhile, the Kelwyns too relax their moral tensions, which they had worked up to a high pitch, threatening, finally, to dispossess the Kites. Instead they move out themselves, taking a place nearby which promises not to plunge them into the tensions of moral ideology but to be merely a pleasant and livable place for the rest of the summer. The whole novel thus moves away from the taut clash of moral abstractions and self-righteous aggressions to an idyllic celebration of the mere pleasure of contentedness with life, the vital quotidian nourishment the characters find by relaxing into the easier conditions of their being. There is often a festal tone to the book. A dancing bear, to which Parthenope feeds coffee after it has been stunned by lightning, gypsy fortunetellers, and other odd and picturesque wanderers come in every once in a while as if from some enchanted realm just over the horizon. The novel loses nothing of its sharp edge by leaving even the exasperating Kites in something of a soft glow.

In Chapter 19 of the novel the larger issues Howells has in mind are presented in almost allegorical form. "The simple idyl of the passing days" has become blissful for Parthenope and Emerance because, without yet declaring themselves to each other, they know now that they are in love. As Howells says, "the understanding of their pastoral situation" is "tacit between them." Their idyl is given variety and point by the itinerants who significantly come and go. First there are some Italians from near Genoa, who play a hand organ and impress Parthenope with their old-world beauty and grace, so different, as she reflects, from the "mannerless uncouthness of the Yankee country-folk." The Italians are followed by an Irish linen peddler, who enters surly but exits benign. He is followed by a "sailorlike Frenchman," whom Parthenope sketches and who accepts a ten-cent note with "charming effusion." And then one day, seeming to "rise from the ground like a human cloud," a gigantic Negro "with a sullen, bestial face" and "vast, naked feet" appears on the scene to glare with bloodshot eyes at Parthenope and Emerance, before lurking away into the shadow of the woods.

The time is 1876, and the centennial, as Howells stresses in later chapters, is a time for national as well as personal stock-taking and soul-searching. Things are not well. The tramps and wanderers who come and go may be picturesque, but they have taken to the road because there is a depression, as there must be every now and then in an economy which Howells calls "as little regulated as the weather." In this centennial summer "men without work were prowling the country everywhere." Parthenope and Emerance reflect on the fact that the old life of rural New England is in decay. The Shaker communities consist entirely of the wistful aged. The local population has fallen off in recent years, and the woods and fields show many abandoned and tumbled-down houses. The old-line Americans have got out of touch with life; their emotional life has hardened, shriveled, and dried up. In the local farmers the once vital Puritanism has become a mean-minded, sardonic pessimism. The practical hardiness and adaptability of the old New Englander has become, in the Kites, merely inefficiency, guile, and stupidity. The Kelwyns are genteel and finicking almost to the point of futility. The immigrant Europeans and the gigantic Negro are more vivid and more powerfully alive than the Anglo-Saxons who have gone to seed in the New World.

The idyl of Parthenope and Emerance is thus given an undercurrent of ominousness by the hints and portents of trouble in the land. Yet because of their marriage, a marriage of principle and impulse, we understand that all will be well. That this is the way they themselves understand their union is made clear at the end of Chapter 15. In Parthenope impulse has hardened into a too tense ethical idealism, into principles too rigidly held. In Emerance impulse flows strong and fresh but without direction or purpose. Howells is saying that American life is characterized by this kind of split, that when it occurs in exacerbated form, desiccation and aimlessness ensue, and that ever new modes of reconciliation must be found. Howells's novel is justly called "an idyl" because all the emphasis is on the need for the fresh surge of impulse, the creative, genial welling-up of emotion, the relaxation of willed principle (of which he thinks there will never be a lack).

*The Vacation of the Kelwyns* imparts a strong sense of the importance of actualities and of the intricate circuit of life that passes from the real to the ideal, from impulse to principle. This sense of things, which we identified with James at the end of Chapter I, is common in the English novel, but not at all common in the American novel, where the real and ideal are characteristically forced far apart into a striking opposition. Nor is Howells's fine sense of human involvement common in the American novel,* few charac-

---

* On this score and others, Lionel Trilling has praised *The Vacation of the Kelwyns* briefly in his essay on Howells, and although I do not seem to make so much of Howells in general as Mr.

ters in which will be found sharing this reflection of Kelwyn's: "It is strange how difficult it is to withdraw from any human relation, no matter how provisional. There is always an unexpected wrench, a rending of fibers, a pang of remorse . . . I think that at the end of every relation in life there is a sort of blind desire, unreasonable and illogical, to have it on again. If it ends abruptly or inimically this is especially the case." Howells speaks here of what may be called the normality of "human relation," the dramatization of which makes the substance of so many great English novels. By contrast the assumption of many of the best American novels is that the escape from "human relation," which Kelwyn calls a "rending of fibres," is an easy and fortunate thing. Unless, that is, as in the archetypal case of Chillingworth and Dimmesdale, the relation is obsessive and fatal. (It endears Howells to us to think that his most moving expression of the strange difficulty of withdrawing from human relation should have been published in his advanced age, in the year he died.)

Because of its symbolic reconciliations and harmonies *The Vacation of the Kelwyns* is akin to romance as we find it in Shakespeare's late plays. But, for the same reason, it is somewhat anomalous in American romance. American romance, as I have been saying in this book, does not bank much on the harmonies and reconciliations which pastoral idyl may bring into human life, or on the spiritual health it may bestow upon the future. Pastoral feeling in Cooper, Melville, Mark Twain, and Faulkner is elegiac; the pastoral experience is elusive, momentary, always receding into the past. When it is momentarily recaptured—in the forests with Natty Bumppo, in Typee, on the raft with Huck Finn, in

---

Trilling does, it remains true that the book is, as he says, a remarkable one. The main arguments of Mr. Trilling's essays in *The Liberal Imagination* prepare one for a sympathetic reading of Howells's novel, as they do for many greater novels. These essays implicitly answer, much better than I could, the objections that are likely to be raised against *The Vacation of the Kelwyns*.

the Mississippi hunting camp with Ike McCaslin—it is restorative, it recruits the benign emotions, it may even bring about a moral regeneration. But the pastoral experience is rather an escape from society and the complexities of one's own being than the source of ideals and practices which are capable of unifying and healing society, or one's own being.

Despite the elements of romance in the three novels we have been looking at in this chapter—the tragicomic legend in *Gatsby,* the high melodramatic coloring in *The Grandissimes* and the idyllic allegory of *The Vacation of the Kelwyns*—they are all concerned with the realities of man's life in society. They all concern themselves with the processes by which distorted or exaggerated ideals either lead to the defeat of the individual in society or are modified and chastened in him by disillusion and social education. The chastisement of distorted ideals is, as was observed above, a common theme in American literature, beginning with Hawthorne and Melville. But it has not often been memorably presented in the tones of social comedy.

# Chapter IX

# NORRIS AND
# NATURALISM

"NATURALISM" is a necessary word in discussing the novel, but since it is used in different ways, a definition may be in order. For example, one often finds it convenient to speak of the "naturalistic detail" or "level" of a novel, meaning simply its aggregation of things in nature or in the inanimate setting, as distinguished from the ideas, metaphors, symbols, and perhaps the emotions also to be found in the book. Related to this usage is the more technically metaphysical meaning assigned to the word "naturalism" by Allen Tate and Caroline Gordon in their *The House of Fiction*. Thus naturalism becomes the opposite of supernaturalism. But since this makes James and Howells as much naturalists as Zola, Frank Norris and Jack London, it seems preferable, for our purposes, to apply the word to those American writers who are in the general tradition of Zola—such as Norris, London, Dreiser, and Farrell.*

*2 senses of naturalism (1) natural vs. supernatural (2) naturalism (Zola)*

---

* I am assuming that the novel is realistic by definition, so that

For, like Norris himself, the American naturalist movement ostensibly takes its departure from the attempt of Zola and his contemporaries to write a new kind of scientific fiction. In the theory of the French school, the ideal was to exercise a free "experimental" method—to place one's characters in a certain environment, as one places specimens in a laboratory experiment, and to observe and report without fear or favor how they acted according to natural laws. Zola's shocking and highly imaginative novels, however, are only loosely "scientific," and as Philip Rahv has said, the invocation of science by the French naturalists came primarily out of a desire to attach to the novel the prestige rather than the method of science. But the French naturalistic novel—the American less so—had a genuine relation to science in the sense that it did often succeed by means of a massive and careful research, by a ruthless, "experimental" truth-telling, and by attention to forces, principles of behavior, and the influence of the environment and of heredity. Also, like nineteenth-century science, the naturalistic novel took a bleakly pessimistic view when considering the ability of the individual to control his fate.

Many of these tendencies were taken over from Zola by Norris in his first novel, *McTeague*. Dreiser was a student of science and we hear a good deal in his books about the "chemisms" which it is alleged, often unconvincingly, direct his characters to their fates. But we hear very little about science from Norris. And although French naturalism

---

the term "realism" can never have much utility when we are discriminating among different novels and novelists. One cannot say that Dreiser is realistic and James not; it is a question of distinguishing between Dreiser's realism and James's realism. Thus, naturalism is a special case of realism. And although it is often identified with its interest in unusually sordid reality, it actually becomes a special case of realism by adhering to a necessitarian ideology. In aesthetic terms this ideology becomes a metaphor of fate and of man's situation in the universe, and so, although naturalism begins as a special emphasis within the limits of realism, it culminates in a form of poetry.

proclaimed itself in revolt against romanticism, Norris presents his naturalism as a new form of romance.

In *The Responsibilities of the Novelist* he tells us that his own novels are intended to oppose "realism," by which he means the realism of Howells and perhaps of James. This realism he describes as too "minute," and he goes on to say ironically that "it is the drama of a broken teacup, the tragedy of a walk down the block, the excitement of an afternoon call." The "romance" with which Norris intends to oppose what he regards as the pettiness of realism is not very clearly defined. But he tells us that unlike realism, which "confines itself to the type of normal life," romance "is the kind of fiction that takes cognizance of variations from the type of normal life." Again, unlike realism, romance sees deeply and exposes the most hidden passions. According to Norris, romance is close to the imagination of the "People" and neither springs from nor appeals to the mere "Artist," "Amateur," or "Aesthete." The meaning of this important idea I shall consider later.

What strikes the historically-minded reader is the general similarity of Norris's plea for romance to the earlier pleas made by Brown, Cooper, Simms, Hawthorne, and Melville. The significance of this similarity has not been understood, and Norris's description of his fiction as romance has been taken to be merely vague and eccentric, if not positively perverse—at least, as applied to books like *McTeague* and *The Octopus,* rather than to *Moran of the Lady Letty,* which is more obviously "romantic." Yet the youthful father of fictional naturalism in this country was in dead earnest in describing his works as romances, as he was in everything he did and said. And in the brief years of his growing maturity, before he died in 1900 at the age of thirty, he wrote books that departed from realism by becoming in a unified act of the imagination at once romances and naturalistic novels.

## McTeague

Norris's first novel was mostly written in 1892 but it was not finished and published until 1899 (it was thus preceded by another important early document in American naturalism, Stephen Crane's *Maggie*, which was published earlier but made little impression). McTeague, the hero of the book, is an illiterate dentist in San Francisco, an innocent animal-like man who falls victim to the corrupt ways of city life. In telling the story Norris sticks close to the heredity-environment-degeneration theme. Marcus Schouler, Mc-Teague's supposed friend, informs the authorities that McTeague is practicing dentistry without a license. This activates the fatal forces of environment and heredity and starts the hero off on his undeviating path to disaster.

*McTeague* is Norris's best book, having all the hallmarks of young genius and forming in its crude way a genuine art work. Like many American novels, *The Octopus* is all "picture," and the few "scenes" we are given are perfunctory, with the exception of one or two that stick in the mind, like the ranch festival and accompanying jack-rabbit hunt, though even here everything is done with the wide brush. But *McTeague* has several closely observed and adequately dramatized scenes—even though others are so far overdramatized as to exceed the bounds of calculated distortion and to become self-parodies. But we do not easily forget McTeague in his Dental Parlors, the fight at the beach between McTeague and Marcus Schouler, the wedding of McTeague and Trina, the evening at the vaudeville, McTeague's weird and brutal murder of Trina, nor, melodramatic as it is, the final death struggle between McTeague and Marcus. Norris had an eye for social behavior when he chose to use it—although his overt comments on human manners are likely to be banal ("no people have a keener eye for the amenities than those whose social position is not assured"). He often gets off passages of quiet and effective factual observation:

> Then Trina and the dentist were married. The guests stood in constrained attitudes, looking furtively out of the corners of their eyes. Mr. Sieppe never moved a muscle; Mrs. Sieppe cried into her handkerchief all the time. At the melodeon Selina played "Call Me Thine Own," very softly, the tremulo stop pulled out. She looked over her shoulder from time to time. Between the pauses of the music one could hear the low tones of the minister, the responses of the participants, and the suppressed sounds of Mrs. Sieppe's weeping. Outside the noises of the street rose to the windows in muffled undertones, a cable car rumbled past, a newsboy went by chanting the evening papers; from somewhere in the building itself came a persistent noise of sawing.
>
> Trina and McTeague knelt. The dentist's knees thudded on the floor and he presented to view the soles of his shoes, painfully new and unworn, the leather still yellow, the brass nail heads still glittering. Trina sank at his side very gracefully, setting her dress and train with a little gesture of her hand.

Having come to know McTeague and Trina in the circumstances of their ordinary lives, we are able to feel for them as their story unfolds. Thus they have an existence apart from the puppets they become as the pressure of their Fate, in the latter parts of the book, hurries them on to their annihilation.

These scenes are more successful in telling us about the characters than are Norris's theoretical devices. One of these latter is the trick of giving everyone a sort of Darwinian double existence, so that on the surface people are domesticated and conventionalized, whereas underneath they are carnivorous beasts. In the naturalistic novel the beast shows through the human exterior as in the older fiction the devil did; the modern Mephistopheles is a were-wolf or, more likely, an apeman. There is a rampant animal imagery in *McTeague*, and often it occurs where people are being metaphorically hustled up and down the evolutionary ladder, between the animal and the human levels. There is a memorable moment in the book when, before she is married to McTeague, Trina reclines prettily in the dentist's chair. She is under ether, and McTeague's emotions are described thus:

> Suddenly the animal in the man stirred and woke; the evil instincts that in him were so close to the surface leaped to life, shouting and clamoring.
>
> It was a crisis—a crisis that had arisen all in an instant; a crisis for which he was totally unprepared. Blindly, and without knowing why, McTeague fought against it, moved by an unreasoned instinct of resistance. Within him, a certain second self, another better McTeague rose with the brute; both were strong, with the huge crude strength of the man himself. The two were at grapples. There in that cheap and shabby "Dental Parlor" a dreaded struggle began. It was the old battle, old as the world, wide as the world—the sudden panther leap of the animal, lips drawn, fangs aflash, hideous, monstrous, not to be resisted, and the simultaneous arousing of the other man, the better self that cries, "Down, down," without knowing why; that grips the monster; that fights to strangle it, to thrust it down and back.

To quote from the several passages of this sort is really unfair, because they tend to be rather trashy expressions of what, taking the book as a whole, is a satisfactory poetic metaphor. But it is certainly not much of a device of characterization. Nor are the pseudo-Homeric epithets Norris attaches to his people, repeating over and over again that Trina's hair is "moist" and "regal," that her ear lobes are "anemic" (though she herself does not seem to be), or that McTeague has "the hands of the old car boy" (the boy, that is, who pushes cars in mine tunnels, as McTeague had done before learning dentistry). There is little attempt to characterize lesser figures like Zerkow, the junk man, and Maria Macapa, the demented Mexican woman whom Zerkow marries in the hope of finding a solid gold table service she crazily remembers as having been once in her family's possession. Zerkow and Maria are only slightly less absurd than the pathetic Dickensian comic lovers, Miss Baker and Old Grannis.

Over against the scenic realism and the characterization of the main figures, however, there is a powerful tendency towards abstraction. In *McTeague* the circuit of life between the real and the ideal often ceases to operate and the two fly wildly asunder. One reason for the abstractness that makes so notable a part of the book is that McTeague himself is semilegendary; we should have to change our feeling about him if his name were Joe McTeague, say, instead of apparently just plain McTeague. He is of the confraternity of the blond beast, the "Nietzschean" or "Darwinian" Adam, so much admired by Norris and Jack London. In this respect McTeague is the spiritual father of mass-media heroes like Edgar Rice Burroughs's Tarzan. Also we feel blowing through the novel the cold ideology of the era of Herbert Spencer, as when Norris poetically exclaims of McTeague and Trina that "chance had brought them face to face, and mysterious instincts as ungovernable as the winds of heaven were at work knitting their lives together."

And we come to see that Norris is moved most deeply (this is more obvious in *The Octopus* than in *McTeague*) not by people and their daily tragedies and adventures but by abstractions, by Forces, Environments, Accidents, and Influences.

Like almost every other interesting American naturalistic novel one might name, from the works of Norris himself to those of Faulkner, *McTeague* succeeds because the author is able to write instinctively out of his natural genius and with his considerable grasp of ordinary novelistic procedures. When he obtrudes his pet ideas and prejudices, his writing begins to be meretricious. The effects are forced, and the language sounds faked. The strong parts of *Mc-Teague* are the dramatic scenes and the central fable of degeneration, melodramatic as this is. There is also a kind of crude but effective poetry that lends its somber color to the whole. The concluding lines of *McTeague* are in Norris's characteristic convention of romance, with its broadly effective symbolism of fate (the handcuffs) and of greed (the canary that McTeague has absurdly carried in its gold cage, even in the extremity of his flight into Death Valley):

Suddenly the men grappled, and in another instant were rolling and struggling upon the hot white ground. McTeague thrust Marcus backward until he tripped and fell over the body of the dead mule. The little bird cage broke from the saddle with the violence of their fall, and rolled out upon the ground, the flour bags slipping from it. McTeague tore the revolver from Marcus' grip and struck out with it blindly. Clouds of alkali dust, fine and pungent, enveloped the two fighting men, all but strangling them.

McTeague did not know how he killed his enemy, but all at once Marcus grew still beneath his blows. Then there was a sudden last return of energy. McTeague's right wrist was caught, something locked upon it, then the struggling body fell limp and motionless with a long breath.

As McTeague rose to his feet, he felt a pull at his right wrist; something held it fast. Looking down, he saw that Marcus in that last struggle had found strength to handcuff their wrists together. Marcus was dead now; Mc-Teague was locked to the body. All about him, vast, interminable, stretched the measureless leagues of Death Valley.

McTeague remained stupidly looking around him, now at the distant horizon, now at the ground, now at the half-dead canary chittering feebly in its gilt prison.

## The Octopus

Published in 1901, *The Octopus* was the first volume of a projected trilogy to be called *The Epic of the Wheat*. Norris later published a pale sequel called *The Pit* but did not live to write *The Wolf*, which was to have been the third of the series. The trilogy was planned on a grandiose scale. The first novel is subtitled "A Story of California" and concerns "production"; the second is "A Story of Chicago" and concerns "distribution"; the third was to be called "A Story of Europe" and was to concern "consumption." The octopus is the railroad, which had so profoundly reorganized the West in the latter part of the last century. The action of the book has to do with the struggle between a group of wheat ranchers and the rapacious railroad interests and chronicles the inevitable victory of the railroad.

There are so many people in the book that it may be well simply to describe some of them in turn. There is Magnus Derrick, an upright man on the large scale, as his name suggests. Now a wheat farmer, he had been a politician and a miner. He is a gentlemanly American of the old school; he is forensic, Roman, dignified, honest, and his hero is Calhoun. Norris describes his gradual corruption, telling us how he finally consents to enter into a scheme to bribe the commissioners who determine the railway rates, and in Magnus Derrick's moral anguish and shame, we see the failure and decline of an older America, very much as we do in similar characters in the Nebraska novels of Willa Cather.

Then we have Derrick's wife, Annie; she is an easterner, and therefore effete. She reads Pater and poetry and recoils from western manners. She is frightened by the mere vast fecundity of the limitless wheat fields. Norris clearly dislikes her because of her refinement. The Derricks have two sons: Lyman, who moves to San Francisco, and Harran, who remains faithful to his father. The city (even San Francisco) is the abode of evil and decay, like the East, in Norris's Populist mythology; and so Lyman quickly becomes corrupt. He is a member of the commission, and being covertly in the pay of the railroad, betrays the wheat ranchers. Harran, although he fights "the interests" along with his father, is more up-to-date; he takes to bribing and suborning as the way of the world.

The most appealing character in the novel, and the only one who is developed novelistically, so that we understand the inner strains of the man and can carefully watch the changes that take place in him, is another rancher named Annixter. He is a brilliant, irritable man with chronic indigestion who eats prunes all day and is reading *David Copperfield* throughout *The Octopus*. He is a maverick, a cynic, and has a raw, distrustful contempt for human beings. He is a strong woman-hater but is finally brought out of his misanthropy by his love for Hilma Tree, a kind of Eternal Woman or Goddess of the Wheat who works in Annixter's dairy. Through his love for her he is newly made a member of the human race, before being killed in an encounter with the marshal and the railroad agents. The story of Annixter and Hilma Tree departs from the canons of naturalism—according to which any character involved in life must degenerate in a straight line of descent and defeat. A tragic note is struck in his humanization and subsequent death, and his life is implied to be a kind of triumph, rather than just another bleak and meaningless episode in the spectacle of human fate, which is the usual impression Norris leaves about the meaning of individual lives.

Among the villains of the piece there is Genslinger, the venal editor of the local paper; he is in the pay of the ubiquitous railroad, and he blackmails and then double-crosses Magnus Derrick. The star villain, however, is S. Behrman, a caricature of the capitalist. He seems obviously to be a Jew, although this is never said to be so. He is the local banker and general agent of the railroad and finally becomes the owner of Magnus Derrick's ten-thousand-acre ranch. He meets a spectacular end when he is buried alive by the wheat in the hold of a ship.

Among the other minor characters there is Dyke, the well-meaning train engineer and now small-time farmer who is hounded and ruined by S. Behrman. There is Caraher, the Irish saloon keeper, an anarchist of bomb-throwing tendencies, and the only character in the book who has any meaningful political ideas at all, with the exception of the archaic Calhoun conservatism of Magnus Derrick. Then there is Vanamee, a character on whom the author seems to bank rather heavily as a representative of the mysterious and occult branches of experience. A kind of Ishmael, a wandering shepherd and range rider, Vanamee is a mystic who resembles, as Norris keeps saying, "the younger Hebrew prophets." Vanamee's life has been blighted by the fate of Angèle Varian, a girl he had been in love with but who had been raped and had died. He has discovered that by pressing his hands to his temples and concentrating he can turn people into automata and call them to him, which he frequently does. Vanamee spends his agonized nights trying to call back the spirit of Angèle. He finally finds peace of mind in the Christian-pagan message that may be derived from the book—namely that death, injustice, and suffering are redeemed and recompensed in the eternal rebirth of Life, symbolized by the cycle of the wheat.

But much the most portentous character in *The Octopus* is Presley, who is in an odd way one side of Norris himself and who acts fitfully as the book's center of intelligence. Presley is rather abstractly conceived as a poet and an intellectual. In keeping with the clichés of lowbrow literature, which *The Octopus* is, he is presented as *the* poet, *the* intellectual. It seems clear that in the figure of Presley, Norris is shriving himself of one aspect of his own personality—for he too was a poet and intellectual or might have been had he not escaped the early influences of his education in France and at Harvard.

Trained in an eastern university, Presley has come West to write a great poem on the romance of the frontier "where," as he says, "a new race, a new people—hardy, brave, passionate—were building an empire; where the tumultuous life ran like fire from dawn to dark and from dark to dawn again, primitive, brutal, honest, and without fear." Presley, as we see, has the makings of an epic poet of the West. Yet there is an inner uncertainty in the man, which grows worse as he stays on in California and watches the struggle between railroad and rancher. Searching for the "true Romance," as he calls it, he finds only the sordid machinations of the railroad. Believing himself to belong with "the People" he nevertheless tends to find them rather repulsive as individuals. And so we find Presley saying to himself "the romance, the real romance, is here somewhere. I'll get hold of it yet." Presley seems finally on the verge of a great poetic vision, however, when he exclaims to Vanamee: "The great poem of the West. It is that which I want to write. Oh, to put it all into hexameters; strike the great iron note; sing the vast terrible song; the song of the People; the forerunners of empire!" "Vanamee," Norris adds, "understood him perfectly"—which seems to prove that Vanamee is a man of supreme intelligence. Presley finally begins to write his projected epic, "Song of the West." Vanamee finds it great, but Mrs. Derrick, who reads "the little toy magazines, full of the flaccid banalities of the 'Minor Poets'" says that it "is not literature"—to which Presley replies "between his teeth" that he thanks God it is not. The epic does not work out however, and in the end Presley becomes a famous writer only because of a "Socialistic poem" he has written called "The Toilers." But Presley is destined to discover that literature is unsatisfactory; he abandons his writing and becomes an anarchist, declaring to the saloon keeper Caraher, "By God, I too, I'm a Red!"

He then throws a bomb at S. Behrman, but, like a true intellectual, he misses.

Norris thus makes out of Presley a prototype of a whole series of "intellectuals" and "poets" who are imagined in modern liberal idealism to have given up literature for political action or for a closer contact with reality, because of their sense of social injustice and their perception of the impotence of literature to affect the reality into which they try to hurl themselves. Presley seems, however, to be operating in a vacuum; for he never has any real involvement with or knowledge of either literature or politics. Perhaps we may call Presley a subintellectual, as his friend Vanamee is a submystic. This is nothing against them—the only point being that Norris takes each of them for the genuine article.

Although Vanamee finds a religious significance in the life cycle of the wheat, Norris himself derives a different lesson and the book concludes with a declaration of the naturalist creed:

> Men—motes in the sunshine—perished, were shot down in the very noon of life, hearts were broken, little children started in life lamentably handicapped; young girls were brought to a life of shame; old women died . . . for lack of food. In the little, isolated group of human insects, misery, death, and anguish spun like a wheel of fire.
>
> *But the* WHEAT *remained.* Untouched, unassailable, undefiled, that mighty world-force, that nourisher of nations, wrapped in Nirvanic calm, indifferent to the human swarm, gigantic, resistless . . .
>
> The larger view always and through all shams, all wickednesses, discovers the Truth that will, in the end, prevail, and all things, surely, inevitably, resistlessly work together for good.

It is possible to suppose momentarily that Norris is presenting something like Henry Adams's symbolic Virgin and

Dynamo. The Wheat, that is, might be the benignant nourishing force which in the end overcomes the inhuman and destructive force symbolized by the railroad. But in Norris's mind there is no differentiation of forces; there is only Force, and although *The Octopus* seems to be a liberal diatribe against capitalist reaction, the railroad and every injustice it brings with it, down to the last foreclosure on the most miserable property, are finally said to be as exempt from moral evaluation as the wheat itself. Both are irresistible manifestations of the "world-force." This irrationalism comes into play, however, only when Norris is trying to make ultimate formulations or when he breaks over into his particular kind of impassioned poetic insight (the same may be said of other naturalistic writers, particularly Norris's fellow Californians Jack London and Robinson Jeffers).

There is thus all through his work a tension between Norris the liberal humanist and ardent democrat and Norris the protofascist, complete with a racist view of Anglo-Saxon supremacy, a myth of the superman, and a portentous nihilism (some of Norris's anti-intellectual and reactionary views seem to have been derived from reading Kipling and from misreading Nietzsche, as well as from nativist sources). By way of contrast one might recall the more sympathetic view of Melville who shares Norris's love of the sheer poetry of power and death. At the end of *The Octopus* we are left to contemplate an irresistible force which supposedly works for "good"—but for the good of whom or what? is it the "human swarm"?—whereas in *Moby-Dick* we are left with Ishmael on the coffin-lifebuoy, a man in his plight as an individual.

## Norris Historically Viewed

What we usually have, then, in the novels of Norris (and this would apply to Zola as well) is the chronicle of the degeneration of characters under the pressure of heredity and environment, the tone of the story varying from straight novelistic realism to melodrama, epic, and grotesque comedy. Norris makes of his naturalism, even though it may seem to be merely a ruthless realism, a means of restoring to the novel some of the dramatic actions, mysteries, colorful events, and extreme situations, along with the mythic and symbolic motives, that used to be brought into the novel under other auspices. He does not, in other words, abandon the romance or romance-novel; he merely re-creates it and reconstitutes it on new grounds.

Different as he was in temperament and background from the older American romancers, and limited though his genius was, Norris continued in certain respects the tradition of Brockden Brown, Hawthorne, and Melville, a process that was inherent in his attempt to adapt the practice of Zola to American conditions. Historians have often observed how easily in many people's minds Calvinism modified itself during the nineteenth century into the philosophical determinism that stood behind the naturalistic movement in fiction. The "dark necessity" that rules Hawthorne's Chillingworth and Melville's Ahab differs from that which rules Norris's McTeague, because Hawthorne and Melville understand fate as being an inner or psychic predisposition. The ruin of the hero, or hero-villain as he often is, comes about as a result of the clash between his will and the adamant circumstances he finds himself in. Naturalistic doctrine, on the other hand, assumes that fate is something imposed on the individual from the outside. The protagonist of a naturalistic novel is therefore at the mercy of circumstances rather than of himself, indeed he often seems to *have* no self. Psychologically he is a simplified character compared even with the already simplified characters in the older romances, although by way of compensation his life is more richly endowed with concrete detail than is theirs. Nevertheless the sense of the dark necessity that controls human actions is vividly caught by both the naturalists and the older romancers. And despite the shifting of the spotlight from the inner mind to the outer world, it is often caught by the same procedures. Norris, for example, shares with the older writers a melodramatic extravagance, a tendency towards a stiff and abstract conventionalism of plot, a tendency toward the tone if not the actual method of allegory, and an interest in symbols (cf. the gold symbolism in *McTeague*).

To be sure, much had happened to the American novelist since the time of Cooper, Hawthorne, and Melville. What had happened can be suggested by the words realism and anti-intellectualism. The realism which was introduced into the older romance-novels only sporadically became after the Civil War the primary prerequisite of the serious novel, whether as practiced by James, Howells, Mark Twain, Stephen Crane, or Norris. With the advent of these writers an era began which has not yet been superseded, and perhaps never will be—an era in which all the imaginative dimensions of the novel begin on the operational base of realism. Historically involved with this realism, although not logically necessitated by it, is the anti- or non-intellectualism shown by most of the important modern novelists except those who belong to the school of James and Howells. The older writers, from Brown and Cooper to Melville, thought of themselves, not perhaps as "intellectuals" in any of the modern senses of this term, but at least as writers a part of whose task it was to have a commerce with the life of ideas and with certain traditional values. Norris is a classic case of the modern lowbrow novelist, something of an intellectual himself to be sure, and yet a lowbrow because of his native temperament and conviction—but also because, let us not fail to add, lowbrowism is one of the most successful literary poses in modern America.

Compared with Cooper and Melville, nurtured as they were on a fairly complex Anglo-American culture, Frank Norris is a semibarbarian out of the new West. And yet nothing so confirms one's belief in the existence of an American tradition of the romance-novel as the fact that

*Calvinism*
↓
*naturalistic determinism*

Norris's background and upbringing furnish him with an imagination which is so similar to that derived from quite different sources by the older writers. Take, for example, two of the leading imaginative ideas of Melville: first, the golden age with its simple life of innocence and genial emotions, which he generically calls "Typee"; and, second, his idea of Evil, the "great power of blackness" which, as we have noted in an earlier chapter, he finds in Hawthorne's tales and which he thinks "derives its force from its appeals to that Calvinistic sense of Innate Depravity and Original Sin, from whose visitations, in some shape or other, no deeply thinking mind is always and wholly free." To a considerable extent Melville consciously derives these two leading ideas from literary and intellectual tradition, however native they may have been to the demands of his temperament.

One finds new versions of Melville's ideas in the novels of Frank Norris. But they have been derived not so much from reflection and reading as from Norris's instinctive imaginative sympathy with the doctrines of American Populism, the movement of agrarian protest and revolt which was in its heyday when Norris was forming his ideas in the 1880's and 1890's. The importance of Populist doctrine in understanding the art of Frank Norris is suggested by his own remark, cited above, that romance derives from the "People."

It was not really the plain facts and concrete injustices behind the Populist protest that appealed to Norris. Rather, it was what Richard Hofstadter calls (in *The Age of Reform*) "the folklore of Populism." For our purposes, this folklore may be understood as having two origins. First, there is what Mr. Hofstadter calls the "agrarian myth" that ever since the time of Jefferson has haunted the mind, not of the vast commercialized middle class or perhaps after the earliest times the farmers either, but of reformers and intellectuals. This "myth" involves the idea of a pastoral golden age—a time of plain living, independence, self-sufficiency and closeness to the soil—an idea which has been celebrated in various ways by innumerable American writers. Second, there is the mythology of Calvinism which especially in the rural West and South has always infused Protestantism, even the non-Calvinist sects, with its particular kind of Manichaean demonology.

If, as we have been saying in this book, American fiction has traditionally enhanced realism with nostalgic idyl and with melodrama, it is evidently akin in its imagination to "the folklore of Populism," which has always done the same. This is pointed up sharply when we perceive how close a writer like Norris actually is to Populism—not, it must be re-emphasized, to its genuinely liberal or its genuinely realistic reformist program but to its vaunting, mythic ideology (an ideology often reactionary in its political implication). In Norris's *McTeague* and *The Octopus* one finds this ideology more or less exactly represented; one finds what Mr. Hofstadter calls "the idea of a golden age. . . . the dualistic version of social struggles; the conspiracy theory of history; and the doctrine of the primacy of money."

McTeague is not literally an agrarian hero; yet he does come out of a simple rural America, and he is corrupted and defeated by the customs and laws of the evil city. The fact that nature is thoroughly Darwinized in Norris's imagination and that McTeague, though appealing in his masculine simplicity, is not far above the brute, does not quite conceal the underlying myth of Adam and the fall from Eden that makes McTeague a sort of brutalized Billy Budd. The dualistic version of social struggles is apparent in *McTeague*, though not nearly so strongly dramatized as it is in *The Octopus*. In both books the social question is conceived as a clear-cut, black-and-white war between the grasping capitalist and the plain American. And although Norris does not campaign for silver, he accepts the idea of the primacy of money. Gold is shown, especially in *Mc-Teague*, to be as fertile a source of evil and misery as the devil himself and its sinister powers are melodramatized with an exaggerated symbolism. In *The Octopus* we find a full use of the conspiracy theory of history—the theory that all would be well with American life if only it were not for the machinations of the money power—the bankers, the railroad magnates, and their panoply of venal journalists and lawyers, suborned marshals, and hired assassins.

The main difference between the folklore of Populism and the imagination of Frank Norris is that naturalist doctrine has given him an underlying pessimism about nature itself and man's place in it. Norris appears to accept what Mr. Hofstadter calls "the concept of natural harmonies," a utopian faith in the natural order and in the virtue of man's living in harmony with it; but this view of things always has to contend in Norris's mind with a radically pessimistic view. As with most American naturalistic novelists, the pessimism wins out in the end, but in doing so it seems to take over from the idyl of nature some of its poetic, utopian quality, so that what we have is not hardheaded Darwinism but romantic nihilism, the final implication of which is that death itself is utopia.

*Martin Eden!*

Norris's romance-novels succeeded in reclaiming for American fiction an imaginative profundity that the age of Howells was leaving out—a fact which Norris's crudity and passages of bad writing cannot conceal. *McTeague* introduced to the novel a new animal vitality and a new subject matter drawn from lower-class life. From a moral and intellectual point of view, *The Octopus* has to be called a sort of subnovel. Yet no sympathetic reader can forget its enormous panoramic power. The book has, as D. H. Lawrence says, a brooding, primitive tone, an astonishing sense of a world instinct with sinister forces, that remind one of Cooper's *The Prairie*.

In view of their imaginative achievement one does not worry too much, in reading Norris's books, about their sentence-to-sentence faults of syntax and language, although like Dreiser, Norris was unable to tell whether the English he himself wrote was good or bad. *McTeague* and

*The Octopus* prove again that it is possible to master certain fundamental aspects of the art of prose fiction despite the imperfection of the language in which the feat is achieved. One does not destroy either Norris or Dreiser by pointing out their bad grammar and their false rhetoric. On the other hand neither can you write a very great novel unless you are master of your language, as Hawthorne, Melville, Mark Twain, James, and Faulkner are masters. And then again you may be the perfect master of your language without being a great master of the art of the novel; Hemingway is an example.

Many later writers, the two greatest being Dreiser and Faulkner, have shown that naturalism remains a usable technique. Dreiser performed the considerable service of adapting the colorful poetry of Norris to the more exacting tasks imposed upon the social novelist—very much as James assimilated Hawthorne's imagination of romance into his novels. Faulkner, a more universal genius than Dreiser and less specifically deriving from Norris, allies the naturalistic procedures with certain of the classic motives of fiction. But it is in Norris that we see the glories and perils of naturalism in their sheerest form.

Chapter X

# FAULKNER—THE GREAT YEARS

ALTHOUGH Faulkner has written fine things in the last twenty years, his best period was that between 1929 and 1932, when he wrote *The Sound and the Fury, As I Lay Dying, Sanctuary,* and *Light in August.* These are among the best novels of the twentieth century.

There will always be a certain kind of reader who dismisses Faulkner as an irresponsible sensationalist, a sadist, a muddled thinker, a charlatan, a man who never mastered English, and so on. There have always been readers who felt the same way about Dostoevski. Faulkner is not in a class with Dostoevski, but he is an authentic genius, and after James one of the two or three greatest of American novelists. One may note also that he is by instinct and practice *a novelist,* a master (if sometimes an unruly one) of the large concerted novelistic effect. He is also a great fabulist and writer of tales or short stories, but it is in the general tradition of the naturalistic novel that he flourishes best.

For present purposes *Sanctuary* may be dismissed with a brief note (but see Appendix I). It is a brilliant *tour de force,* combining the abstract intellectual swiftness of melodrama, the mechanically emblematic moralism of allegory, and the realistic detail and evocation of fate one associates with naturalism. This combination of elements lends plausibility to Malraux's comparison of *Sanctuary* with the Greek drama. Faulkner's novel offers, also, passages of humor that give it a place among the modern novels of grotesque comedy as practiced in their various ways by Conrad, Kafka, Nathanael West, and others who have brought to the older comic tradition of Dickens and Dostoevski a modern or "existentialist" tone. But for all its brilliance, there is a certain amount of fakery in *Sanctuary,* as in all *tours de force,* which is happily not present in Faulkner's best work.

*The Sound and the Fury* (1929) is Faulkner's masterpiece. *As I Lay Dying* (1930) is the simplest and most unified of his longer fictions and has certain fine successes of language. *Light in August* (1932) contains in larger profusion than do any of his other books the essential elements, good and bad, of the author's genius. It may be profitable to consider these novels out of their chronological sequence, so that they illustrate different stages of the difficult art of the novel. From this point of view we might think of *As I Lay Dying,* despite its apparently elaborate technique, as a relatively simple and limited form, really an extended tale. *Light in August* is more ambitious and is a classic example of what is meant by speaking of an American novel as distinguished from a European one. *The Sound and the Fury* is one of the few American novels that rise to a truly tragic art, bringing the possibilities of the novel form to their fulfillment.

## As I Lay Dying

Faulkner's story of the Bundren family is a short comic novel which reminds one a good deal of folk tale and fable. With a few superficial changes the author might have used the convention of a humorous narrator who would spin the whole episodic, richly colloquial tale in his own voice. Faulkner's trick of making each character speak in turn has been called the "multiple point of view." But a multiple point of view, if it is multiple enough, of necessity becomes simply the point of view of the omniscient author, and it is hard to see that outside of one or two of the sections devoted to the introspective, analytical Darl much has been gained by Faulkner's elaborate procedure. On the other hand not much has been lost, and once the reader is prepared to accept or ignore the few surrealistic excesses of image and language, there is little to disconcert him and much to excite his admiration. (By surrealistic excesses I mean such attempts at "art" as making one of the characters repeat, "My mother is a fish." Faulkner has always had a weakness for this kind of sophistication, with its suggestion of recondite symbolism.)

If the story is a fable as well as a comic tall tale, it must have a moral, and indeed the hazardous and hair-raising journey of the Bundrens in order to bury the mother of the family in the cemetery at Jefferson as they had promised her they would seems to give the tale the moral solemnity of a religious ritual. It makes us think of the myths of burial and the sacredness of the dead. But the ritual feeling, we note, is not hieratic or theological or even tragic. It is tinged with comedy as in Mark Twain, Melville, and Faulkner ritual feeling usually is.

*As I Lay Dying*, then, is a comic fable about piety towards the dead and the sacredness of promises to the dead,

a view of the significance of the story which is not nulli-
fied by the desire of the Bundrens to lay the mother's ghost
and have done with the powerful will and assertive mind
the family has had to put up with all these years—the only
such temperament among the Bundrens. Nor is the moral of
the tale destroyed, as many readers too easily conclude, by
the fact that the characters have other sorts of mixed motives for going to Jefferson—Anse, the father of the family,
needs a new set of false teeth, not to mention a new wife.
But it is human to have mixed motives and a novelist's mistake not to show them that way. Perhaps the book is also
a fable, as I suggested in an earlier chapter, showing the
peculiar precariousness with which Americans meet a common obligation through momentarily concerted action. At
any rate Europeans sometimes see in *As I Lay Dying* an
example of the unstable moral intensity which drives
Americans on rare occasions to a grotesque, Quixotic gal-
lantry.

These large significances are present and to be ac-
counted for. Even so they remain a kind of shadowy super-
structure to the only moral Faulkner, through the voice of
Addie Bundren (the mother), overtly insists on. Faulkner
preaches the act over the word, the concrete over the abstract. Addie, as she explains herself, had been unreason-
ing, willful, passionate, vital, realistic; the creed she adheres
to in short is a Mississippi hill-country version of the
activist creed of American writers from Emerson and William James to Stephen Crane and Hemingway.* There is
no doubt either that her irrational activism is meant to impress us as being more genuinely religious and profound
than doctrinal religion, which in the persons of the Reverend Whitfield and Cora Tull is shown to be self-righteous
and hypocritical. Furthermore the fact that the family is
acting in common seems more important than their reasons

* The language of this passage, which makes relations among
"blood," consciousness, and individuality, suggests that Faulkner
has been impressed by D. H. Lawrence.

for doing so. Addie's soliloquy (beginning on p. 461 of the Modern Library Edition) is the moral center of the book and its essence is in these words:

> And so when Cora Tull would tell me I was not a true mother, I would think how words go straight up in a thin line, quick and harmless; and how terribly doing goes along the earth, clinging to it, so that after a while the two lines are too far apart for the same person to straddle from one to the other; and that sin and love and fear are just sounds that people who never sinned nor loved nor feared have for what they never had and cannot have until they forget the words.

As in *Huckleberry Finn, Moby-Dick,* and "Song of the Open Road," we find in *As I Lay Dying* the theme of the strenuous journey and the quest that gives it meaning. The quest involves the search for identity, and Darl being the intellectual of the family—rustic and waif though he is—reflects this. It involves the discovery of kinship, of one's common humanity, and this is best illustrated, if only in muted tones, by the newly released compassion and genial emotions of the hitherto rigidly secretive Cash. Above all it involves the rediscovery of the self by breaking out of the circle of selfhood. As Addie says, remembering her marriage and the birth of her first child: "My aloneness had been violated and then made whole again by the violation: time, Anse, love, what you will, outside the circle." This century-old theme of American literature was to be used more fully, though perhaps with less concentrated effectiveness, in *Light in August.* It also appears in *The Sound and the Fury.*

It would be tiresome to try to analyze the style of *As I Lay Dying.* At its best the language is the purest and most beautiful in Faulkner. It is almost as good as that in *Huckleberry Finn,* which it so much resembles. As in *Huckleberry Finn* the modulations from vernacular to high literary language are what count most. A passage near the end,

where Cash is remembering that Darl has had to be put in
the asylum, is as good as any:

> And then I see that the grip she was carrying was one
> of them little graphophones. It was for a fact, all shut
> up as pretty as a picture, and every time a new record
> would come from the mail order and us sitting in the
> house in the winter, listening to it, I would think what a
> shame Darl couldn't be to enjoy it too. But it is better
> so for him. This world is not his world; this life his life.

## Light in August

There could hardly be a more characteristically American
novel than *Light in August*—with its realism; its loose structure; its few characters who though vividly presented are
never quite convincingly related to each other; its tendency
to become a romance by taking on a legendary quality
and by alternating violent melodramatic actions with comic
interludes and scenes of pastoral idyl; its concern with the
isolated self; its awareness of contradictions, racial and
other; its symbolism of light and dark. Generally speaking,
*Light in August* is in these respects akin to books apparently
as diverse as *The Prairie, The House of the Seven Gables,
Moby-Dick, The Grandissimes,* and *Huckleberry Finn,* not
to mention *Uncle Tom's Cabin* and many others, including
such novels of more recent vintage as Robert Penn Warren's
*Night Rider* and Ralph Ellison's *The Invisible Man.*

In *Light in August* things are perceived in space rather
than temporally as they are in *The Sound and the Fury.*
Except for the Reverend Hightower, one of Faulkner's characters who are ruined by time, no one is particularly aware
of time; and the surviving, enduring character, Lena Grove,
lives in a timeless realm which seems to be at once eternity and the present moment. The Mississippi landscape

spreads out before us and the faculty of vision becomes very important as we are shown the town of Jefferson, the houses of Hightower and Miss Burden, or the smoke on the horizon as Miss Burden's house burns. There is much use of the painter's art (even the sculptor's, as when Faulkner makes a wagon slowly passing through the countryside look like part of a frieze, or a seated person—Lena Grove or Hightower—resemble a statue). The art style is not cubist or otherwise modernist as it sometimes is in Faulkner's writing (*Pylon*, for example); it is serene, harmonious, and always aware, even in the midst of dark and violent actions, of a luminousness and spatial harmony that suggest an eternal order.

A simple and somewhat disconnected story emerges from the "abundance of representation," which, as Irving Howe correctly says, constitutes the splendor of *Light in August*. Lena Grove, a poor and ignorant farm girl from Alabama, painfully wends her way into northern Mississippi in pursuit of Lucas Burch, with whose child she is pregnant. Hearing that her ne'er-do-well lover has got a job at a sawmill near Jefferson, she goes there and finds Byron Bunch and Joe Christmas. But Burch has left; as the story goes on, Lena has her child and at the end is still on the road, an example apparently of perpetual motion. Now she is accompanied not by Burch but by Bunch; which one accompanies her she seems to regard as a matter of indifference.

Meanwhile in a long and exhaustive flash-back we are told the history of Joe Christmas, an orphan and (as everyone including himself assumes) part Negro. We are told how Christmas murders Miss Burden, a descendant of New England abolitionists, and how he is caught, escapes, and is finally murdered himself in the Reverend Hightower's kitchen by Percy Grimm. We are also told a good deal about the life of Hightower, particularly how he ruined his career and lost his wife because of his fantasy of identification with his Confederate grandfather, an officer in the army who had been killed in Jefferson during the Civil War. As the story unfolds, Hightower is now an old man isolated from the world, but before he dies he gets more or less involved with Lena and Joe Christmas and serves rather loosely as the unifying figure and center of intelligence of the last sections of the novel. There are thus three separate strands of narrative in *Light in August*, each having its central character. The book makes a kind of triptych.

Lena Grove is one of those intensely female females we meet in Faulkner's books, like Eula Varner in *The Hamlet*. A somewhat bovine earth mother, she has all those womanly qualities which, as Faulkner likes to point out, baffle, fascinate, outrage, and finally defeat men. According to Faulkner's gynecological demonology (it constitutes a sort of Mississippi Manichaeism) men are more interesting and valuable than women but the dark or Satanic principle of the universe decrees that they are the weaker sex and are doomed to be frustrated and ephemeral. Faulkner appears to agree both with folk superstition and Henry Adams that compared with women men are in Adams's word "epiphenomenal."

The bovine woman brings to Faulkner's mind echoes of ancient myth and ritual (hence the name, Lena Grove—cf. Hilma Tree in *The Octopus*) and he treats her alternately with gravity and with a measure of humorously grandiose fantasy and mockery. Lena's placidity is not only that of the cow but unmistakably that of the gods in their eternity. Hence Faulkner has given her a ritual office by associating her with the religious procession depicted in Keats's "Ode on a Grecian Urn," a favorite poem of Faulkner of which there are several echoes in *Light in August*. In Lena's unvarying inner harmony (and here Faulkner is serious rather than mocking) all opposites and disparates are reconciled or perhaps rendered meaningless. In the words of Keats's poem, beauty is truth and truth beauty. By implying that Lena Grove somehow symbolizes this ideal unity Faulkner suggests no metaphysical reconciliation. He merely praises again the quiet enduring stoicism and wisdom of the heart which he finds among the poor whites, Negroes, and other socially marginal types.

The first thing to be said about Joe Christmas is that he is not a villain, as is sometimes thought. Nor, except in a distantly symbolic way, is he a tragic hero or a "Christ-figure." He has many of the qualities Faulkner admires. He suffers, he is a divided man, he is marginal and bereaved; he is "outraged." He asks merely to live, to share the human experience, and to be an individual. Like the slave in "Red Leaves," he "runs well"—he has in other words some power of giving his doomed life meaning by insisting as long as he can on his right to be human. All this outbalances his being a criminal. It even outbalances his being a murderer.

It is the custom of some traditionalist critics to say, in the words of one of them, that "sentimentalists and sociologists are bound to regard Christmas solely as a victim," whereas actually he is a tragic figure akin to Oedipus. But the main difference between Joe Christmas and Oedipus (or any other tragic hero in the full classic sense) is that Christmas really *is* a victim; he never has a chance, and a chance, or at least the illusion of a chance, a tragic hero must have. It is true that in *The Sound and the Fury* and perhaps elsewhere Faulkner achieves a genuine tragic vision of life and evokes the profound and harmonious emotions that tragedy evokes. But on the whole his vision of things is more akin to that of "sentimentalists and sociologists" than to that of Sophocles—if by this we mean that, like many modern novelists, he takes a rather darkly naturalistic view of things but finds a saving grace in the simplest sentiments of men. Joe Christmas, as Faulkner presents him, is a character conceived not in the manner of the tragedian but of the naturalistic novelist. There is no mystery, no disastrous choice, no noble action, no tragic recognition. Instead there are heredity, environment, neurotic causation, social maladjustment. What happens later to Joe Christmas is made inevitable by the circumstances of his boyhood in the orphanage. In fact one may be very specific about the origin of the train of causes. Christmas's life is given its definitive bias by his encounter with the dietitian, described near the beginning of Chapter 6. Hiding in a closet and eating toothpaste, he has seen the dietitian making illicit love. When she discovers this, Christmas expects, and *desires*, to be whipped. Instead she offers him a silver dollar:

> He was waiting to get whipped and then be released. Her voice went on, urgent, tense, fast: "A whole dollar. See? How much you could buy. Some to eat every day for a week. And next month maybe I'll give you another one."
>
> He did not move or speak. He might have been carven, as a large toy: small, still, round headed and round eyed, in overalls. He was still with astonishment, shock, outrage.

What the boy wants is recognition, acceptance as a human being, if only through physical punishment. A whipping would establish the passionate, human contact. Instead he is given a silver dollar, and he sees his doom in its adamant, abstract, circular form. He has now been given an irresistible compulsion to destroy every human relationship that he gets involved in. And this compulsion includes the suicidal desire to destroy himself.

Joe Christmas thus joins the long procession of isolated, doomed heroes that begin to appear in the American novel with Brockden Brown, Hawthorne, and Melville. This is not the place to discuss the complex picture of Protestantism that emerges from *Light in August;* yet one may note that in the isolation of Christmas (and others in the book) Calvinism is still strongly felt as an influence, despite the fact that the psychology Faulkner has applied is generally "Freudian," in the popular behavioristic sense. Apparently nothing appears to our American novelists to be more terrible than to have become isolated or to have fallen victim to a cold, abstract hatred of life—nor, we must admit, does any doom call forth a more spontaneous admiration or require a more arduous repudiation.

But if Christmas has his American ancestors, Faulkner has also made some attempt at modernizing him by making him in effect a Conradian or postromantic, existentialist hero. The portrait of Kurtz, the ultimately lost, rootless, and alienated man in Conrad's *Heart of Darkness,* is a distant model for Christmas. The Reverend Hightower, too, is a kind of Marlow (the narrator of Conrad's story), if only in the tone of his voice and in his physical appearance ("Hightower sits again in the attitude of an Eastern idol, between his parallel arms on the armrests of the chair"). And it is clear that Faulkner has learned some of his more florid rhetoric from Conrad. The following passage might have come from the pen of either Conrad or Faulkner; it is from *Heart of Darkness:*

> And in the hush that had fallen suddenly on the whole sorrowful land, the immense wilderness, the colossal body of the fecund and mysterious life seemed to look at her, pensive, as though it had been looking at the image of its own tenebrous and passionate soul.

This sort of thing has its own rhetorical magnificence, although both Conrad and Faulkner are perhaps a little too easily moved by the fecund, the pensive and the tenebrous. And there is no doubt that these authors—melodramatists both—tend to construct a rhetoric of doom and darkness in excess of what the occasion demands.

The Reverend Hightower is one of Faulkner's best characters. He appeals to us in many ways—first and most importantly in the sad everyday conditions of his life: the decaying house with the weather-beaten sign in front saying "Art Lessons Christmas Cards Photographs Developed"; the swivel chair in which he sits before the desk with the green shaded reading lamp as he gazes fixedly out the window; his moving colloquies with Byron Bunch, who, though

his companion, is so different from him in heritage and intellect—as different as Sancho Panza is from Don Quixote
(a parallel which is very much in Faulkner's mind). Only
because Hightower is established in novelistic detail do we
become interested in the fantastic obsession that has
ruined his life. Like Quentin Compson and Horace Benbow
(see *Sartoris* and *Sanctuary*), Hightower is one of Faulkner's intellectuals—he is fastidious, genteel, frightened by
life. Haunted by the glory and crime of the past, he is incapable of living in the present. Like Quentin Compson he
tries willfully to impose a kind of order on the irrational
flow of time and nature. His view of things, however, is not
metaphysical or theological like Quentin's; it is purely
mythic and aesthetic, the product of a mind immersed in
Keats and Tennyson. A careful reading of the pages at the
end of Chapter 20 will show that Hightower does not return to his earlier Christian belief in his moment of ultimate insight before he dies. The turn of his mind is to
grasp truth aesthetically; truth is for him an ecstatic perception of a supreme moment in the natural, historical
order, a moment in which, to employ the Keatsian vocabu-
lary Faulkner encourages us to use, beauty is grasped as
truth and truth as beauty. Before he dies he sees the truth
about himself—"I have not been clay"—which is merely a
way of admitting finally that neither truth nor beauty can
be perceived by the mind that remains inverted and
solipsistic and denies man's common fate in nature and
time. This is the truth that finally comes to Hightower; and
it is what allows him to see for the first time, and patheti-
cally for the last, the full beauty of the myth he has lived
by. For a moment he can now be free, for the first time
and the last. The progression of his views has thus taken
him beyond his Christianity and his pure aestheticism to a
full, profound, perhaps tragic naturalism (to use the word
in its philosophical rather than strictly novelistic reference).

A good deal has been written about the symbolism of
*Light in August,* and although much of this criticism has

been predictably beside the main points, it remains true that this novel has in it a much more complicated symbolism than *The Sound and the Fury* or *As I Lay Dying*. The most obviously conscious and willed symbolism is the least successful—such as the attributes of Christ Faulkner associates with Joe Christmas; these have an artificial, inorganic, even an arty quality about them. The symbolism that seems most profoundly organic with the action and meaning of the book is that of the circle, and I would judge that, like any interesting symbol, this was half consciously intended by the author but has implications within the book of which he was probably not entirely conscious when he wrote it.

Three circles should be kept in mind; they are associated with the three main characters. Remembering the theme of solitude vs. society, alienation vs. community that we noticed in *As I Lay Dying*, we remember also that Faulkner spoke of Addie Bundren's aloneness as a circle that had to be violated in order to be made whole. Although this is a literary idea that Faulkner might have absorbed from many sources, among them Yeats, the symbol of the circle of selfhood may be taken as an archetype of the modern imagination, and especially wherever Puritanism has made itself felt. Lena Grove's circle, then, since she is a kind of earth goddess, is simply that of the death and renewal of nature. She is also associated with the urn of Keats's ode and the ritual procession of its encircling frieze. In the circle of her being truth and beauty are perpetually absorbed into each other. In Lena selfhood is whole; it is congruous with experience, with nature and with time.

The circle associated with Joe Christmas is the fatalistic, repetitive pattern of his life; in actual symbolization it varies from the silver dollar the dietitian gives him to the pattern of his flight from the sheriff and his dogs. He wants, of course, to break out of his circle—"to define himself as human," in the words of Robert Penn Warren. Yet whenever this becomes possible, usually in relation to a woman

217

he has become involved with, he succumbs to the irresistible compulsion to preserve his isolation. Finally, virtual suicide is the only solution. One might add that his circle is also racial; he is doomed to oscillate helplessly between the white world and the black.

If Christmas's imprisoning circle is imposed on him by circumstance, the Reverend Hightower's is imposed by himself, forged by his own intellect and neurotic fantasy. Only at the end when for a moment he is released from the isolation and stagnation of his life does the wheel that is a part of his obsessive fantasy finally spin free:

> The wheel whirls on. It is going fast and smooth now, because it is freed now of burden, of vehicle, axle, all. In the lambent suspension of August into which night is about to fully come, it seems to engender and surround itself with a faint glow like a halo. The halo is full of faces. The faces are not shaped with suffering, not shaped with anything: not horror, pain, not even reproach. They are peaceful, as though they have escaped into an apotheosis; his own is among them.

Despite the religious overtones of the language, this ultimate vision of Hightower seems to be a purely naturalistic intuition of his own solidarity with the other people he has known. It is this intuition that finally frees him.

The symbolism we have been noticing runs fairly deep, but it remains of the natural order, as, on the whole, does similar symbolism having to do with the self and its isolation in the writings of Hawthorne, Melville, and James. The specifically Christian symbolism in *Light in August* is not made deeply significant. It seems impossible to be much impressed with the fact that Faulkner calls one of his characters "Joe Christmas," and that he is thirty-three years old, has his feet votively bathed, and is in a manner crucified. The symbolism of the circle would certainly, if we had here a specifically Christian novel, include the traditional symbolism of death and the newborn spiritual life. But this central mystery of Christianity is not present. And *Light in August* reminds us that Faulkner's imagination is not characteristically stirred by incarnation, catharsis, and harmony, but rather by separation, alienation, and contradiction. If *Light in August* were a Christian novel it might use the symbolism of the book as it stands—the circle, the opposition of light and dark, and so on. But in some way it would have to employ the idea that life comes about *through* death, that in some way a new spiritual life had come to the community of Jefferson through the death of Joe Christmas. But this does not happen; there is no new life, no transfiguration anywhere that would not have occurred without Joe Christmas. There is no new religious consciousness or knowledge. In Joe Christmas we do not celebrate the death and rebirth of the hero.

Light and dark, good and evil, life and death, Eros and Thanatos are postulated in *Light in August* as eternal and autonomous contradictions. There is no possibility of absorbing and reconciling these contradictions in a whole view of life that is in any specific sense religious, or, for that matter, tragic. There are only two courses open: 1) to commit some transcendent act of horror or violence or suicide, 2) to find reattachment to the simple concrete conditions of life, through love, stoic patience, or humor, for in this way one may, as it were, temporarily step aside from the eternal contradictions in which humanity is involved and give the world the appearance of harmony.


## The Sound and the Fury

*The Sound and the Fury* is the eloquent testimony to the truth (when we are considering the art of the novel) of James's remark about Hawthorne "that the flower of art blooms only where the soil is deep, that it takes a great deal of history to produce a little literature, that it needs a complex social machinery to set a writer in motion." Before such a book as *The Sound and the Fury* could be written there had to be, of course, a funded history in the South. There had to be not only a past but a sense of the past. There had to be also, else such a book as Faulkner's might actually have been written in the South in the nineteenth century, a modern mind to write it—and by a modern mind I mean a divided, realistic, ironic mind with a sense of the tragedy of history.

No book as rich and resonant or so concertedly powerful in its tragic impact as *The Sound and the Fury* could have been written, given the subject, by an American writer of the nineteenth century, southern *or* northern. Among novels about the decline of a family Melville's *Pierre* suffers by comparison with Faulkner's book by the diffusion of its effect, the consequence of Melville's morbid introspectiveness and inability to embody his genuine historical sense in the daily fate of his characters. Even *The House of the Seven Gables,* a more distinguished and authentically historical chronicle of a family curse, lacks the tragic consistency of *The Sound and the Fury,* although it has certain sturdy pictorial virtues which we do not find in Faulkner's novel. Nevertheless, the non-Emersonian tradition of Hawthorne and Melville prepared the way for Faulkner by introducing the strain of dark and somber drama which characterizes so much of the best American fiction. And indeed Faulkner's kinship is as much with these northern writers as it is with the ante-bellum southern romancer William Gilmore Simms, although in Simms's lurid tales of seduction, revenge, violence, and murder, like *Charlemont, Beauchampe,* and *Confession,* one may find dimly forecast some of the themes of Faulkner (cf. Chapter I).

But there had to intervene between the older American traditions and Faulkner the naturalistic novel with its license as to subject matter and the promise it offers—so infrequently fulfilled—of reviving a genuine tragic art by evoking fate in terms of heredity and environment. Perhaps

Marx, certainly Freud, had to intervene. Dostoevski had also to intervene, for indeed there is a distinctly Russian quality about *The Sound and the Fury*, and like *The Brothers Karamazov*, which also concerns the dissolution of a family, it is able to incorporate in its grandiose novelistic way a sort of hidden Greek tragedy, reminiscent of Aeschylus's chronicles of the house of Atreus or Sophocles's of the house of Thebes. Above all there had to intervene Joyce's *Ulysses*, as we shall see in a minute.

But first let us recall the main elements of the book. Its subject is what happens to the last generation of the Compson family, a family whose ups and downs are representative of the experience of the South over the two hundred and more years after the first immigrant Compson settled in Faulkner's partly imaginary Yoknapatawpha County in Mississippi. The father and mother of the family do not figure prominently. Mr. Compson (Jason III) is an ineffectual lawyer who devotes himself mainly to whiskey and the Latin authors and dies young. Mrs. Compson is one of those wraiths one meets in southern novels, of whom it is said (as in *Absalom, Absalom!*) that "the War made ghosts of our ladies"; she is sickly, whining, neurasthenic.

Their four children are the main characters, except for Dilsey, the Negro servant. In Jason IV, the businessman of the family, the older southern traditions of the genteel property-holding class are seen to disappear in favor of a purely materialistic way of life. He finally disposes of the family holdings, so that what was once a fine estate becomes, as Faulkner says, a square mile "intact again in row after row of small crowded jerry-built individually owned demiurban bungalows." Jason has two brothers. The first is Quentin, whose overpowering sense of family honor and pride and whose neurotic love of his sister, the promiscuous Candace, leads him to commit suicide at the end of his year at Harvard. There is also Benjy, the idiot of the family. There is Quentin, the daughter of Candace (Caddy) and a local Lothario named Dalton Ames. She runs off with a pitchman

from a visiting carnival, taking with her a considerable sum
of money which Jason has misappropriated from Caddy.
The characters do not do very much; the plot is meager.
But the evocation of character and of situation is both full
and dramatic.

One can hardly hope to trace the process by which so
rich a book as *The Sound and the Fury* was conceived. A
clue may be discovered, however, in the evolution in Faulkner's work of the doomed, alienated, more or less intellectual
young man who seems clearly to be one projection of the
author himself and who finds fullest expression in Quentin
Compson.*

The first version of Faulkner's doomed young man is
Donald Mahon, the wounded veteran of the "Lost-
Generation" novel, *Soldiers' Pay.* Yet he is so mortally
wounded and so vaguely understood by the author that he
is hardly more than an inanimate object. In *Sartoris*, Faulkner's third novel (*Mosquitoes* is the second), we have
young Bayard Sartoris whose fate is given meaning partly
by the fact that he is a member of one of the old families

* He is present again, to be sure, as Darl Bundren in *As I Lay
Dying*, but after that book Faulkner lost interest in the sensitive,
doomed young man, although Gavin Stevens, who figures in later
books as the small-town intellectual who is both alienated from
and spokesman for his fellow citizens, may once have resembled
the suffering young men of the early books. It should be noted,
by the way, that in keeping with his characteristically American
myth about himself—according to which he is not a writer or a
literary man but only "a farmer"—Faulkner never projects himself as an artist. The nearest he gets to it is a reference to a man
called William Faulkner in *Mosquitoes;* he is described rather
coyly as "a little blackman . . . a liar by profession." Faulkner
projects himself as a reckless, doomed, guilty young man or as
the Gavin Stevens type, the Dixiecrat lawyer who went to
Harvard. Or, if he is identifying with a skill it is not that of
writing; it is the stunt flying of aviators, the precise and loving
carpentry of Cash Bundren, the forest skill of hunters, or the
monologues of poor-white humorists and raconteurs like Ratliffe,
the sewing machine agent (see especially *The Hamlet*).

that were to figure in the chronicle of Yoknapatawpha County. In *Sartoris* Faulkner was shedding his emulation of Hemingway, Fitzgerald, Lawrence, and Huxley and discovering his true subject. But although Bayard is given a historical dimension, he is nevertheless drawn rather conventionally as having the desperate gaiety and sadness of the World War I veteran. He never has any very interesting feelings or thoughts.

But in Quentin Compson we have a fuller representation. Not only does he have the history of his family and of Yoknapatawpha County behind him, so that this is richly felt in whatever he does; but now Faulkner has discovered how to *do* this character. He makes this discovery to a certain extent by reading *Ulysses* and by perceiving the plausibility of modeling Quentin on Stephen Daedalus. The similarities are obvious enough—they are both Hamlet-like young men; they are alienated from yet feel powerfully attached to their homelands; they are preoccupied by time and the symbolic significance of passing episodes in their lives and Stephen Daedalus's idea that "history is a nightmare from which I am trying to awake" expresses Quentin Compson's own state of mind; both young men are haunted by guilt: Quentin tries to believe he has committed incest with his sister, as Stephen tries to believe he has killed his mother.

Joyce's influence on *The Sound and the Fury*, as every reader must see, affects not only Quentin Compson but the very structure and language of the book. In the first two sections especially, it is not narrative but (as in *Ulysses*) the association of the symbols and ideas that forms the continuity. We soon become aware, as we begin to understand the unconventional technique of *The Sound and the Fury*, that the book contains a fairly sustained if meagre narrative of the conventional sort. But it is important to perceive that the action of the book extends beyond the narrative which recounts the dissolution of the Compson family and includes a gradual revelation in detail of a whole culture, a representative episode in history. This revelation, like revelations in the novels of James as well as of Joyce, is really itself the main action; it is dramatic; it is "rendered." It is not, in other words, merely a by-product of the action; it *is* the action.

*The Sound and the Fury* meets the Jamesian requirements of drama, "solidity of specification," and presentation of characters. The calculated alternation of "picture" and "scene," the dramatic rendition of a way of life, the painting of "portraits," the "rich passion for extremes"—all these elements of the Jamesian novel are present, as the reader easily sees, provided he is not thrown off by the sometimes difficult language and the modernist freedom with chronology. One need not stress the Joycean devices Faulkner uses: the interior monologue and stream of consciousness, the cinematic montage effect, the free, lyric, punning language. These are merely particulars in the complicated conjunction of forces that produced Faulkner's first great book.

What happened to Faulkner is roughly what happened to Melville in writing *Moby-Dick*. Melville discovered simultaneously how to use Shakespeare and how to represent in their fullest meaning the native and personal materials he had been trying to use in his earlier books. Faulkner's simultaneous discovery of Joyce (to put aside for the moment other influences on *The Sound and the Fury*) and of the full significance, as a literary idea, of Yoknapatawpha County is closely analogous to Melville's discoveries. So that *Moby-Dick* and *The Sound and the Fury* are classic examples of the successful union of American with European genius. In each book the author has discovered and appropriated for the first time his authentic native subject and has been able to bring to it a subtle and original art. But in each book the trick has been turned by enlisting an artistry quite foreign to the author's own.

It will be recalled that *The Sound and the Fury* consists of four portraits, one section of the book being devoted to each: Benjy, April 7, 1928; Quentin, June 2, 1910; Jason, April 6, 1928; Dilsey, April 8, 1928. Faulkner has not made it easier for us by putting the most difficult section first and many potential readers have been disconcerted not only by the language and the rapid time-shifts of the opening pages but also by the fact that the main character, who is also the point of view, is an idiot. Of this last circumstance the first thing to say is that, as Lionel Trilling has put it, the cardinal fact about Benjy is not that he is an idiot but that he is human. There is a pathos about Benjy which is unparalleled in the American novel; little Pip in *Moby-Dick*, for example, is by comparison to the humanity of Benjy a mere literary idea. One would have to turn to a novelist like Dostoevski to find an episode as moving as that which recounts how Benjy, at the age of eighteen, gets out of the yard and molests some schoolchildren because he mistakes one of them for his beloved sister Caddy.

"I'm scared."

"He won't hurt you. I pass here every day. He just runs along the fence."

They came on. I opened the gate and they stopped, turning. I was trying to say, and I caught her, trying to say, and she screamed and I was trying to say and trying and the bright shapes began to stop and I tried to get out. I tried to get it off my face, but the bright shapes were going away. They were going up the hill to where it fell away and I tried to cry. But when I breathed in, I couldn't breathe out again to cry, and I tried to keep from falling off the hill into the bright, whirling shapes.

*Here, loony, Luster said. Here come some. Hush your slobbering and moaning, now.*

Benjy is human, then; certainly there is much of the human fate in his "I was trying to say, and I caught her, trying to say, and she screamed and I was trying to say." In many essential ways Benjy's fate is recognizably ours, which is what we basically require of any character in a novel.

But what is to be said of using an idiot not only as a character but as the point of view, of asking us to see things and comprehend them as an idiot may be supposed to do? First, one should note that the voice which speaks to us is not that of an idiot but of a skillful and resourceful novelist using for the moment a carefully limited and contrived convention. Second, that there are certain aesthetic advantages in perceiving experience more or less as it may be supposed an idiot perceives it. It is not true, as is sometimes said, that the general flow of chaotic experience passes through Benjy's mind. His experience is severely limited to a few things—Caddy and the other members of the family, his cemetery, the picket fence around the front yard, the golf players, the "branch" and outbuildings elsewhere on the property, the smell of leaves, the firelight and mirror into which he loves to gaze. These and a few other images play before his mind. But although Benjy's experience is limited to a few archetypes, these are perceived and rendered without the intervention of the intellect or the moralizing faculty which would inevitably be present in any other perceiving mind, except that of a child. Thus Faulkner is able to give us a sense of experience in all its native immediacy and primitive freshness and innocence. There are plenty of other characters in the book to convey the same experiences to us with all the peculiar bias of their temperaments. But we gain by having them from Benjy first. And we see that Faulkner has done in the Benjy section what every accomplished novelist has to be able to do. He eats his cake and has it too. That is, he establishes a character; he uses this character as his point of view; but Benjy as point of view is merely the dramatic convention of the piece. The actual point of view is still the author's, and his mind envelops the whole. The dramatic convention, however, is all-important and the Benjy section is a more accomplished piece of writing than it would be if the omniscient author were content to appear merely as such.

What Benjy sees, then, is immediate and emergent. But

it is not chaotic. A very skillful control is at work in this first section, and, in many ways, what happens epitomizes and forecasts the rest of the novel. The characters are already suggested in their entirety, even while they are still children. Thus, on pp. 42–43 of the Modern Library Edition, we have Quentin already meditative, aloof, and entranced by the mystery of death or at least by a mystery that will later turn out to be the mystery of death—"Quentin was still standing there by the branch. He was chunking into the shadows where the branch was." Caddy is already independent and reckless:

"I don't care," Caddy said. "I'll walk right in the parlor where they are."
"I'll bet your pappy whip you if you do," Versh said.
"I don't care," Caddy said.

Jason is already the mean-spirited materialist who, with his hands in his pockets, says, "I'm hungry" and tattles to their father that "Caddy and Quentin threw water on each other."

Given Faulkner's intention to upset the normal sequence of time, there is a further advantage in Benjy's idiocy, assuming, as Faulkner does, that the mind of an idiot, like the unconscious itself, is timeless. For Benjy what happened in 1902 is as vivid and immediate as what happened in 1910 or 1928. Again Faulkner is able to have his cake and eat it too, for he is able to evoke past events with vivid freshness and at the same time give the reader a powerful sense of the passing, as well as the pathos, of time.

It is not hard to follow with sufficient accuracy the shifts of time in the Benjy section. Each shift is indicated by the use of italics. The shift is usually made by an association of images. For example, at the opening of the book Benjy hears the golfers calling "caddie," and he begins to moan because he is reminded of his sister, who left home in 1910, eighteen years ago. Or he catches his clothes on a nail in the fence, and this takes him farther back, to 1898 or 1900, when he had crawled through the fence at Christmas time and had gotten his hands cold. The time levels shift mainly among a few crucial years—the period around 1900, when the children are still small; 1910, the marriage of Caddy and suicide of Quentin; 1913, the year Benjy is gelded after frightening the schoolchildren; 1928, the present time, when Quentin, the girl, is planning to run off with the carnival man.

In the Quentin section of *The Sound and the Fury* we find some of the same evocativeness of the Benjy section. Events we have already learned about assume new dimensions, because now they are called forth in a fairly complicated and sophisticated mind. Quentin's mind, like Benjy's in this respect, is obsessive and returns again and again to a few images and ideas; and this gives a necessary consistency to what might otherwise be an inchoate flow of reminiscence and perception. Quentin's mind broods on the ideas and events that are stated, like the themes of a musical composition, in the opening pages: his father's melancholy (not to say platitudinous) thoughts about the meaning of time, the marriage of Caddy, his willful belief that in some symbolic way he has committed incest with Caddy, his preoccupation with death, his approaching suicide.

One had better admit immediately that the Quentin episode is not so successful as the others. If, taking the book generally, the Joycean influence is beneficial, it is nevertheless true that Quentin, like Stephen Daedalus himself, is rather abstract. It is also true, however, that in relation to Quentin, as in relation to Stephen, *other* characters become vividly real. Thus if we can't quite believe that an abstract desire to step aside from time can move anyone as much as it is said to move Quentin, we can easily believe in Caddy and in Quentin's neurotic love for her. If we can't quite accept either Faulkner's or Quentin's solemnity about such symbolic acts as twisting the hands off Quentin's watch, we can accept Quentin's elegiac meditations about the fate of his family, and the pathos of his memories. If we sometimes get a little tired of Quentin's sententious utterances and his morbid introspection, we are rewarded by getting brief glimpses (all too brief indeed) of other characters. Among these are Gerald Bland, the gilded youth from Kentucky, with his brassy doting mother, his hard straw hat, and his racing shell; the Deacon, a marvelous northernized Negro with a Brooks Brothers suit, and a collection of preposterous pretensions; Herbert Head, who had cheated at Harvard and to whom Caddy is hastily married when it is found that she is pregnant with another man's child.

The episode of the little Italian girl who follows Quentin and gets him in trouble with the authorities is very successful. The allegorical overtone—since to Quentin she represents his "Little Sister Death"—is not amiss, for the simple reason that the episode is rendered in full realistic detail and does not strike us, as most of the time symbols do, as being bootlegged into the book. The episode of the trout succeeds rather by a certain Whitmanesque mysticism of water, dissolution, and death than by the somewhat portentous symbolism, according to which the trout, "delicate and motionless among the wavering shadows," represents (apparently) the capacity to find an equilibrium in the stream of time. Quentin, on the other hand, wants only to escape time and the sound and fury of life. He has therefore tried to believe that he has committed incest with Caddy and that this sin, like a purifying flame, removes them to a transcendent realm and immolates their gross natural existence: "it was to isolate her out of the loud world so that it would have to flee us of necessity and then the sound of it would be as if it had never been." One may note the beauty of Quentin's meditations about his sister whenever these take the form of actual memory, as in the long passage on their abortive suicide pact. The dialogue between Quentin and his father at the end of the section is also impressive, and neither the morbid abstractness of Quentin's mind nor the mean and cliché philosophizings of his father can spoil the elegiac tone—"was the saddest word of all there is nothing else in the world its not despair until time its not even time until it was."

In Faulkner how a character talks makes all the difference. Although Henry James shows more knowledge of vernacular speech than is commonly supposed, it is still relatively true that all his characters talk Henry James language. That is James's literary convention. But when Faulkner does not hear the individual language of one of his characters, that character does not seem real. Faulkner clearly does not know how Quentin sounds—sometimes Quentin talks Joyce; sometimes he uses an ornate rhetoric about time and the South; sometimes he speaks with an unexpected sardonic vulgarity.

The first words of the Jason section are all-revealing: "Once a bitch always a bitch, what I say." Faulkner knows exactly how Jason sounds, and this goes a long way towards explaining why Jason is an authentic, original, and memorable character. He is a novelist's triumph by comparison to whom Benjy and Quentin, though probably not Dilsey, seem a little too much the product of moralistic, philosophic, or symbolic calculation. We are always relieved when the others are shown as they actually think, feel, and live rather than as they illustrate the idea the author has about them. We do not have to look for this relief in the case of Jason.

To be sure, the unconscious mind of Jason is not very interesting. The musing flow of his thoughts is not much richer than the salty language in which they are overtly expressed. Hence, although Faulkner goes on, in the Jason section, with the convention of the point of view, the interior monologue falls sharply off. Jason's ideas and his experience, like those of Benjy and Quentin, are obsessively limited. But he lives more than they among material things and quotidian events and if this makes him less pure, it also makes him more real.

Readers who follow the traditionalist view of Faulkner will have trouble seeing Jason as Faulkner sees him. I mean by the "traditionalist view" that kind of conservative criticism that divides Faulkner's characters into Sartorises (good) and Snopeses (bad). The good people, according to this account, retain the southern ideals of honor and justice; they believe in a society based on tradition, religion, and the sense of community. The bad people are individualistic materialists who have no conception of honor, tradition, or the sanctity of family and community, whose only notion of community is, in fact, the cash nexus.

There is no doubt that these moral distinctions are important to Faulkner, as they are for any thinking person. Presumably he would like to accept them in their pristine "Confederate" innocence, were he not too modern, too realistic, and too honest to do so. He accepts them, one may think, but with all the reservation and irony which a divided and contradictory mind is likely to exhibit.

Thus Jason appears at first to be a Snopes in all but name. He is mean-spirited, obscene, rapacious, anti-Semitic. But he also suffers. He has his frustrations and his neurotic headaches. And there are at least two things about him which always engage Faulkner's sympathy. First, he has humor. Second, he suffers from the peculiar masculine "outrage," at portraying which Faulkner is a master, possibly the greatest master of all time. Jason is bedeviled by the self-pity, treachery, libidinousness, and animal success of women. He is also, in the person of Dilsey, bedeviled by woman's moral superiority. His inner agony is vividly suggested by his frantic race over the countryside in his car, his headache getting worse all the time, in pursuit of his niece Quentin, who has taken the money and run off with the pitchman. Here is ultimate defeat in all its Sunday-morning particularity. And of his humor, one has to admit its callousness; at the same time it is impossible not to be moved by it.

I says no I never had university advantages because at Harvard they teach you how to go for a swim at night without knowing how to swim. . . . I haven't got much

pride, I can't afford it with a kitchen full of niggers to
feed and robbing the state asylum of its star freshman.
Blood, I says, governors and generals [in early genera-
tions of the Compson family, that is]. It's a damn good
thing we never had any kings and presidents; we'd all
be down there at Jackson chasing butterflies.

Jason's flow of native language makes him what he is, allowing us to see him (nowhere better than at the very end of
his part of the book) in all his unforgivable cruelty, vulgarity, and human appeal:

Like I say once a bitch always a bitch. And just let me
have twenty-four hours without any damn New York jew
to advise me what it's going to do. I don't want to make
a killing; save that to suck in the smart gamblers with. I
just want an even chance to get my money back. And
once I've done that they can bring all Beale Street and
all bedlam in here and two of them can sleep in my bed
and another one can have my place at the table too.

The first three sections of *The Sound and the Fury* open
with the sound of a voice or the procession of someone's
inner thoughts. But in the Dilsey section we see the main
character before we hear her. The portrait of Dilsey enlists
the painter's art and the portrait at the beginning is marvelously done, once we accept the fact that the painter is
of the modern school and something of an expressionist:

She wore a thin black straw hat perched upon her tur-
ban, and a maroon velvet cape with a border of mangy
and anonymous fur above a dress of purple silk, and she
stood in the door for awhile with her myriad and sunken
face lifted to the weather. . . . She had been a big
woman once but now her skeleton rose, draped loosely
in unpadded skin that tightened again upon a paunch
almost dropsical, as though muscle and tissue had been
courage or fortitude which the days or the years had con-
sumed until only the indomitable skeleton was left rising
like a ruin or a landmark above the somnolent and im-

pervious guts, and above that the collapsed face that gave the impression of the bones themselves being outside the flesh, lifted into the drawing day with an expression at once fatalistic and of a child's astonished disappointment, until she turned and entered the house again and closed the door.

If we see Dilsey graphically, we are no less struck by her speech, which in nearly every utterance is inevitably real and full of tragic significance. For Dilsey appeals to us both as an individual and as the tragic chorus of the piece. There is never even the slightest note of falsity in anything she says—never the faintest hint of the comic Negro of stage convention nor of romantic idolization of primitive wisdom. Her tone is assured and consistent whether her words are colloquial or Biblical, and no one in American literature has spoken more memorably—whether we hear her abstractedly saying, "Eight o'clock," when the broken-down kitchen clock with one hand strikes five or (as Dilsey, Frony, and Benjy return from the Reverend Shegog's sermon and approach the "square, paintless house with its rotting portico"):

"I've seed de first en de last," Dilsey said. "Never you mind me."

"First en last whut?" Frony said.

"Never you mind," Dilsey said. "I see de beginnin, en now I sees de endin."

It is not an accident that Dilsey is made to appeal to our senses more fully and variously than any of the other characters. She lives in the world, as they do not. Her acceptance of things as they are is tragic, which means that it is tolerably complete and includes an awareness of the human condition none of the other characters can bear. Not having Dilsey's tragic awareness, they all panic at a point where Dilsey would be able to remain morally active. Thus the tremendous conclusion of the book, in which Benjy terrifyingly roars because Luster has driven the carriage around the square to the left instead of to the right, is an epitome of the whole:

> Ben's voice roared and roared. Queenie moved again [this time around the square to the right], her feet began to clop-clop steadily again, and at once Ben hushed. Luster looked quickly back over his shoulder, then he drove on. The broken flower drooped over Ben's fist and his eyes were empty and blue and serene again as cornice and façade flowed smoothly once more from left to right; post and tree, window and doorway, and signboard, each in its ordered place.

And so the violence and irrationality recede, leaving us with the starkly effective stage-set which a southern county seat, with its square, its Confederate statue and neo-classic courthouse, provides.

In reading *The Sound and the Fury* it is important to remember that the book is a novel and not, structurally, a symbolic poem of any sort, except as any profound narrative is; its structure in every fundamental respect is novelistic. Yet one would never gather that this is true from most of the extant criticism. Carvel Collins, for example, discusses two "structural systems" in *The Sound and the Fury*, while suggesting that there are others not yet vouchsafed. He believes that one of these "structural systems" is an association of symbols derived from the passage in *Macbeth* from which Faulkner takes his title:

> Out, out brief candle!
> Life's but a walking shadow, a poor player
> That struts and frets his hour upon the stage
> And then is heard no more: it is a tale
> Told by an idiot, full of sound and fury,
> Signifying nothing.

Well, Benjy is an idiot and the tale is first told by him (but it *signifies*—oh, immensely!). There are candles in the book; Benjy likes them. Quentin uses the word "shadow" a good deal and lives among them. Jason is a poor player; he frets;

*+ "Christian" system too*

he even struts. But there is no structural system here—only verbal echoes that enrich the general music.

The other "structural system" is based on Freud. Benjy is the Id, Quentin the Ego, Jason the Super-Ego, Candace a sort of Libido, Dilsey the "warm, loving nature," perhaps the integrated personality. As Mr. Collins works it out, there is more to this formulation than one might at first think. But it does not point to a principle of structure. And what Mr. Collins succeeds in saying is only that both Faulkner and Freud are profound psychologists.

Because she remembers that *The Sound and the Fury* is a novel, and therefore deals with the kinds of experience people have, Olga W. Vickery is more convincing in her account of the structure of the book, even though she largely confines herself to discussing the sequence of the four sections. The four sections, she says, are four ways of perceiving experience and they are arranged so as to dramatize the passage from a private to a public world. Thus Benjy with his tightly organized system of sensations, Quentin with his obsessive abstractions, and Jason with his total utilitarianism cling to views of experience which prove inadequate to cope with the irrationality and unpredictableness of reality. In this sense they resemble the many characters in Hawthorne, Melville, and James who try disastrously to impose a narrow theory on a wide world. But Dilsey, Mrs. Vickery goes on, not being in defiance of circumstance is able to create order out of it; she *lives* experience and is aware of its tragic implications and so she can control it through morally significant action, keeping the family going when, without her, it would collapse.

In this way *The Sound and the Fury* would seem to meet Philip Rahv's requirement for the novel: that the novelist, if he is as good as "the great European authors," will use experience "as a concrete medium for the testing and creation of values." Mr. Rahv fears that too often Faulkner merely parodies experience and that this accounts for the violence and excess of his writing. Mr. Rahv has his point, and it will perhaps apply to other Faulkner novels, the impressive and indeed amazing *Absalom, Absalom!* among them. But *The Sound and the Fury* presents experience at a level of completeness, fidelity, and significance which is close to the high point of possibility in the novel.

*The Sound and the Fury* is the most "novelistic" of Faulkner's works, and, as in the fictions of Henry James, the element of romance is complexly assimilated and sublimated, so that it becomes a suffused poetry of language, metaphor, and event. In Faulkner's other novels the element of romance is more obtrusive and autonomous—most richly so in *Light in August* and *As I Lay Dying*.

In his Introduction to *The Portable Faulkner*, Malcolm Cowley has written that Faulkner combines "two of the principal traditions in American letters: the tradition of psychological horror, often close to symbolism, that begins with Charles Brockden Brown, our first professional novelist, and extends through Poe, Melville, Henry James (in his later stories), Stephen Crane, and Hemingway; and the other tradition of frontier humor and realism, beginning with Augustus Longstreet's *Georgia Scenes* and having Mark Twain as its best example." This is true and illuminating. But (as Mr. Cowley himself suggests) it does not include all the various aspects of Faulkner's fiction. There is, besides realism, naturalism. And as a tradition complementary to the melodrama of Charles Brockden Brown and the other writers Mr. Cowley mentions, there is, besides frontier humor, frontier nostalgia and the tradition of pastoral idyl that leaves so memorable a mark on the fiction of such writers as Cooper, Mark Twain, and Hemingway.

The many-sided genius of Faulkner—loose, uneven, and wasteful as his way of writing sometimes is—has performed so far the greatest feat of twentieth-century American fiction. And at the heart of that accomplishment one observes taking place, with rich amplification and ever fresh discovery, the characteristic process of the American novelist by which he brings to the novel the perennial poetry of romance.

# Appendix I

*Sanctuary* vs. *The Turn of the Screw*

THE difference between allegory and symbolism can perhaps be made clear by further illustration. Faulkner's *Sanctuary* is first of all a social novel, poised on the eve of the Depression years and in the naturalist tradition. Henry James's *The Turn of the Screw* is a tale of psychological horror. Both are related to the Gothic tradition, depending as they do on the well-known devices of terror, sinister locale, abnormal psychology and victimization.

Like all extreme melodrama *Sanctuary* projects its meanings into an abstract and mechanical articulation of persons and events. And since these persons and events so often strike us as symbols for readily recognizable social phenomena, we are led to think of *Sanctuary*, in Irving Howe's phrase, as a "social charade." In fact it is a sort of muffled sociological allegory.

George Marion O'Donnell's account of *Sanctuary* as an allegory is (I believe) generally thought to be unacceptable, even though by calling it an allegory his purpose was to distinguish this book from Faulkner's greater work, such as *The Sound and the Fury*. Mr. O'Donnell's pioneering essay conceived of Faulkner as a "traditional," "mythic," and "tragic" writer who, himself in the best tradition of the aristocratic South, was portraying and lamenting in his novels the decline of this South.

O'Donnell's idea of Faulkner's imagination as mythic, tragic, and traditional is similar to Mrs. Leavis's idea of Hawthorne, and like Mrs. Leavis's view it fails to take account of the many contradictory aspects of Faulkner's imagination and overstates a half-truth. But it will be enough now to quote Mr. O'Donnell's interpretation of *Sanctuary:*

> In simple terms the pattern of the allegory is something like this: Southern Womanhood Corrupted but Undefiled (Temple Drake), in the company of Corrupted Tradition (Gowan Stevens, a professional Virginian), falls into the clutches of Amoral Modernism (Popeye), which is itself impotent, but which with the aid of its strong ally Natural Lust ("Red") rapes Southern Womanhood unnaturally and then seduces her so satisfactorily that her corruption is total, and she becomes the tacit ally of Modernism. Meanwhile Pore White Trash (Goodwin) has been accused of the crime which he, with the aid of the Naif Faithful (Tawmmy), actually tried to prevent. The Formalized Tradition (Horace Benbow), perceiving the true state of affairs, tries vainly to defend Pore White Trash. However, Southern Womanhood is so hopelessly corrupted that she wilfully sees Pore White Trash convicted and lynched; she is then carried off by Wealth (Judge Drake) to meaningless escape in European luxury. Modernism, carrying in it from birth its own impotence and doom, submits with masochistic pleasure to its own destruction for the one crime that it has not yet committed—Revolutionary Destruction of Order (the murder of the Alabama policeman, for which the innocent Popeye is executed).

This interpretation, with all of its ridiculous personifications, strikes me as essentially correct. It illustrates the fact that Faulkner's mind, like Hawthorne's, is less discriminating than many Faulkner devotees want to admit—at least in the sense that it entertains the lowest of lowbrow fantasies. At the top of Faulkner's imagination there is great refinement and distinction. But into its lower reaches there readily flow the crude archetypes of the folk imagination, the very archetypes which may constitute a good part of the conscious or unconscious mental machinery of a state senator, let us say, in Faulkner's native Mississippi.

*The Scarlet Letter* is a greater work than *Sanctuary* because (to confine ourselves to the language we are at present using) the allegory includes but is larger and more significant than the folk archetypes. In *Sanctuary*, on the other hand, the allegory is merely a picturesque arrangement of the archetypes. There is more to this brilliantly concise book than the allegory, however, and *Sanctuary* is closer to the best genius of Faulkner than Mr. O'Donnell thought.

By contrast *The Turn of the Screw* is symbolistic rather than allegorical. In using the Gothic convention for psychological purposes, rather than sociological as in *Sanctuary*, James makes his symbols stand for what is *not* known, except by suggestion and indirection. The ghosts of Peter Quint and Miss Jessel, considered as symbols, are ambiguous. Deviously they lead us to seek the truths they always seem about to reveal. We never find these truths and are left with the symbols themselves in all their mysterious and terrible suggestiveness. James's tale is not an exposition of truth but an exploration of truth's ultimate mysteries.

In his essay "The Ambiguity of Henry James" Edmund Wilson outlines the meanings *The Turn of the Screw* would have if it *were* an allegory. The allegory would be Freudian, and we should read the story and understand the ghosts as the neurotic sex fantasy of the repressed governess. Wilson's account of the tale, which appeared in the 1930's, was a necessary correction to the older view that the ghosts were real diabolic agencies and that the governess, about whom there was nothing demented or sinister, was simply trying to protect the children from them.

Furthermore, it is astonishing how literally James uses the Freudian dream symbols. But a careful reading of the tale convinces us that the ghosts may really be there, marvelously adapted to but finally independent of the governess's fantasies. There are things about them, such as the physical appearance of Peter Quint, which the governess could not know and could not project out of her unconscious. The universe of meanings is bigger than the governess's own distraught mind, and the drama of the tale lies in her attempt to foresee and interpret with her frantic consciousness everything that can happen to her. Of course, she cannot do this, and if there is a moral in the book, it is that the attempt to live in a totally cognized world, in which all ambiguities are rationalized and symbolized according to the bias of one's own mind, is madness. However alert and imaginative it may be, the mind is narrow and obsessive compared with the infinite variety of experience. In the story James provides a tremendous dramatic irony by showing us reality in a guise that seems only slightly to vary from the governess's conception of it—but the variation is enough to suggest the abyss of difference.

Since the story deals with "meaning," with knowledge and its limits, with the symbolizing processes of the mind as it seeks to rationalize the world, it is symbolistic; and all the potentially allegorical elements are broken down into the subtler ambiguities of the poetic symbol.

Still, *The Turn of the Screw* is eminently a novel, or at least a *novella*. And one's final sense of it does not arise from its being a symbolistic poem or a drama of meaning. By the end of the tale the governess has emerged, not as a mere point of view for delving into psychological and metaphysical mysteries but as a human being whose pathos is that of everyone—namely, that she has in terror, joy, and anxiety spun out in her mind a precious image of reality. She has constructed for herself a richly eventful inner world and she has staked everything on possessing and inhabiting this world. In her case, this is a momentary madness—and yet the governess is not a lunatic or more than temporarily psychotic. The narrator of the first pages of the story, whom James calls Douglas and who strongly resembles Conrad's Marlow, speaks glowingly of the governess as he had known her in later years. She was "awfully clever and nice." She was "the most agreeable woman I've ever known in her position; she would have been worthy of any whatever."

Her fantasied version of reality is only in degree different from the false but precious and jealously guarded version we all form in our minds. And in its desperate sensibility and intense cultivation it is particularly like the imagination of Henry James. This may account for the tremendous pathos of the final paragraph, where we are told that the immense fantasy which, mad and misguided as it is, has cost so much human effort and projected so much vicarious life, has been suddenly destroyed and there is nothing left for the governess but to stare "at the quiet day."

# Appendix II

## Romance, the Folk Imagination, and Myth Criticism

IN the preceding chapters there have been several occasions for referring to the folk mind or folk imagination, especially whenever the question of romance has come up. It is not a good idea to try to define too closely either the archetypes of the folk mind or the romance that sometimes embodies them. Neither, fortunately, is capable of being reduced to a single formula. The closest I have come to a formula is to speak repeatedly, though I think by no means exclusively, of a presumed archetypal symbolic drama of light and dark which has certainly been always widespread if not universal in folklore. The conflicts thus symbolized have been many; they may be suggested by such contraries as life and death, good and evil, male and female, angel and demon, God and Satan, summer and winter. This formula has the imprecision which is inevitable if it is to remain relevant to the manifold uses of the folk imagination in the American romance-novels. That the light-dark archetype *is* relevant to the American romance-novels I have tried to show not only by examining some of them but by following the lead of those critics, like D. H. Lawrence, Yvor Winters, and Leslie Fiedler, who have thought that certain forces and institutions in American society have tended to confirm and sustain, and yet to modify in the life of the imagination, this archetype. I am only too painfully aware, in all this, of the necessity of sacrificing a semblance of specific clarity of definition in order that what I have had to say should refer, illuminatingly as I hope, to many different facets of the novel—and to many different kinds of novel.

In order to suggest what would be lost by a more limited formula, I now confront the objection to my procedure which, as I am well aware, will be brought against it by what have become known as the "myth critics." (I am not myself a "myth critic," although I have been interested in myth, as in one way or another every student of literature must be, and although my first book, *Quest for Myth*, was a historical study of the subject.) These critics, whose influence has been considerable in the last fifteen years, will immediately and mistakenly equate romance with myth. In the critical practice of this school of thought, if not strictly in theory, there is only one myth—namely, the death and rebirth of a god. This archetype is thought to constitute the essential action of tragedy especially, but also of comedy, elegy, and perhaps ultimately all valuable literary forms. It is thought, as one gathers, to be eternally recreated in man's unconscious, and also to be prescribed, in some unexplained manner, by the nature of literature itself—so that in various guises it is always cropping up in different writers and different cultures, irrespective of context, time, or routes of transmission. The characteristic American form of the mythic archetype is thought to be the fall from innocence and the initiation into life—an action of the soul that entails a symbolic dying and rebirth.

I think it has already been sufficiently shown in the preceding chapters that American literature does not often mirror forth this dramatic action. Instead it pictures human life in a context of unresolved contradictions—contradictions which, for better or for worse, are not absorbed, reconciled, or transcended.

The myth critic gets from the rigidity and formal abstractness of his approach a very biased view of American literature. He seems to know only the "late" works of a given author, which are also, by comparison, the lesser and more eccentric works. He is interested in *The Marble Faun* but not *The Scarlet Letter*, *Billy Budd* but not *Moby-Dick*, *The Golden Bowl* but not *The Bostonians*, *The Old Man and the Sea* but not *A Farewell to Arms*, *The Bear* but not *The Sound and the Fury*. The special gains of this approach are outweighed by its apparent denigration of the greater and more characteristic work of whatever author may be in question. Many readers have in recent years formed a distaste for works of literature which are radically involved with the dilemmas of their time and their place and which draw too directly on the reality and the moral contradictions of human experience. As I pointed out in the Introduction, romance as the American novelists have used it does not necessarily incapacitate the novel for a radical involvement with human dilemmas and may in fact enhance this involvement. On the other hand, an exclusive interest in myth, as defined by the myth critics, seems infallibly to lead to an exaggerated opinion of works which avoid this involvement and promise the immanence of grace, of final harmony and reconciliation, in a world whose contradictions it seems no longer possible to bear.

A corollary tendency of the myth critic is that he always sees a novel from above. According to his theory the novel is merely one more of the several literary forms in which the mythic archetype has manifested itself, more or less as God is said to embody Himself in the temporal order. Although there is some historical justification for this idea, in the sense that a novel of Scott or Fielding may be regarded as a descendant of medieval romance or ancient myth, generalizations of this sort lead to little but themselves. They ignore the whole reality of time and place and the whole illuminating cultural context, which more than other literary forms the novel reflects. I have been mindful of this in saying that realism is the fundamental distinguishing quality of the novel and in going on to speak of romance as something that in the novel arises from and modifies realism rather than of realism as something that in the novel romance condescends to become. This procedure is not historical in the most general sense. But it is in the limited and concrete sense, and that is the one that counts in our appreciation and judgment of the novel.

# Works Cited

Anderson, Quentin, *The American Henry James* (1957)

Arthos, John, "Ritual and Humor in the Writing of William Faulkner," *William Faulkner: Two Decades of Criticism*, ed. by Frederick J. Hoffman and Olga Vickery (1951)

Arvin, Newton, *Herman Melville* (1950)

Barzun, Jacques, "Henry James, Melodramatist," *The Question of Henry James*, ed. by F. W. Dupee (1945)

Bewley, Marius, "Fenimore Cooper and the Economic Age," *American Literature* (May 1954)

Brooks, Van Wyck, *The Ordeal of Mark Twain* (1920)

Chase, Richard, "The Stone and the Crucifixion," *Kenyon Review* (Autumn 1948)

Collins, Carvel, "The Interior Monologues of *The Sound and the Fury*," *English Institute Essays: 1952*, ed. by Alan S. Downer (1954)

Cowley, Malcolm, Introduction to *The Portable Hawthorne* (1948)

De Voto, Bernard, Introduction to *The Portable Mark Twain* (1946)

——, *Mark Twain at Work* (1942)

Edel, Leon, Introduction to *The Portrait of a Lady*, Riverside Editions (1955)

Eliot, T. S., Introduction to *The Adventures of Huckleberry Finn* (1950)

Fiedler, Leslie A., "As Free as Any Cretur . . .", *New Republic* (August 15 and 22, 1955)

Fogle, R. H., *Hawthorne's Fiction: The Light and the Dark* (1952)

Grossman, James, *James Fenimore Cooper* (1949)

Jacobs, Robert D., "Faulkner's Tragedy of Isolation," *Southern Renascence*, ed. by Louis D. Rubin, Jr. and Robert D. Jacobs (1953)

James, Henry, "The Art of Fiction," *Henry James, Selected Fiction*, ed. by Leon Edel (1953)

——, *The Art of the Novel*, ed. by R. P. Blackmur (1934)

Leavis, F. R., Introduction to *Pudd'nhead Wilson*, Grove Press (1955)

——, *The Great Tradition*, Anchor Books (1954)

Leavis, Q. D., "Hawthorne as Poet," *Sewanee Review* (Spring–Summer 1951)

Lubbock, Percy, *The Craft of Fiction* (1921)

O'Donnell, George Marion, "Faulkner's Mythology," *Two Decades of Criticism, op. cit.*

Rahv, Philip, "The Cult of Experience in American Writing," *Image and Idea* (1949)

Rourke, Constance, *American Humor* (1931)

Schorer, Mark, "Technique as Discovery," *Hudson Review* (Spring 1948)

Smith, Henry Nash, Introduction to *The Prairie*, Rinehart Editions (1950)

Spender, Stephen, *The Destructive Element* (1935)

Stewart, George R., "The Two Moby-Dicks," *American Literature* (January 1954)

Tate, Allen, "Techniques of Fiction," *Sewanee Review* (Spring 1944)

Trilling, Lionel, Introduction to *The Adventures of Huckleberry Finn*, Rinehart Editions (1948)

——, *The Liberal Imagination* (1950)

Vickery, Olga, "*The Sound and the Fury*: A Study in Perspective," *PMLA* (December 1954)

Wilson, Edmund, "The Ambiguity of Henry James," *The Question of Henry James, op. cit.*

——, "Citizen of the Union," *The Shores of Light* (1952)

Winters, Yvor, *Maule's Curse* (1938)

Mahon, Donald, character of, 222

*Main Currents of American Thought* (Parrington), 37–38

Malraux, on *Sanctuary*, 206

Manners, Cable's power of presenting, 168; ideas of in America, 159; lack of in *The Great Gatsby*, 162

*Marble Faun, The* (Hawthorne), preface to, 18

*Mardi*, basis of, 93

Marquand, J. P., as a novelist of manners, 158

Marquesas Islands, 93

Marx, Karl, influence of on Faulkner, 221

Masquerade, in *The Grandissimes*, 169

Materialism, of Bush family, 61

Matthews, Brander, on Cooper, 44

Matthiessen, F. O., on *Billy Budd*, 113

Maturin, romances of, 16

McCaslin, Ike, 61

*McTeague* (Norris), animal imagery in, 190; appraisal of, 188ff.; circuit of life in, 191; dualism in, 202; heredity-environment-degeneration theme of, 188; naturalistic tendencies in, 186; poetry in, 192; reason for success of, 191–92; as a romance, 187; social question in, 202; as a "sport," 4; symbol of gold in, 202–3; symbolism in, 192; and tendency towards abstraction, 191

Melodrama, and "Gothic," 37; in *The Grandissimes*, 161;

in *Huckleberry Finn*, 148–49; Parrington on, 37–38; in *The Spy*, 14–15; uses of, 39–41; in *Wieland*, 38–39

Melville, Herman, as an artist, 90; Arvin on, 100–1; on Calvinistic sense of sin, 201; as celebrant of masculine life, 64; characters in, 160; contrasted with Norris, 198; on creation of art, 95–96; culture of, 200; dilemma of, 92–93; on Hawthorne, 89–90; and idea of Evil, 201; imagination of, 89–91, 112–13, 201; influence of on Faulkner, 220; as an intellectual, 200; language of, 140, 150; as master of novel, 204; morality of, 106–9; on the Nantucketers, 97–99; as a novelist of manners, 158; pastoral feeling in, 183; and plea for romance, 187; poetic humor of, 120; and quest for truth, 90–91; source of moral values in, 159; as a thinker, 90; and use of humor, 102–4; and use of native legends, 102; and use of Shakespeare, 224

*Memoirs of Carwin, the Biloquist* (Brown), 34

Metaphor, use of in *Portrait of a Lady*, 119–22; use of in *The Prairie*, 60

*Middle of the Journey, The* (Trilling), Hawthorne's influence on, 84

Middlebrow literature, 10

*Middlemarch* (Eliot), poetry in, 118; tradition in, 4

Middleton, character of, 59

Mississippi River, De Voto on, 143; as a symbol, 143

of Populism on, 202; and influence of Zola, 186; irrationalism of, 198; as a lowbrow, 200; naturalistic creed
of, 197; pessimism of, 203;
Populist ideology of, 202;
portrayal of social behavior
of, 188–89; as a protofascist,
198; on realism, 187, 200;
on romance, 187; and earlier
American romancers, 200;
source of movement in, 191;
and sympathy with Ameri-
can Populism, 201–3; de-
vices of, 189–90; treatment
of romance of, 199; and use
of naturalism, 199; and wor-
ship of Force, 198
Nostalgia, frontier, in Faulkner, 236
*Notions of the Americans*
(Cooper), 14–15; on American fiction, 46–47; on "poverty of materials," 50
Novel, American, art-conscious-
ness in, 4; disunity in, 6–7;
exploring quality of, 4
Novel, definition of, 12–13;
moral significance of, 24;
and poetry, 82
Novel, English, classic tragedy
in, 2; as imperial enterprise,
4; influence of Christianity
in, 2; naturalism in, 2; qualities of, 2
Novel of manners, affinity with
dramatic high comedy, 158;
as in Jane Austen, 158; classic situation of, 169; "common sense" in, 158; definition of, 157–58; European,
159; moral standards in, 158
Novels of manners, American,
159–60; and environment,
160; as a romance, 160

*Oasis, The* (McCarthy), Hawthorne's influence on, 83–84
*Octopus, The* (Norris), characters in, 193–96; compared
with *The Prairie*, 203; plan
of, 193; as a romance, 187;
social question in, 202–3
O'Donnell, G. M., on Faulkner's imagination, 238–39;
on *Sanctuary* as an allegory,
237
O'Hara, John, as a novelist of
manners, 158
*Old Creole Days* (Cable),
mystification of, 169
Osmond, Gilbert, character of,
125–27, 130–34
*Other House, The* (James),
135–36
*Our Mutual Friend* (Dickens),
complexity of, 5

Painter's art, use of, 211
Parody, use of, 145
Parrington, on melodrama, 37–
38
Pastoral feeling, in American
novels, 183–84
Pearl, character of, 75, 78–79
*Père Goriot* (Balzac), legend
in, 163; Rastignac's challenge in, 164
Pessimism, of Norris, 203
Philosophe, Palmyre, nature of,
173
*Pierre* (Melville), ambiguities
in, 92; as a novel of manners, 158; as a "sport," 4
Piety, moral question of, 62–
63
*Pioneers, The* (Cooper), use
of myth in, 54
Pip, role of in *Moby-Dick*,
110; and Benjy Compson,
225

Richard Chase was born in New England in 1914 and graduated from Dartmouth College. He received his M.A. and Ph.D. degrees from Columbia University, where he was a member of the English faculty until his death in 1962. Aside from numerous articles in literary journals, Mr. Chase's published works of criticism are *Quest for Myth* (1949), *Herman Melville* (1949), *Emily Dickinson* (1951), and *Walt Whitman Reconsidered* (1955).